UNLEASHING
THE SECOND
AMERICAN
CENTURY

UNLEASHING
THE SECOND
AMERICAN
CENTURY

FOUR FORCES
FOR ECONOMIC DOMINANCE

Joel Kurtzman

PublicAffairs
New York

PublicAffairs books are available at special discounts for bulk purchases in the US
by corporations, institutions, and other organizations. For more information, please
contact the Special Markets Department at the Perseus Books Group, 2300 Chestnut
Street, Suite 200, Philadelphia, PA 19103, call (800) 810-4145, ext. 5000, or e-mail
special.markets@perseusbooks.com.

Book Design by Jack Lenzo

Kurtzman, Joel.
Unleashing the second American century : four forces for economic dominance / Joel
Kurtzman.
pages cm
Includes bibliographical references and index.
ISBN 978-1-61039-309-6 (hardcover)—ISBN 978-1-61039-310-2 (ebook) 1. Economic
forecasting—United States. 2. United States—Economic conditions—21st century. 3.
Manufactures—United States. I. Title.
HC106.83.K87 2014
330.973—dc23
2013033299
10 9 8 7 6 5 4 3 2 1

To Robert L. Dilenschneider,
a man who always sees the bigger picture.

CONTENTS

PREFACE

The term "the American Century" was coined by Henry R. Luce, co-founder of *Time* magazine, in the run-up to America's involvement in World War II. It was a term meant to reflect America taking its place at the center of the world's stage, and not a span of time. But as the first American Century wore on, the country became dependent on other nations for its energy—especially its oil—and ultimately for finances, too. Energy and finance are usually intertwined.

The second American Century is different from the first. It begins with America headed down the path toward energy independence, and ultimately to becoming an energy-exporting nation. It begins with America still leading the world in innovation, an America rich with capital in private hands and with a rapidly growing, highly productive industrial and manufacturing base. It begins with many other powerful but largely unappreciated attributes as well.

What will the second American Century be like?

If you take America's powerful agricultural, industrial, high-tech, biotech, university, research, and military strengths, and graft onto them the energy abundance of, say, Russia or Saudi Arabia, you start to get a picture of what this new era will be like. As energy starts to flow in abundance from our wells, manufacturing will be returning to our shores at an ever-increasing pace. As an increased number of manufactured goods begin to be exported from the United States to the rest of the world, money will begin pouring back into the country. With that, over the long haul, America's finances will rebound.

If you add to what I just described the resources of our two North American Free Trade Agreement (NAFTA) partners, Canada and Mexico, it really gets interesting. As George P. Shultz, former secretary of labor, treasury, and state, and distinguished fellow at Stanford University's Hoover Institution, has said, "North America, with the U.S. in the lead, is the world's center of creativity and innovation. Any measure will do: new companies formed, Nobel Prizes received, R&D spending, attractiveness to high talent from anywhere, patents issued, and numbers of great universities." Add to that the fact that "North America is on its way to being a net exporter of energy," Shultz said, and "the implications for geopolitical developments are vast. North America will have security of supply no matter what happens in the Middle East or elsewhere."[1]

The unimaginable wealth of the United States is about to be unleashed—again. It happened in the twentieth century, particularly in the aftermath of World War II, and it is beginning to happen now. Back then, as our troops came home from a horrendous overseas war, they returned to a country whose national debt was a staggering 120 percent of gross domestic product—an all-time high—as a result of the Great Depression and World War II. Our soldiers returned home in need of jobs, places to live, and education. They returned to a country in need of a new infrastructure of roads, bridges, rail lines, airports, pipelines, and ports. They returned, that is, to a country that is much like America today.

So what happened next?

A massive wave of growth, for roughly sixty years, with only brief interruptions. Along with that growth, there was the unprecedented development of our universities and of our scientific and technological capabilities, the emergence of brand new industries, the exploration of space and of the worlds inside our bodies and our cells. During that time, America was transformed.

As we go forward, America's future looks just as bright. The Great Recession and the housing crisis caused tremendous pain and disruption, but they also cleansed the system of excess. The government may be burdened by debt, but the private sector, and millions of Americans, have been sitting on their cash. A lot of cash. And soon they will begin to spend. In place of recession and crisis, we will face a period of renewed growth, with a new sense of optimism about the future.

So when will that growth start happening?

It is happening now in some parts of the country. Take a trip to North Dakota, or Cambridge, Massachusetts, or Silicon Valley and San Francisco, or Austin or Houston, or New York City, and you will see the seeds of growth taking root. Soon that growth will be happening everywhere.

That growth—and the new century it will usher in—is the subject of this book.

INTRODUCTION

"NO ONE EVER MADE A PLUGGED NICKEL BETTING AGAINST THE USA"

This book was conceived out of my frustration with the ill-informed statements made by so many of the candidates for office during the 2012 election cycle. It's not the first time people have made erroneous assessments regarding the United States and its prospects. Almost from the start there were politicians and pundits who counted us out. But during those recent campaigns—the national one for the presidency as well as ones conducted on the state and local level—we heard claim after claim that our best days were behind us. One phrase in particular—"We don't make anything here anymore"—made me extremely weary.

Candidates who should have known better, who should have understood more about the American economy and our role in the world, were mindlessly repeating a statement that made people nervous, made them doubt our place in the world, and made them pessimistic about the future. Worse, it just wasn't true. Commentators, pundits, and other so-called opinion leaders repeated it as if it were a mantra.

China was surpassing us—"eating our lunch" was how a lot of them put it—and the United States, and perhaps all of the Western world, was more or less doomed. Then, of course, they added that all of our ills were to be blamed on the people and policies of the other political party. It's difficult to remember another time when so many cheap shots were fired and so many uninformed statements made.

While all of this nonsense was taking place, the streets were filled with protesters of all ages in lawn chairs (apparently the preferred method of protest these days). Members of the Tea Party vied with members of Occupy Wall Street for media time.

But as I listened to their arguments, and in a couple of instances talked to members of these groups, it soon became apparent to me that none of them really knew what they were talking about. Their own situations may have ranged from difficult to wretched, but did the personal difficulties of some people mean that an entire country, all of the United States of America, was wretched as well? Was the United States really in as bad a shape as these people said it was?

From where I sit, as a senior fellow at the Milken Institute, a non-profit, nonpartisan, economic think tank (although the opinions in this book are entirely my own), and from my board-level relationship to The Wharton School's SEI Center for Advanced Studies in Management, I have access to an unusual array of data, facts, and other kinds of information, and, most importantly, to some of the most brilliant and insightful people in the world.

But I wasn't born yesterday; nor did I just start gathering information about the United States and its prospects. I have been an "economy watcher" most of my professional life and have studied the economy from the time I was in graduate school, including the period when I was a practicing international economist at the United Nations, the years when I covered economics and business at the *New York Times*, and the years I spent as editor-in-chief of the *Harvard Business Review*. I have authored or coauthored hundreds of articles and dozens of books on the global and US economy. Over the years I've interviewed hundreds of CEOs and other business executives and a wide range of leaders in politics and economics. If you talked to any of my colleagues or friends, they would tell you that understanding where the economy is headed has been a passion of mine. I love uncovering long- and short-term trends.

So, I decided to see if the assertions making their way through the public's collective consciousness were correct. Was America really out of time? Was our power waning? Was the debt really crippling us? Would China soon surpass us? Were we truly a spent power? Will our children be worse off than we are? Are our creative and innovative fires ebbing? And, of course, is it really true that we don't make anything here anymore?

Thankfully, the answer to all these questions is no. America is not a spent power, not by a long shot. In fact, as I hope this book shows, the United States is poised for what my mother used to call a "growth spurt." It is about to unleash its second American Century, to play on Henry Luce's famous phrase, and this second century is likely to be better than the first. Many people ask me where the country is headed. And as a result of all my fact finding and research, I can answer with a single word: "Up."

It goes without saying that America has plenty of problems. We need to do a much better job of educating kids from all economic backgrounds, to make sure they can earn decent livings and get ahead. We need to invest in our infrastructure, and collectively we could drop a few pounds, since obesity has become epidemic. But can you name a country that doesn't have problems? Problems are part of the human condition, and when they are solved, and barriers are removed, life gets better—and some smart person somewhere usually makes a buck. Because of the incentives our economic system offers, combined with our enterprising culture, I believe that if you could put America's problems on one side of a balance scale, and our opportunities on the other, the opportunities would carry the day. I'm not saying our problems will be cleaned up overnight, or that they will be easy to solve. What I am saying is that they will be solved over time.

I do not say this lightly. Nor have I always been an optimist. I believe the future will be rosy for America, rosier than for China, India, Russia, Brazil, most of Europe, and much of the world, because a lot of things have shifted in our favor. America may have talent, as the name of a popular TV show implies, but it also has resources, ability, and more than its share of luck. Simply put, the geographical area of the world we occupy is teeming with wealth—including massive quantities of energy and other rare and highly prized resources, such as solar and wind resources, bodies of water and waterways, forests, and some of the best arable land in the world.

After poring over spreadsheets filled with facts and digesting enough statistics to make me drowsy, I can report back with a very high level of confidence that America's best days are ahead of us and that, despite their bellyaching, our kids—*if they do the work and get a college education*—will have it better than we do. America is not about to lose its economic dominance.

The United States is not in decline—far from it. We may be temporarily, uh, hysterical, more than a little ill informed, occasionally wrong-headed, and sometimes outright nuts. But in decline? Like the sign says when you exit Brooklyn, *Forgetaboutit.*

Depending on how you read the numbers, and believe me, there are lots of ways to read them, the United States is either the world's largest manufacturer or about tied with China for the number-one spot. If you add up the value of everything made in the world each year by all 7 billion people living on the planet, Americans produce about 20 percent of all that *stuff.* Given that we are just 4.5 percent of the world's population, and China is 19 percent, that's quite an achievement. America's productivity, measured on a per capita basis, remains the world standard. China, India, Russia, and Brazil may work hard—well, maybe not Russia—but believe it or not, America works smart. America's top-tier factories are second to none.

But that's hardly the end of it. American companies manufacture huge quantities of a wide variety of products in other countries around the world, including China and the rest of Asia, Europe, Latin America, Africa, and Australia. Understanding the numbers behind these facts is tricky, so I'll give you some anecdotal evidence. Cincinnati-based Procter & Gamble manufactures products at more than fifty locations around the world as well as in the United States. Back-from-the-dead General Motors builds Vauxhalls in Britain; Opels in Germany; Holdens in Australia; and Jiefangs, Buicks, and Cadillacs in China and also assembles cars in Brazil, Mexico, and Canada, all in addition to what it makes in the United States. San Jose–based Intel manufactures its sophisticated computer chips in Israel, Ireland, China, Malaysia, Vietnam, and—of course—the United States. The list goes on. American companies grew inside the United States, and then they branched out and planted their flags around the world. We make a lot of things here, but we also make a lot *there*, if there means everywhere.

So why am I bringing this up? Because of the quirky way the statistics are kept. American companies produce 20 percent of the world's goods in the United States, *and perhaps as much as another 15 to 20 percent of the world's goods outside of our country.* That means that when you count up China's share of manufacturing, and compare it to ours, you are including in China's figures a lot of items made there by American firms doing business in China. The iPhones, iPods, Macs, and components made in China for Apple produce profits for the company in Cupertino, California.[1]

And, while the same is true in reverse, since dozens of non-US companies make things within our shores, the foreign share of America's manufacturing might is still smaller.

That means that while the United States produces 20 percent of the world's goods within our shores, American companies collectively produce somewhere between 30 and 40 percent of everything produced in the world. What's more, since a lot of the money these companies earn comes from their overseas operations, that cash stays offshore thanks to the idiotic way our companies are taxed. When our corporate tax laws are finally (hopefully) reformed, that money is likely to come rushing back to America. As a result, as this book will show, our corporations are sitting on an extraordinary amount of cash, and that cash is just waiting to be deployed.

The United States is a global power with an economy that long ago grew and expanded beyond our shores and now lies stretched out around the globe. No other country is as global as we are.

Let me illustrate what I mean. A couple of years ago I was asked to give a talk about globalization to an association of small- to medium-sized American companies called Vistage International. The group met in Boston that year, and there were leaders from roughly eight hundred companies in the audience.

I had dozens of PowerPoint slides focusing on global trade and investment, labor costs, the relative size of markets, investment opportunities, and so on. My guess is that almost everyone in the audience had read, at some point, *The World Is Flat*, by Tom Friedman—or another book like that. The leaders of these companies were very well informed.

At the beginning of my talk, I asked for a show of hands. "How many companies here are doing business internationally?" I asked. Surprisingly, almost every person in the room raised a hand. The group assembled in the room did not include General Electric or General Motors or IBM or Apple, or any other Fortune 50 or Fortune 500 company.

These were, for the most part, smaller companies headquartered in the northeastern part of the country or in New England. My guess is that out of the eight hundred companies represented, no more than a small handful had revenues of $1 billion or more. How could they all be global?

Rather than give a dry speech, I decided to make my session interactive, so I asked the people in the room to share with each other how they went global. The answer was simple. They read that there were opportunities around the world that they were not taking advantage of, and they went after them. Mostly, their main tool was the Internet. They used it to find partners, distributors, suppliers, and investors.

Members of the group volunteered their stories. A small industrial valve maker in Rhode Island distributed its products in Europe through a German valve maker that it found surfing the web. Europe wasn't this company's biggest market, the United States and Canada were, but its European sales were growing, despite the continent's slowdown. A surgical instrument maker outside of Boston sold its products in Asia through a distributor in Singapore that it also found on the web. Ditto for an automobile parts maker that sourced parts from Mexico.

By big company standards, these companies were small potatoes. But they illustrate a point. America's commercial culture is not sitting idly by, waiting to be overtaken. Big companies are proactive, and so are little ones. No American business is volunteering to go extinct. They are taking measures to succeed, and they are doing it on their own and without much fanfare. These companies have grit.

The fact is, American products and influence are everywhere—in people's homes, garages, and offices, in the skies, on the rails, in government buildings, and in their heads, thanks to our attainments in art, entertainment, literature, and music.

German, Canadian, and French students may throw rocks at the police during antiglobalization demonstrations, but they do it with American rock 'n' roll or rap on their iPhones and iPods, listening to their music using Beats headphones made by Dr. Dre. They wear Levi's jeans and Nike running shoes (the perfect shoes to wear when you're protesting against America) while digesting Big Macs and fries or Crunchwraps from Taco Bell. When they get home, they do their homework on Dell or Apple computers and take American medicines to make sure their police-inflicted bruises do not get infected. They do this while the police, who try to stop the demonstrations, talk on Motorola emergency radios, fly American-made helicopters, and— if need be—spray American-made pepper and tear gas to clear the gatherings.

I'm recounting all these rather bizarre facts for a reason. If American companies made everything in the United States that they sold, all 30 to 40 percent of the world's stuff, the rest of the world would not only be up in arms; it wouldn't have enough money to buy what we make. As it stands, even with many of our manufacturing plants distributed around the globe, depending on how you measure it, the US economy still accounts for between 21 and 23 percent of the world's gross domestic product (GDP). That's a pretty good measure of how well our 4.5 percent of the world's population is doing.[2]

Even so, a lot of our manufacturing is coming back to our shores. But don't expect the factories that we built in China or Malaysia or Mexico to come back the same as when they left. When new factories are built, or old ones are refurbished and expanded, they won't be the same labor-intensive places that went away. In the intervening years, manufacturing went to college—you might even say it studied abroad. The factories that are coming back home will be highly automated and amazingly productive, making very high-quality goods and getting them to customers sometimes within hours of when they are built. The people who work in these factories will have to have some college behind them or even a college degree. Brawn may be important at the gym or on the field, but it's no longer needed at industrial jobsites.

Of course, America's political candidates, along with the people protesting from their lawn chairs, don't seem to get any of this. Can a country with 4.5 percent of the world's population, that produces a quarter of the world's goods, really be a spent power?

Really? If you said yes, then please tell me how.

The fact is, it's not twilight in America. For years, a number of big, positive trends have been getting underway that were interrupted, but not stopped, by the so-called Great Recession and financial crisis. Some of those trends were happening off-camera and out of view. But they were happening. Other trends, like our newfound ability to exploit previously inaccessible reserves of oil and natural gas, are finally getting a little attention, but more as a curiosity than as a force that will transform our country and the world. The truth is, the United States is something akin to a laboratory experiment that more often than not produces the right result.

My purpose in this book is to separate fact from fiction and provide a realistic assessment of where America stands now and where it is going in a fast-changing world. I'm going to make the case for a second American Century by putting some important but often overlooked facts on the table, presenting them in a way that makes sense and that hopefully will enable you to see things in a new light. Here is just one of those facts: American businesses are sitting on some $4 trillion in cash that is waiting to be invested in a productive way when the time is right. To put this in perspective, that amount is equal to the entire GDP of Germany, the world's fourth-largest economy. That's how much money our companies have in the bank.[3]

Facts alone, however, do not make for much of a story. Over the years I've met many incredible "only-in-America" type people, and I tell their story as a way that I think illustrates my thesis in a vivid, personal way.

Most of all, though, this book is meant to be an antidote to all of those self-serving naysayers who repeat, sometimes without thinking and sometimes to further their own selfish causes, that our best days are behind us. As my immigrant father used to say, "no one ever made a plugged nickel betting against the USA." That was true when he arrived on our shores, and it is certainly true now.

MY PERSPECTIVE

I've spent years analyzing and reporting on the economy, the markets, and business, looking, in particular, for our strengths and weaknesses. What's clear, after painstakingly assessing our prospects over a long period of time, is that all the talk about the imminent collapse of the United States is not only baseless, it's dead wrong. We've all heard the arguments before, for at least a hundred years, as a matter of fact. They were as wrongheaded and false a century ago as they are today.

Even so, doom saying is big business. Since the collapse of the housing markets and the Great Recession of 2008, there have been articles, books, and websites ad nauseum devoted to future depressions. Since 2008, forecasters of one type or another—most self-taught— have predicted that depressions like the one we experienced after the 1929 stock-market collapse would occur in 2009, 2010, 2011, 2012, and 2013.

One of those doomsayers, Gerald Celente, publisher of *Trends Journal*, wrote that the economy would fall into a depression in 2011, and when that didn't happen, simply moved his prediction to 2012. Other doomsayers, such as Harry S. Dent, have written scores of books over the decades forecasting economic collapse. One of them, A. Gary Shilling, an economist and beekeeper, has been writing about economic catastrophe since at least the 1980s.[4]

With so much political negativity, and with the specter of the economic and financial crises of 2008 still lingering (I call that period a Rich Man's Depression, for reasons I will explain later in this book), Americans are understandably nervous and find it difficult to trust their leaders. As a result, they have gone from optimistic to wary about the future.

As they commute to and from work in their cars, many find the airwaves clogged with the rants of media hosts who like to frighten their listeners with nonsensical charges against our leaders. True, some of our leaders justifiably deserve our scorn—especially those who distort facts for their own purposes, or whose only ambition is for themselves, not the country, or those who use their office for their own gain.

But the combined effect of our negative, politically polarized media and our say-anything-to-get-votes form of politics is taking its toll. In 2011, a CNN poll showed that 48 percent of Americans thought a 1930s-style Great Depression, with unemployment above 20 percent, was imminent.[5]

Such negativity has even given rise to a weird new movement— doomsday preppers. These sad, terrified people are hoarding food, water, weapons, and ammo in advance of what they believe to be the coming economic, political, and/or ecological catastrophe. The National Geographic channel has gotten high ratings for a reality TV show that follows these people as they make their preparations. It also shows how "preppers" practice fleeing their residences—"bugging out," in prepper's parlance—to take safety in makeshift underground or remote locations.

Not everyone is panicked like the preppers, and not everyone thinks a depression is imminent. But a great many people are scared stiff by what they read and what they hear.

Badmouthing the future is not a crime. Neither is fear-mongering. If it were, our prisons would be even fuller, starting with Glenn Beck. But while it isn't a crime, in my view, hell has a special region reserved for media hosts who terrify their audiences with fantasies and paranoid lies and then try to sell them investments in gold and remote parcels of land where they will never be found.

America is strong. Anyone who objectively looks across the world's economic horizon knows this. In many ways it is even insulated from all those economic troubles abroad—Europe's debt crisis and Asia's potential for a slowdown. It is my view that even in an ailing world, America will grow stronger still—significantly so, for reasons I will explain.

The United States is far from a spent power, and while our problems are real, they are manageable. This is not just my opinion. Numbers and trends back up my claims. America is a wealthy, accomplished, dynamic country, and it is better positioned to shape the future than any other nation on earth. Not that we can rest on our laurels. But the facts are the facts.

One reason is the luck of geography and geology, but not all of it is luck. Our strengths are immense. In our downwardly spiraling discussions about our fate, we have done the economic equivalent of mistaking weather for climate. There may be economic clouds in the sky today, and perhaps a few tomorrow, but the clouds are fleeting and the long-term outlook is bright. In fact, the farther out in time we focus our gaze, the better it looks.

There are four transformational forces that I believe will propel the United States to new heights. They have been mostly overlooked in the gloomy aftermath of the 2008 financial disaster and in our contentious, overly partisan hair-pulling and debates. Other countries have one or two of these forces working in their favor. Only the United States has all four.

We have a choice. We can wring our hands—or we can open our eyes. And if we do the latter, we will be pleased with what we see. To build on Henry Luce's famous phrase, we are heading into the second American Century, and the wind is at our backs.

▼▼▼▼

When people accuse the United States of no longer making anything, it is largely because what we make they don't see—or don't often buy. The United States no longer makes flip flops or beach balls or frills. We're not like China—we make very little clothing, not many shoes, and hardly any toys—especially those tainted with arsenic or lead.

What we make are electric generators and gas turbines, jetliners and bulldozers, trucks, cranes, military goods, software, and computer products. We make medical devices, pharmaceuticals, and instruments for analyzing your heart, blood, and genes. We make all kinds of radar equipment. America makes fertilizers, pesticides, and plastics—some of which it even makes from soybeans and corn. We make fewer vehicles than China—although a lot of what China makes would not be allowed on our roads—but more vehicles than Japan, Germany, and South Korea. We make twice as many tractors as Japan, three times as many as Italy, and almost five times more than China. We are the largest producer of electricity from wind. America produces food and exports more of it than any other nation in the world. The list of what America makes is long.

Americans are—at the time of this writing—remotely driving a six-wheeled, 2,000-pound truck that is filled with lab equipment, powered by a plutonium power source, and carrying lasers, ovens, science experiments, and imaging devices of all types, and this truck is on the surface of Mars, roughly 350 million miles away. At the same time, rocket entrepreneurs in California, New Mexico, and Florida are sending payloads to the International Space Station orbiting the earth. These relatively inexpensive rockets are based on new designs.

The products I just listed are only a tiny fraction of what America makes. People actually need what America makes, and they need those things rain or shine. In many cases, America is the only place in the world where you can buy certain types of goods and services.

But because the average American doesn't buy gas turbines, or firefighting helicopters, or Abrams tanks, or jet fighters, they mindlessly repeat the phrase, "We don't make anything here anymore." Let's banish this phrase from daily usage, and especially in the media, because it's simply not true.

But even more importantly, we are likely to make much more than this in America soon, because it is the new "best place" to locate factories, as a result of productivity, cost, access to markets, quality, creativity, and our newly accessible reserves of abundant, cheap, relatively clean energy.

FOUR FORCES OF CHANGE

Over the years, most of what I wrote about the American economy in books, articles, columns, and blogs (not to mention on Facebook) was about the headwinds we faced. In fact, my late colleague at the *New York Times*, William Safire, in his *On Language* column in the *New York Times Magazine*, credited me with coining the term "economic headwinds."[6] That's how deeply the concept resonated with me. In fact, when I left my job as a business editor and columnist at the *Times* to become editor-in-chief of the *Harvard Business Review*, one of my colleagues stood on a desk in the newsroom during my farewell party and read the titles of a few of my books, columns, and articles—*The Decline and Crash of the American Economy*, *The Death of Money*, "Dancing Past the Recession," "Eating Our Seed Corn," and so on down the list. The laughter was uproarious as people thought about the gloominess of my outlook. And yet, those books, articles, and columns, *at the time*, turned out to be much more true than false.

I mention all this because it still feels a little odd for me to write a book of outright optimism, especially when so many other people—*people who are supposed to know these things*—think we are headed toward some form of economic abyss. And yet, my facts are correct.

In my view, the United States, a nation so many of us consider *favored* (though probably for different reasons), is about to be favored again for the following reasons:

1. *Soaring levels of creativity*—No other country in the world, in such a short time, has created so many scientific, technological, industrial, commercial, financial, and artistic innovations. Not only has America's creativity changed science and business, it has changed world culture.

2. *Massive new energy reserves*—America is headed for energy independence around 2020, and it is on track to be a net energy exporting nation by 2025.[7] These new sources of energy can be used as fuels or turned into products. Imagine a future in which oil and natural gas wealth flows to our shores and not to the Middle East, Russia, or Venezuela.

3. *Gigantic amounts of capital*—As a result of the Great Recession, business has renegotiated its debt, and businesses and individuals have become ultraconservative with capital. Trillions of dollars of investment funds are in private hands, waiting for the go-ahead to be deployed.

4. *Unrivaled manufacturing depth*—America makes a myriad of things, and now it will make more as businesses move to the United States to take advantage of abundant energy and capital and to tap into our vast reserves of intelligence and creativity.

Think about it. Israel is a creative nation that just found large deposits of natural gas, but it is a small country without much capital and without much expertise in manufacturing or commerce. Canada has energy and capital, and it is blessed with some of the world's most creative entrepreneurs, but it has a small population, and most of its manufacturing is pointed south, at the United States. Canada makes great components, but hardly any finished products. Japan has capital and people, and it's great at manufacturing, but it hasn't proved to be a creative country, and it has no energy resources at all. China has resources and capital, but it hasn't shown itself to be creative, and its manufacturing sector, while large, is nowhere near as efficient or as advanced as ours. In addition, most of its new energy reserves are in areas where water is scarce, and water is needed to tease natural gas and oil out of rock. Europe has some resources, and some small, wonderful concentrations of creativity, but it has hardly any entrepreneurs, and it has uneven manufacturing depth. Moreover, its capital is not readily accessible. I could go on.

Creativity is important. If it wasn't, no one would marvel at Apple, or be impressed with innovations from Pfizer, IBM, Tesla, or

Boeing. If it wasn't, no one would listen to our rock 'n' roll, rap, and country and western songs; watch our movies and TV shows; or come to the United States to study or work.

I doubt creativity is in our genes. We're too diverse a nation to say that anything about America is in our genes. But creativity is in our culture. In the Cold War, Russia trained many genius-level scientists and mathematicians, many with an innovative bent. But it wasn't until they immigrated to the United States, Israel, or Canada that they were able to shine in biotech, engineering, or information technology, or—dare I say it—in the backrooms of Wall Street, where they created so many of those algorithms used by investment and hedge funds.

To be sure, the United States is a big country, and other factors are also at play, with many that are not all that positive. But if we are prudent, and if we apply a little wisdom to the task, we will watch the United States soar.

Let me explain a little more about the forces I am referring to by taking a visit to what I call the innovation corridor.

CHAPTER ONE

A STROLL THROUGH THE INNOVATION CORRIDOR

Come walk with me . . .

If we proceed southwest on Third Street, which until recently was an empty, overgrown-with-weeds street in the Kendall Square area of Cambridge, Massachusetts, we will see the future laid out before our eyes. The old rubber and metal-bending factories in this part of town are long gone—bulldozed flat forty years ago to make way for a giant National Aeronautics and Space Administration research facility that was planned and laid out, but never built. Interest in returning to the moon waned, budget deficits grew, and, let's face it, America has always been a country with a preposterously short attention span.

For decades, this crumbling area of Kendall Square was known for its vacant lots, food trucks, and gritty brick warehouses. And yet, it is adjacent to the sprawling campus of the Massachusetts Institute of Technology. MIT, with its (how shall I put this?) less-than-gorgeous jumble of geeky, radar-domed buildings, is one of the world's greatest, if not the greatest, and most selective research universities. Separating MIT from the empty lots of Third Street were rotting plywood fences covered with notices for lost dogs and apartments for rent. You could find neighborhoods that looked like this in any old, eastern-seaboard city.

And then something remarkable happened. This Cambridge neighborhood became home to a new wave of American-led innovation that is transforming the world. Many different factors drove this transformation—including advances in digital, robotic, space, and aeronautic technology. But my tour will focus on just one aspect of what is now taking shape—the biomedical corridor.

That means I will ignore Amazon's newly leased 100,000 square feet of research space, and Google's 40,000 square feet of research space, and Microsoft's, IBM's, and Nokia's research centers. These are the still-vibrant remnants of a previous age of American-led invention and creativity. That era spawned a myriad of software and hardware companies, chip developers, the Internet, the electronic economy, ATMs, smartphones, GPS, electron microscopes, and a multitude of "apps." For the United States, most of that is now a little less than cutting edge.

What's going on now is different from what went on in the 1990s. What is taking place now in the Kendall Square area of Cambridge, a city of just 100,000 people across the Charles River from Boston, is happening on a new level. And if in previous eras America's ferocious creative outbursts changed the world, well, you ain't seen nothing yet. Not by a long shot.

A HOTBED OF RESEARCH

The empty lots in the area around Third Street—the few that remain— are now surrounded by millions of square feet of new construction. Not the type of construction you would find just anywhere. The buildings built on these lots are crammed with high-tech laboratories and billions of dollars' worth of equipment. More importantly, these buildings are not staffed by Boston's version of *The Office*, but with some of the world's smartest, most creative and driven scientists. A new generation of innovators is in charge. So far they have been largely ignored, as we Americans ignorantly deride ourselves about our fading powers of innovation and our lost prominence in the world.

Here's what I mean.

If we continue walking in Kendall Square toward the Charles River, we come to the gleaming, environmentally friendly (LEED-Platinum certified), glass and steel, 344,000-square-foot, twelve-story research and corporate headquarters of the Genzyme Corporation. With 12,000 employees, a large number of them scientists, it is one of the biggest and most productive biotechnology firms in the world. Working there are hundreds of MDs and PhDs, almost all of whom have done academic work beyond their lofty degrees. In addition, there are large handfuls of what they call *dual-degree* people who earned *both* an MD and a PhD, sometimes simultaneously. These people might not get the kind of airplay that Honey Boo Boo or the Kardashians get, but they are pushing the frontiers of invention. These dual-degree folks are the kind of people who add advanced work in engineering, mathematics, chemistry, biology, computer science, and other subjects to their already formidable medical degrees. And, while we worry out loud about our neighbors who can't find Kansas on a map, the United States has more dual-degree researchers than any other country on earth. In fact, the United States still leads the world when it comes to the number of *qualified* (as opposed to people who simply studied a subject) engineers, computer scientists, mathematicians, chemists, and other technical professionals.[1]

In 2011, Genzyme was acquired by the world's fourth-largest pharmaceutical company, the French firm Sanofi, for what would ultimately be $20 billion. Why such a high price for a company that had less than $5 billion in revenue, and a little over $420 million in net income, when Sanofi bought it? "That's the cost of moving to Cambridge," said Chris Viehbacher, Sanofi's chief executive.

My interpretation of Viehbacher's remark, and remarks made by other leaders I talked to at other major pharmaceutical and biotech companies, is that the United States is undeniably ahead of every other country when it comes to research relating to human, animal, and plant biology and the ability to turn that research into practical products. That lead—the result of our long-term investments in our colleges and universities—will affect other sectors of the economy, thereby creating jobs. As more researchers are employed at Cambridge (and at other American innovation hubs), thanks to domestic and foreign investment in America's innovators, gains will continue to cascade through the economy. That will happen when our most talented and inventive thinkers purchase or rent places to live, buy cars, eat out at restaurants, shop in supermarkets, attend movies, and send their kids to school. We don't all have to be MD- or PhD-level researchers to benefit from the rush to invest in the United States.

Cambridge real estate may be pricey, but that's not what Viehbacher meant. What he meant was that no other country in the world has come close to matching the brainpower, creativity, and boldness that presently exist in the United States. No other country has invested so much money in its scientific elite—many of them foreign born—and in its homegrown students as well. No other country has been as successful in breaking down barriers between academic departments, and thereby promoting the kind of multidisciplinary collaboration that produces innovation. "The universe, and life, are not organized by departments the way our universities are. God does not have a separate department of physics, biology, chemistry, and mathematics," the mathematician and inventor R. Buckminster Fuller once told me decades ago. "So, if everything works together, why do we separate it into different disciplines when we get to school?"

In addition, no other country has been as successful as we have in eradicating the boundaries between academic science and business— which explains why so many companies support MIT and other American research universities, and why that's not the case in, say, Europe. And no other country has come close to getting as much for its money and its efforts in these collaborations as the United States.

Though we chastise ourselves constantly and pick over our flaws, particularly (and justifiably) with regard to the shameful state of public primary and secondary education, America's major universities, including large state universities and elite private colleges, remain (with few exceptions) the best in the world. (This explains why about 764,000 foreign students are hard at work studying at our universities.)

It's not that other countries don't have excellent schools for, say, computer science. Most major, developed countries have a school or two with a very credible reputation and a strong faculty. But the claim to fame of American universities is that they pretty much invented, or greatly expanded, the fields in which they teach. Researchers in the United Kingdom may have been early pioneers in the development of computers, jet engines, and biology, but the most advanced work in these fields is taking place in the United States.

In 2012, when *US News & World Report* ranked the world's top twenty-five schools for computer science, the top five were

American—MIT, Stanford, Carnegie Mellon, the University of California at Berkeley, and Harvard. Of the remaining twenty schools, half were located in the United States.[2] And if you take any other technical field—such as engineering, biology, or medicine—the rankings are equally skewed toward the United States.

Given that we account for a very small percentage of the global population (4.5 percent, as mentioned in the Introduction), it's amazing that so many of the world's best schools are here. And yet, it is because of these schools that the United States continues to be the world's most formidable science-and-technology superpower. Keeping our scientific lead intact will protect our economic lead as well.

In fact, our economy is built on science and technology, and it will continue to be built on science and technology, which are the country's true engines of growth and among its most important advantages—I will get into our other advantages later. In addition, it's not just *that* we do science, it's *how* we do science that gives the United States this formidable edge.

The United States has accomplished a lot scientifically, but the good news is that the era of science-based creativity is just getting started. The world is at the beginning of a new period of invention, and the United States has already taken the lead. It has done so by pulling in investment, such as Sanofi's; by attracting talented investigators from around the world; and by producing marketable products. And, although not everything is rosy—it costs more to produce a drug, for example, than it ever did before, and the chances of failing are higher than in the past—the bio-pharma industry is aware of its problems and is tackling them. Besides, as I will discuss in later chapters, the scientific elite of the United States is doing work that is much harder and more complex than ever before and that requires more people than ever before to accomplish. If you're making a fourth-generation antibiotic, that's hard. But if you're trying to eradicate, or even reverse, Alzheimer's disease, that's *really* hard. It requires bringing together experts from dozens of different disciplines.

The bio-pharma sector is but one area of the economy where the United States not only leads, but is advancing its lead. And, despite what the pundits and politicians say, despite their arguments and misremembered or misapplied statistics, despite all the doom-and-gloom talk, the United States is not falling behind, it is moving farther ahead. This is not wishful thinking, and I am not being Pollyannaish. I am simply stating the facts, as I will show.

SCIENCE MEETS BUSINESS

Cambridge's Genzyme has pioneered the development of genetically based cancer treatments as well as treatments for kidney diseases, autoimmune diseases, and many other maladies that befall us. It is saving lives today by making medicines using advanced genetic-engineering techniques that until recently existed only in the minds of a few science-fiction writers.

Genzyme's roots are similar to those of many other American companies. It was founded by George Whitesides, a distinguished academic chemist from Harvard University (a ten-minute bicycle ride from Kendall Square and MIT), and Sheridan Snyder, a venture capital pioneer. The firm was awarded the National Medal of Technology by President George W. Bush in 2005. And yet, despite the accolades and profits, the company has never slowed down. In fact, one of the reasons Sanofi purchased Genzyme was to use its creativity and dynamism to transform the culture of Sanofi itself—to infuse this smart-but-staid French pharmaceutical company with a little American juice. By purchasing Genzyme, Sanofi acquired, if not a new corporate research center, an important driver of new ways of thinking.

▼▼▼▼

If we walk a little farther down Third Street, with its new layers of asphalt and its freshly painted traffic lanes (including mandatory bicycle lanes), we pass a number of new restaurants and cafés where there were none before. These places capture the creative electricity of the area, with names like Za, Evoo, Kika, and Voltage. For the first time in this part of Cambridge, there is a café culture, albeit one that embodies the intellectual spirit of Kendall Square. Here, you can see gray-haired Nobel Prize winners conversing with young researchers and entrepreneurs while they sip lattes and eat designer pizzas. To create a syllogism worthy of tests like the SAT (I am talking about MIT, after all), the restaurants on Third Street are to the geeks and nerds of Kendall Square what the Ivy, The Grill on the Alley, and Craft are to the sharks of Hollywood, and what Les Deux Margots, Le Dome, and the Café Montmartre were to the writers and artists of Paris. These are places where a lot of things get done: concepts and ideas are developed, refined, and exchanged, and wisdom is passed down—in an informal way. Sipping double espressos with your mentor, or downing a few craft beers with a colleague, is how a great deal of knowledge is transferred.

As we walk past these restaurants, we turn right onto Main Street. There, you might notice some not-very-mature trees and shrubs in front of the gleaming, ten-story McGovern Institute for Brain Research at MIT. The institute represents the first installment on a $350 million gift from high-tech publishing pioneer Patrick J. McGovern and his wife, Lore Harp McGovern. The aim of the institute is to accelerate neurological research around the world from a base in Cambridge (institutes in China and Europe are also being planned), and to do it in an interdisciplinary way. Creative investigators have the resources they need to make gains against diseases affecting the brain and to push forward our understanding of how the brain works. About a third of the institute's principal investigators—its highest-level scientists—moved to Cambridge from other parts of the world to pursue their work. They will form an important part of President Barack Obama's initiative to map and understand how our brains work.

Figure 1.1. The McGovern Institute for Brain Research at MIT, in a once rundown part of Cambridge, Massachusetts. Ed Brodzinsky.

Behind the McGovern Institute is the fifteen-story, ultra-modern, 180,000-square-foot brick and glass building where the David H. Koch Institute for Integrative Cancer Research at MIT is located.

Say what you will about the Koch brothers and their Tea Party politics, David's new research facility brings together about six hundred of the best research scientists from around the world in a variety of disciplines to defeat cancer in creative new ways at the cellular and genetic levels. At a recent meeting, Koch told me that the institute is nicknamed the "happy building" by the scientists who work there because budgets are almost unlimited, the twenty-five main labs are the best in the world, the teams of investigators are interdisciplinary, and the outcomes will have so much impact on so many people's lives. "People who work in the building," Koch said, "are just happy to be there to pursue their work." Having talked to several researchers working at the Koch Institute, I got the impression that he is right.

As we continue our walk, we come to an elegant and tastefully designed five-story, smoke-colored building, the Broad Institute of MIT and Harvard. This center began with a $400 million gift from Eli and Edythe Broad. Eli is a determined, trim, gray-haired, Los Angeles–based entrepreneur who is known for getting his way despite his soft-spoken demeanor. He built a thriving homebuilding company, which he sold, then bought and sold an insurance company. The Broads are multibillionaires who have as their goal giving away all of their money before they die, and doing it in bold, thoughtful, high-impact ways.

The institute's aim is not exactly modest—it is to transform medicine. And the institute is doing this by intensifying collaboration between different branches of science. One of its six areas of focus[3]—I love how it is stated—is the following: "*Assemble a complete picture of the molecular components of life*"—which is quite an ambitious goal. Another area of focus is also audacious: "*Transform the process of therapeutic discovery and development.*" Because creativity is central to the institute's efforts, the Broads have insisted that, in addition to its team of scientists, a full-time artist be in residence at the institute. What's the role of an artist at a scientific institute like this one? It's to provide an example for the others who work there—to remind them that creativity takes many forms, pursues many paths, and, perhaps most importantly, is open to new ideas and influences. But an even bigger thought is this: true creativity, whether in science or the arts, means having the courage to take risks. As an inspiration, another Broad philanthropic effort, the Broad Art Foundation, has one of the best art collections in the world, which it lends to museums and art institutes.

The Broad Institute partners with Harvard's five affiliated hospitals and with other hospitals and research centers around the country. Under its founding director, Eric Lander, a professor of biology at MIT, it is at the forefront of the drive to develop "precision medicine," where every person's treatment will be unique, based on their own DNA.

Thanks to the National Institutes of Health, based in Bethesda, Maryland, and other funders, researchers at universities around the country, with a large group in Kendall Square, are pushing science in the same direction. And they are getting results. In 2003, when the Human Genome Project was completed, it took thirteen years and $3 billion to produce a map of a person's full complement of DNA. Today, a similar analysis takes hours, and DNA sequencing is rapidly coming down in price. Two new companies, GnuBio in Cambridge and Ion Torrent Systems in Connecticut, are in the process of introducing machines that can sequence a person's DNA for about $1,000. Not only that, but GnuBio's machine is small enough to fit on a desktop—a far cry from the vast and elaborate laboratory resources required to sequence genes in 2003.

Ion Torrent and GnuBio illustrate just how powerful this new wave of invention will be. Whereas Moore's Law dictates that silicon chips double their computing power every eighteen months, today's gains in the biosciences exceed that pace. That's why the cost of sequencing a person's genome has gone from $3 billion to $1,000, and from thirteen years to hours. It's also the reason why the Broad Institute's success in attaining its goals—assembling a complete picture of the molecular components of life and transforming the process of therapeutic discovery and development—could soon be at hand.

Think about the power of those goals. If the underlying molecular biology of life is fully understood, and the treatment model shifts accordingly, not only will many—or even most—diseases finally be understood, they will succumb to treatment. At that point, doctors wielding tricorders, like the one used to diagnose and treat diseases by the character Bones in the original *Star Trek*, might become a reality. In the new spirit of invention, the San Diego–based $20 billion telecommunications company Qualcomm is offering a $10 million prize to the first researcher to develop one: the competition envisions an instrument like a tricorder that would be "capable of capturing key health metrics and diagnosing a set of 15 diseases."[4]

▼▼▼▼

If we continue walking past the Koch and Broad institutes, we come to the Ragon Institute, a collaboration between MIT, Harvard, and Massachusetts General Hospital (one of the five hospitals affiliated with Harvard), where investigators are working day and night to create an AIDS vaccine. Then, if we turn right on Broadway, we will walk by the Whitehead Institute for Biomedical Research, which collaborates closely with the Broad Institute and has conducted breakthrough research on Alzheimer's, Parkinson's, diabetes, and certain cancers.

As we walk, we will also pass the Cambridge Innovation Center, which is where dozens of high-tech software and biology-based startups are housed. These early-stage companies operate from tiny offices, most with glass walls. They share conference space and other common areas in an effort to foster collaboration and what they call "fast-flow" innovation. More than a hundred companies have gone from fledgling startup to commercialization at the Cambridge Innovation Center, between them raising a total of $1.7 billion.

During a recent visit to the center, I listened to a demo by a would-be entrepreneur who was a neuroscientist at one of MIT's many labs. She showed me her new product—a cap that scans your brain and reads your mood. The device is designed to learn a person's likes and dislikes. And, though it is not exactly a product designed to save the world, like the ideas coming out of the labs at the Broad Institute, for instance, it is designed to make money. "Our market," the inventor said, "is advertising agencies and marketers who want to know in an unbiased way if they are reaching customers with their products and messages."

A hundred companies may seem like a lot to incubate at once, but it is not as many as MIT has incubated already. Since it was founded a century and a half ago, MIT has produced alumni who have started

25,800 companies, producing a total of $2 trillion in annual revenues, and employing 3.3 million people worldwide[5] in a variety of fields, from aviation to telecommunications, computers, and the biosciences. Collectively, these companies (among them Hewlett-Packard, Qualcomm, Texas Instruments, Analog Devices, and the Bose Corporation) are making our lives better and the world a more productive place.

None of this was happenstance, by the way; it was planned. If you read a paper called "Science, the Endless Frontier"[6] by the late Vannevar Bush, a professor at MIT who headed the Office of Scientific Research and Development during World War II, you get an inkling of just how important science was viewed as being. It was seen as an engine of economic growth and overall prosperity as well as a key component of national defense.

During World War II, Bush, a tall, lean man who was the son of a Unitarian minister, was one of the few people who reported directly to President Franklin D. Roosevelt, a good indicator of how important science was to Roosevelt. Not only did his office oversee the Manhattan Project, but it also promoted medical research, especially with regard to battlefield wounds, and the development of jets, rocketry, and radar. In 1945, when the war ended, Bush wrote a paper, first published in *The Atlantic*, which was eerie in its prescience. The paper, called "As We May Think," described a network that would give people unlimited access to knowledge in almost any subject, linking together the world's libraries. It was a pre-computer-era view of what would become the Internet and World Wide Web.

Bush, who also founded Raytheon, the gigantic aerospace company, argued passionately for what we now call "STEM education"—science, technology, engineering, and math. In "Science, the Endless Frontier," he sketched out a plan to use higher education and advanced research to propel the American economy forward. Not only has Bush's plan been working well for MIT for decades, but similar plans, like the one for California's universities that led to the establishment of Silicon Valley, are based on it. Far from being a cost, which is the way too many people think about education, preparing students for careers in science and technology, and educating them at the highest level, is an investment that never fails to pay off.

▼▼▼▼

If, as we walk, we take a two-block detour to Ames Street, we come upon the MIT Media Lab, which, despite its name, conducts inter-disciplinary research into computers, software, biology, and brain science as well as media. The Media Lab is in a constant state of evo-lution and has a new leader, Joichi Ito, who does not exactly have a traditional college professor's credentials. Ito is a college dropout who became a venture-capital investor. He lists among his major accomplishments the fact that he spent years as a "guild leader" for players of the online game World of Warcraft. His appointment to head such an important lab is not just controversial. It shows that MIT is willing to take risks in a quintessentially American way, unlike similar insti-tutions in other countries. It also signals MIT's willingness to go in an entirely new direction if the new world of innovation requires it.

What is that new direction? Rather than assembling a group of scientists and researchers and bringing them into the lab, Ito wants to turn the lab into the center of a web of creativity so that the world's most talented people can collaborate on Media Lab projects wherever they may be. It is a given that not all of these talented people will be in Massachusetts. Massachusetts, after all, is a small state. It's also true that not all these people will be from the United States. But what is true is that the network will be managed from Cambridge, and that the benefits of these networks of collaborators will flow through MIT.

WHAT'S UNDERWAY

Since 2002, 4 million square feet of new research and office space have been built in the Kendall Square area. In addition, $3.2 billion in new construction is in development or underway, which will add almost 4 million additional square feet of space for companies, re-search centers, and new MIT buildings.[7] At the time of this writing, eight massive construction projects were underway in the area around Third Street. All of this indicates the strength of this new chapter of American-led innovation.

One of those construction projects is for Novartis, the giant Swiss pharmaceutical company, the third-largest pharmaceutical company in the world. The largest new building is the Alexandria Center, which will house, among other companies, Biogen Idec. In addition, the Novartis research complex is being expanded as the company continues to move its research headquarters to Cambridge, from Basel, Switzerland. Why move nearly all its researchers to Cambridge? "The main reason is the availability of talent and the closeness to top academic institutions," Daniel Vasella, the company's former chairman and former chief executive, told me.

Sanofi, of course, is also moving researchers to Cambridge so they will be nearer to Genzyme. And Pfizer, the world's largest pharmaceutical company, is building a new, $300 million research facility in Cambridge not far from Sanofi and Novartis.

Next to these large buildings is something that is still rare in the aftermath of the 2008 financial crisis, a speculative project to build laboratory space that companies can lease when they run out of their own space, need to create a "skunk works," or are just starting up. Even with so much building going on, there remains a shortage of research labs in Cambridge.

Figure 1.2. Novartis's new Institute for Biomedical Research, part of the company's $600 million investment in Cambridge, Massachusetts. Used with permission of the photographer.

Near these construction sites is the world headquarters for Biogen Idec, a global biotech company founded in Switzerland by a group that included an American Nobel Prize–winning chemist. Biogen Idec moved its research facilities to Cambridge shortly after its founding, and later moved its headquarters there as well.

A little farther down the street is the world headquarters of Millennium Pharmaceuticals, now part of Japan's Takeda Pharmaceuticals. Millennium is a pioneer biotech company that uses computer modeling to develop new, exquisitely complex molecules for drugs.

In this little part of the world there are more than 250 vibrant startups, in addition to the big companies. Most are members of the Massachusetts Biotech Council—working feverishly, as startups do, to bring new products to market in a variety of fields relating to biology.

Like all "clusters" of expertise and ingenuity, the biosciences corridor that formed in Cambridge follows certain rules. Michael Porter, a professor at Harvard Business School, spent much of his illustrious career studying how these clusters form over time.[8] The process typically begins when new knowledge is employed, usually by a company working in a specific field. That company—perhaps a family-owned business—might do its own research, or it might utilize existing research in a way that gives it an advantage over its rivals. One of the clusters Porter studied was in Italy, where a number of firms manufacture looms and related products.

Competitive knowledge is then transferred when an employee— say it's the son of the founder—thinks he can do a much better job with something than his old man has been doing. He broods on it, he plots, he schemes, he goes to a distant uncle or a faraway bank for money, and then he quits and starts a rival firm.

The son's new ideas are now put into play and the new company grows. Then, as is usually the case, people working at the new company become disenchanted with what they begin to see as the son's old-fashioned ideas. They plot, they scheme, they go to their faraway uncles and banks to raise money, and they start their own firm. The number of firms grows through this process, and people move to the area to take advantage of the growth. As that happens, banks move into the region, and so do lawyers and consultants and accountants. Startup by startup, knowledge is transferred and enhanced at a slow but steady pace.

I'm not doing justice to Porter's theories in this quick summation, but you get the idea. Now, consider what's happening in Cambridge. Instead of an individual, or a small company, developing the knowledge, you have MIT, Harvard, Tufts, Boston University, and so on. In addition, there are all those research centers operated by global pharmaceutical and biotech companies. The area has an extremely well developed financial center, and is teeming with lawyers, consultants, and experts of all sorts.

The concentration of talent and resources in the Boston-Cambridge area, not to mention in the rest of the country, is astounding. But even more important, instead of having to plot and scheme, the universities in the area have long ago come to the conclusion that it is in everybody's interest for their most gifted researchers to take time off from their academic responsibilities to start companies. Not only that, the schools—which typically take a piece of the proceeds from inventions developed in their labs—make money by doing so. And then there are the big biotech and pharmaceutical companies in the area, which sometimes seed new companies with their own talent, or buy companies started by others. Almost all of the big pharmaceutical companies operating in the area have venture capital operations that invest money into startups. This takes the old, slow-paced model of how areas develop and attaches rockets to it.

Keeping the door open between universities and businesses is something Americans do really well. And it serves us well not just in the biotech corridor, but in other areas of the country and in other sectors of the economy. The massive flow of ideas and people between institutions of one kind or another, startups, established companies, and academic and research institutions accelerates change and innovation. It also has the capability of creating strong growth. And, while other countries have tried to replicate what takes place in Cambridge or Silicon Valley—the Chinese, for example—most of these attempts have failed.

Although it's true that some countries have been able to transfer knowledge between universities and business, none of these countries have been able to match our heated level of knowledge transfer. But even if academics in other countries were willing to work with commercial interests, no other country possesses our uniquely American advantage—a pragmatic, highly entrepreneurial, individualist culture.

German, Japanese, and French workers are just as smart as their American counterparts. But they don't storm out of their places of employment to start new companies, confident that sometime in the foreseeable future they will create something bigger, better, and more valuable than the company that employed them. Except for a very small handful of people, researchers in other countries don't mortgage their homes, max out their credit cards, and beg money from their friends to form companies dedicated to commercializing their ideas. That's America's unique form of chutzpah, and it will keep America number one.

But there's more.

ECONOMIC IMPACTS

If we bicycle across the bridge from Cambridge into Boston, a ten-minute journey, our first stop will be Massachusetts General Hospital, a Harvard partner. Mass General, as it is called, is where the ENCODE project was managed. ENCODE, which stands for "Encyclopedia of DNA Elements,"[9] mapped 80 percent of the so-called "junk DNA" in our cells and found that, far from being junk, these strands of genetic material control a host of biological functions. When they go wrong, disease results.

Using the equivalent of 350 years of computer time at 32 research centers around the world, the project, funded by the National Institutes of Health, found 4 million on-and-off switches in our cells that control for normal traits that contribute to our health as well as abnormal ones that cause problems. This project will be yielding insights into our biology for decades.

Near Kendall Square are Harvard University, Boston University, and BU's research and medical complex. Tufts University, with its medical school and research labs, is also nearby. A little farther away are Brandeis University, Northeastern University, and the Boston campus of the University of Massachusetts. All of these are world-class research facilities that collaborate with each other and with other research centers around the country.

Radiating out farther from Cambridge, there are manufacturing plants around the state and the country as well as around the world producing important life-saving drugs based on the findings of the researchers working in the area around MIT. Collectively, the companies in this small section of Cambridge produce and sell hundreds of billions of dollars' worth of products and employ tens of thousands of people in the United States. The biomedical industry is a vital source of high-wage, high-value jobs for the US economy. When the US Department of Labor added up the impact of this research-intensive sector of the economy, it found that it directly accounted for 1.2 million private-sector jobs in 2009, $96 billion in wages, and $213 billion in output. An independent study found that for every $1 spent on research, $2.20 in new revenue was produced, along with seven new jobs.

No other country has anything like the Third Street corridor surrounding MIT. The concentration of knowledge, research experience, brainpower, and passion is without comparison, which is why so many companies, such as Sanofi, Novartis, and Takeda, are paying the often steep prices required to move there. No European country, no country in Asia, Africa, or South America, has anything as advanced as this one-square-mile area of Massachusetts. In fact, no other country even comes close.

THE AMERICAN ADVANTAGE

But here is the truly amazing part. The area around MIT is only *one* of several research and development centers in the United States. Several others have capabilities equal to those in Cambridge. Many of these areas are seeing their own influx of foreign investment and talent from countries hoping to keep their own industries viable by tapping into America's genius for research and innovation.

America's other research centers are scattered around the country. There are impressive concentrations of talent, knowledge, and resources around the University of California's campuses at Berkeley, San Francisco, and San Diego, as well as around the Scripps and Salk institutes in La Jolla, California. These California research centers are a match for Cambridge, and in the aggregate might even surpass it.

But that's not all there is in California. There is another concentration of researchers and startups in Menlo Park, near the Stanford campus on the edge of Silicon Valley, where the first genetics company, Genentech, was started and where it makes (among other things) a synthetic, genetically modified form of insulin to treat diabetes.

There are dozens of research centers and companies along the I-95 corridor in New Jersey, where so many of the world's biggest pharmaceutical companies are located. And, although our images of New Jersey may be colored by close-ups of reality-TV stars such as Snooki and The Situation, New Jersey is much more serious than the fame of these stars would imply. It is the place where dozens of new drugs have been developed, and where health-care giants such as Johnson & Johnson are located.

There are other areas of the country where world-class innovation takes place as well. There is the area in North Carolina around Duke University, called Research Triangle, where Quintile—which organizes, assesses, and statistically analyzes most of the world's drug trials—is located, for example. In addition, there are areas surrounding the University of Texas at Austin, the Houston Medical Complex, Rockefeller University, and the Weill-Cornell Medical Center in New York. New York is also where Pfizer is located.

There is another research cluster near Carnegie Mellon University in Pittsburgh, and a very creative group of biotech researchers in Seattle. Minneapolis is where some of the first implantable pacemakers were invented, and the area around Salt Lake City is where the first kidney dialysis machine was perfected. In the area around Syracuse, New York, GE makes MRIs and CAT scanners, along with handheld sonogram devices.

My point is simply this: the United States is home to one of the world's fastest-growing economic sectors—a sector whose growth shows no signs of letting up. To be the center of this industry requires a mix of things—educational institutions, the brightest minds in the world, the best managers, and venture capital investors, along with a world-class group of service providers and consultants like Quintile.

With all that expertise and dynamism in this sector alone, does it really make sense to say America is on its way to decline? And is it really true that we don't make anything here anymore?

No way.

CREATIVITY, INC.

The scenes above focus on the biotech and pharmaceutical sectors of the economy, which are vibrant, growing quickly, and proving to be powerful engines of economic growth for the country. But they are not alone. In fact this is only one of many sectors in America that are at the top of their own global industries and have their own clusters of innovation and creativity. These other sectors are never mentioned when the pundits talk about our decline.

Computer hardware and software, telecommunications technology, advanced manufacturing, materials science, chemistry, aeronautical and space engineering, electrical engineering, artificial intelligence, "big data" analysis, and many, many other fields—all have their own centers of expertise scattered around the country. Some of them, like the areas around Stanford and Berkeley for advanced computing, are very much like the Third Street area of Cambridge—home to the world's best minds, companies, and educational and research institutions. These areas are fully formed and mature, with cafés and watering holes for the denizens of computing, along with an army of venture capital investors, consultants, and world-class companies—some of which are startups, others of which are mature.

The places I've mentioned for biotech and computing are not just important centers for the United States and our economy. They are central to the world's development in these areas. And, although a number of recent pessimistic books, such as George Packer's *The Unwinding: An Inner History of the New America*, Cullen Murphy's *Are We Rome? The Fall of an Empire and the Fate of America*, Fareed Zakaria's *The Post-American World*, Morris Berman's *Why America Failed: The Roots of Imperial Decline*, and Edward Luce's *It's Time to Start Thinking: America in the Age of Descent* bemoan our decline economically, industrially, and politically, the truth is that the American economy, thanks to our treasured innovators, is increasing its dominance.

And by what yardstick is our economic decline or our innovation descent measured, anyway? Typically, it is by the number of patents issued. Though the United States is still number one in patents, some countries, such as China, appear to be catching up. But if you look a little closer, you see that China is catching up because its patent laws (now that it has acknowledged it's not right to steal our intellectual capital) are far more lenient than ours. In China, products and processes can be patented that would never be granted a patent in the United States because they lack novelty. I am not being defensive when I say this. I am simply communicating a fact. Some countries have rigorous standards for patents—Albert Einstein was a clerk in Switzerland's patent office, after all—and others have much looser standards.

But if you still don't believe we are innovators, ask yourself to name European, Asian, Latin American, or Australian firms or organizations that are equal to Apple, which not only has continued to dazzle us by inventing new products and business concepts and models, such as iTunes, but—lest we forget—developed the first successful personal computer, way back when. Far from running out of gas, Apple continues to amaze.

Or consider the creative atmosphere at Stanford University, where two graduate students, Larry Page and Sergey Brin, started Google.

Then there is Amazon, which pioneered the online sale of books, but has morphed in many new and creative ways. Amazon is a store of stores. Tiny used-book vendors and other small merchants can sell their wares on Amazon's mighty online site. It is also a platform for comparing prices and purchasing goods, and it is a provider of business and commercial services using its cloud computing infrastructure. And, let's not forget the Kindle e-book reader, which was released by Amazon in 2007, almost three years before Apple sold its first iPad. The Kindle transformed the book industry and changed the way we read, study, and learn.

We cannot forget Microsoft, whose software put personal computers on the desks of almost every businessperson in the world, or Intel, which still produces the advanced chips that make computers cheaper, faster, and better each year.

In the biotech world, America's propensity for innovation has drawn the best minds in the world to our shores. Large innovators, such as the multiproduct genetic-engineering companies Genzyme and Amgen, are admired the world over. At the same time, newer, smaller companies—such as Amyris, which is using genetic engineering to fight malaria; Synthetic Genomics, which is making synthetic microbes; Oncogenex, which is developing new ways to fight cancer; and NovaBay, which is creating new types of antibiotics—are recognized as global leaders. They are proof that new companies continue to emerge.

Then there is the venture capital industry, which launched in America. Venture capital has the capacity to find new entrepreneurs, provide capital to them, and help them change the world. Add to this list all of those dozens of biotech companies operating in Cambridge and in California and in Texas, North Carolina, Washington State, and elsewhere, and you have a formidable foundation for the future.

My list of the usual suspects is far from complete, and a number of companies are profiled later in the book. But the fact is that dozens, perhaps hundreds, of uniquely American companies and organizations continue to out-create their competition. The United States is uniquely endowed with creativity and business acumen, enough to keep it in the lead for decades. This is not to suggest that we should be complacent, or that challenges from other nations should be taken lightly. However, even though the United States is being challenged, it is continuing to succeed.

OUR DAY CONTINUES

Investing in America's brightest minds paid off in the past and it will continue to pay off. It is one of our engines of growth, and we must protect it. China, India, Brazil, Russia, and other emerging-market countries will most likely have their day—*just not yet*. Their stars shine brightest to people who have not been there or do not really understand the capabilities and limitations of these countries, or how long it takes to develop world-beating science and technology capabilities and companies.

But there is something else that resides in Cambridge and in other US cities that is very difficult to quantify—raw creativity. People pay lip service to this word as if it were simply a nice-to-have quality. But in fact, creativity provides tremendous advantage.

China may be investing heavily in its labs and universities in the hopes of becoming a research superpower, but so far this investment hasn't panned out. The Chinese have mastered the technical aspects of research, and they've built a lot of labs, but that's all. Breaking new intellectual ground is not the same as making automobiles or railroad cars by licensing (or stealing) other people's patents and designs. Becoming a research superpower requires deep thinking, constant probing for the truth, an incessant questioning of dogma, a toleration of failure—even to the point of rewarding it—and the acceptance of argument and dissent.

The qualities I just mentioned are human qualities and probably widespread. But societies that stress consensus and conformity—for political or social reasons—and that silence their dissidents are more likely to suppress creativity than societies like ours that tolerate and even celebrate raucous debate. Creativity is messy, noisy, and anarchic. Some of the most creative people are also pigheaded, egocentric, and hyperenergetic. They can't sit still, and they're often unwilling to do what they're told. They have wild creative ideas, and sometimes they have wild political ideas. Stated plainly, creative people are often knowledge- and experience-hungry misfits who don't go with the flow. Just as we are a nation of immigrants, we are also a nation of misfits, a quality we celebrate in our art and popular culture.

The creative spirit is much like the artistic spirit—hence the Broad Institute's decision to have an artist in residence. The kind of iconoclasm necessary to be a creative leader may be anathema to the cultures of many countries, but it is the rock upon which this country is built. America doesn't put its creative artists, rock stars, scientists, or politicians in prison, unless they commit an *actual* crime, the way many authoritarian countries do.

If we're honest, we must recognize that becoming a creative nation is not easy. It did not happen in Japan, a nation we once feared, even though Japan devoted trillions of yen to programs fostering innovation (I presented at several of those sessions). Even so, and in spite of those programs, Japan has had difficulty innovating. If that were not the case, Sony, which gave us the Trinitron color TV, the Walkman, and the Sony store in the 1980s, and owns a huge catalog of music and movies, would have also given us the iPod, iTunes, iPad, and stores in which to sell them in the 2000s. But while Japan's innovation engine flagged, the American innovation engine never stopped rocking.

Don't get me wrong. The Japanese have wonderful engineering capabilities, and phenomenal factories. They are smart and very well educated. They are world leaders in automobile and electronics production. But their culture just isn't as creative as ours. They made money in lots of industries, and they increased their market share dramatically. But they did not invent any industries.

Not one.

And the United States? We invented several, from nuclear energy to mainframe and personal computing, the Internet, genetic engineering, e-book publishing, GPS and related businesses, and many others.

BEING CREATIVE

One thing I know from having worked as a consultant to some big Indian technology outsourcing firms, such as Patne and HCL, is that their analysts and technical people are smart, well trained, and extremely capable. The Indian Institutes of Technology (IIT)—the original five campuses, not the more recent additions—are world class and produce some of the best engineers, computer scientists, and technologists in the world. But a familiar lament is that while the IIT's students are gifted, they emerge as technologists, not entrepreneurs. And yet anyone who has looked at the names of the founders of some of Silicon Valley's best-known companies knows that a lot of these companies were started by Indians who immigrated to the United States. In fact, 13.4 percent[10] of all Silicon Valley startups were started by Indian Americans, a group that makes up less than 1 percent of the US population. So what gives?

The answer, from what I've observed, is that when Indian technologists are submerged in America's culture, they become infected with our enthusiasm for entrepreneurial activities. Coming to the United States changes people. India possesses a fascinating, rich, and in some ways very formal culture—or rather, cultures, because India is extremely diverse. Back in India, when inside a company, people rarely use each other's first names. The structure tends to be hierarchical. People get ahead by doing what they are asked to do. Speaking your mind is not encouraged.

But in the United States, our engineers are expected to speak up if they see something wrong—and when they do, progress is made. New York City Mayor Michael Bloomberg knows the value of encouraging people to speak up—that's why he had those signs put up in areas of New York saying, "If you see something, say something." That's an attitude that permeates America, both in its universities and in its business and technology culture. This is not to say that Indian companies are not capable or even competitive. They are. And they are teeming with lots of impressive people—just not with entrepreneurs.

In my work with many companies, I have observed something interesting. When an engineer from a foreign country arrives in the United States, he or she is typically still in the grips of the home nation's hierarchical culture. But after working for a little while in America, these immigrants change. Their creativity emerges, along with an interest in entrepreneurship. Indians living in the United States start businesses at a rate greater than in India, and it's because of our culture.

The loss of talented people in other countries when they come to America is our gain. Our creativity is infectious and draws talented people to our shores. We need to keep them here after they arrive to study or work. Opening our doors to gifted foreigners is good for us. Why? Because 25 percent of the Americans who have won a Nobel Prize were born in another country, because a large percentage of entrepreneurs in Silicon Valley and elsewhere in the United States are immigrants, and because many of the CEOs of Fortune 500 companies are immigrants as well. These people probably would have done okay in their home countries, but in the United States they became superstars. Their creativity was unleashed.[11]

CHAPTER TWO

THE RICH MAN'S DEPRESSION

The scene has been set for America's rebound. We can get a better understanding of why this is the case by backing up a few steps—a few years, actually, to the point just before the financial crisis of 2008. I've noticed something about the economy at that time that no one else has really talked about: that a number of very positive trends were underway when the disaster hit. Exports were rising, investment in American manufacturing was increasing, and new technologies were under development for taking advantage of our vast, but previously unreachable, reserves of energy. In China, the cost of manufacturing goods was rising, while in America it was falling. In India, the cost of writing software was increasing, while in America it was falling. America's productivity was accelerating. In my view, the Great Recession put a number of strongly positive trends on hold, but it didn't stop them. Those developments now have regained their forward thrust—and actually become stronger—in the recession's aftermath. The Great Recession, though intensely painful for so many people, had a cleansing effect on the economy overall. We are stronger now than we were before the recession began. That strength will help us unleash the next American Century.

But make no mistake about it. The Great Recession did temporarily derail us. What's worse, it wasn't an act of nature—an earthquake or tsunami—that put America's growth on hold. We stumbled because of our own stupidity. Let me explain.

In late 2007, a few months before the economic crisis struck, I visited Lehman Brothers' over-the-top Times Square headquarters in New York City. It was a garish building—a gray glass tower belted with a gigantic video display that tastelessly broadcast news highlights, ads for the firm, stock quotes, pictures, maps, *whatever.* Nothing said "We know how to waste your money" more than the gaudy, LCD cummerbund wrapped around that skyscraper's middle.

I went there to have lunch with Ted Janulis, head of the firm's highly profitable (at least at the time) mortgage securitization division. You remember that division. It's the one that collapsed under the weight of a sagging housing market and ended up bringing down Lehman Brothers, followed by the rest of the world economy. That division of Lehman, along with a handful of other firms, a host of independent mortgage brokers, and some brain-dead banks, ran the global economic and financial system into a ditch. But in late 2007, very few of us knew it was all coming down.

I had met the Chicago-born, boyish-looking managing director for mortgage capital at a conference earlier in the year. I had been moderating a panel focused on creating markets for mortgages through the miracle of securitization, and Janulis was one of the speakers.

The idea was that securitizing mortgages would make homeownership grow, which it did—all the way to 68 percent of households in the United States. Securitizing mortgages means putting hundreds of millions (or even billions) of dollars of mortgages into packages that can be sold to pension funds and rich investors by Wall Street firms such as Lehman Brothers. The interest that each mortgage holder pays his or her bank goes to a firm like Lehman, which keeps some and pays the rest to the investors that bought the packages of mortgages. Because these packages behave like bonds—which are securities— the process is called securitization.

Lehman and other financial firms created thousands of these mortgage-backed securities (another name for the same thing) by buying mortgages from the banks and brokers that issued them. Over time, the pool of securitized mortgages grew to be enormous.

Lehman was the biggest, most innovative firm playing in the securitized mortgage market, and Janulis, precise in his speech, highly polished in his manner, ran that group. When I got to Janulis's office, he took me up to floor forty-something of the gaudy tower to a corporate dining room, where we were joined by one of his colleagues, a woman who had just returned from Dubai. Lehman had an office in Dubai, and Janulis was thinking of creating a mortgage securitization business there to serve the Middle Eastern market.

We sat in the dining room, with its muted, off-white walls that, unlike the building itself, were tastefully decorated with artist prints. We were served by a waiter in a white jacket. From this high up, we could see most of Manhattan.

I'll never forget the points we discussed because, in retrospect, they are just so bizarre. We talked at length about building a system for measuring the creditworthiness of mortgage borrowers in the Middle East based on the American system of FICO scores, where 850 is perfect credit and 300 is abysmal. (The mortgages would have to conform to Islamic law.) We also discussed setting up rating agencies, something like Moody's, Fitch, and Standard & Poor's in the United States, to assess the quality of Middle Eastern securities.

Here I was, eating poached sea bass and sipping Perrier with the head of the mortgage division of Lehman Brothers, a few months before that firm collapsed from a steady stream of bad financial decisions, many of which, presumably, were his. And what were we talking about? Replicating America's system of mortgage securitization, credit scoring, and securities rating, all of which failed to do their principal job of predicting risk, in another region of the world. Forty-seven percent of all *subprime* mortgage securities—the word "subprime" defines them as poor credit—were rated AAA, the highest possible rating. And while that went on, some independent mortgage brokers were fabricating the salary levels of their borrowers. The banks that issued the mortgages then sold them to firms like Lehman, fraudulently signed documents ("robo-signing," they called it), and in some cases even lost their records. This was the system we were talking about bringing to the Middle East, and perhaps the world.

In addition, there was the problem of leverage. I knew that Lehman and the other firms borrowed money to buy mortgages, but I had no idea how much they borrowed. After that firm imploded, it turned out it was not uncommon for Lehman to leverage its investment in mortgages at a rate of 30 to 1,* meaning that for every $1 of its own money, Lehman borrowed $30 from someone else. (Other firms borrowed at leverage rates as high as 50 to 1).

Even if everything was accurate and buttoned down—borrowers' credit scores, and the ratings agencies' grading of the securitizations—this much leverage was dangerous. At 30 to 1, the value of a portfolio only has to decline by about 3.3 percent to wipe out the value of the investment (30 × 3.3 percent equals roughly 100 percent). That doesn't allow for much fluctuation. In fact, if Lehman were an individual borrower, the credit agencies might advise its banks to take away its credit cards.

While these shenanigans were going on, mortgage brokers and banks began issuing "no documentation loans." As a result, they could change a gardener's income from $30,000 into $130,000, without having to admit that they saw the gardener's pay stubs, or that his application was incorrectly filled out. Now, because documentation was no longer needed, a broker could get away with saying, "I must have misunderstood what the applicant said." As a result of all this, it was only a matter of time before gardeners—and other low-wage workers living in $232,400 homes (the median price of a home at the time)—would start to get into trouble.

People taking out these mortgages were enticed by very low initial interest rates—rates of, say, 2 percent. At that rate, their mortgages were affordable. But most of these mortgages were adjustable, which meant interest rates could move up and, in some cases, down. When the borrower's low "teaser" rates were replaced by real rates of 6 percent or more, the borrower's monthly mortgage payment could easily go from $900 to $1,800. As a result, thousands of low-wage homebuyers couldn't pay.

I'm bringing all this up to point out how a relatively well-designed system of mortgages and securitizations, along with systems for rating and scoring different kinds of debt, could still fail. They failed because of atrocious management and recordkeeping, bad decision-making (especially with regard to risk), and greed—none of which we discussed at lunch.

▼▼▼▼

When I left the Lehman building, after meeting some other members of Janulis's team, I walked back to my hotel. As I did, I recall feeling a little perplexed. I had the feeling that the people I met did not seem—*how shall I put this?*—as on top of things as they should have been, given that Lehman was the biggest player in the mortgage securitization field. I felt—forgive me for this judgment—that the people I met were polished, well spoken, *but not all that bright*. I'm not saying they couldn't add up a row of numbers—although it turned out some of them couldn't. What I am saying is they didn't seem to have enough intellectual curiosity to stand back, look at the system they had built, and try to pick apart its flaws. My hunch is that their interest in self-criticism waned as their bonus checks rose.

I put my reservations aside as I thought about that meeting. They, not I, were the ones who were credited with revolutionizing home lending. They, not I, were the market leaders. They, not I, were moving billions of dollars into the housing market. For those reasons, I told myself that my first impressions must have been wrong. Clearly, I told myself, these guys were smart, and I must be in error for feeling something was not quite right. Still, to be on the safe side, I sold all the real estate I owned, moved most of my savings out of stocks and into bonds, and sat tight.

But then, a few months later, in the spring of 2008, Ted Janulis started a review process culminating in the elimination of 2,500 people from his department. A little after that, according to reports by Bloomberg, Lehman announced it had $85 billion in mortgage securities that it couldn't sell. By late spring, the stock of the company was in free fall. Then, in August 2008, three and a half weeks before Lehman Brothers, and the world economy, fell to its knees, Janulis "retired."

A CRISIS UNFOLDS

If you watched CNBC, as I did, while the Great Recession unfolded, you were probably struck with fear. We all were. Until September 15, 2008, the world was doing okay. Or so we thought. But on that day in September, Lehman, the nation's fourth-largest investment bank, became the largest Chapter 11 bankruptcy filing ever. At $639 billion, it was a bankruptcy almost twice the size of the economy of Switzerland.

When Treasury Secretary Hank Paulson and others decided that Lehman should not be bailed out, in order to send a strong message to the financial community that bad business practices wouldn't be tolerated, Paulson probably had no idea of the damage that would result. But others did. Christine Lagarde, who was then France's minister of finance, said the decision was "horrendous" and a "genuine error." Nouriel Roubini, a professor of economics at New York University and an economic consultant, said, "It's clear we're one step away from a financial meltdown."[1] Others were equally alarmed.

The problem can best be understood this way. It was like a game of tug of war, with Lehman holding one side of the rope and thousands of homeowners, banks, pension-fund investors, and insurance companies holding the other. When Paulson decided that Lehman should not be bailed out, so the firm could serve as an object lesson, it was as if Lehman suddenly let go of its end of the rope: a very long line of people and institutions on the other side fell backward into the mud.

The damage that resulted from Lehman's bankruptcy took place on a cataclysmic scale. By March 2009, the stock market had fallen about 40 percent. During that period, about 800,000 people a month lost their jobs. The housing market collapsed by as much as 40 percent in some areas, such as Las Vegas and parts of Florida, Arizona, and California.[2] The credit markets and banks seized up—meaning no loans were made. Retail sales plummeted, especially at the middle and high end of the market. World trade contracted. Within hours of Lehman's collapse, Europe's financial system began to unravel. China, worried about the cash it had invested in the United States—a great deal of it in securitized mortgages—sought a guarantee from Paulson that the Treasury Department would protect its funds. Interest rates fell as the unemployment rate rose above 10 percent.

Without credit, people stopped buying cars, and this pushed Chrysler and GM, already weakened by high oil prices and decades of bad management, into bankruptcy. Airline traffic contracted. With so many people out of work, and retail sales tumbling, tax revenue to the states and the federal government fell just as unemployment costs were rising. For the first time in a generation, government workers were laid off or asked to accept wage givebacks and work furloughs. The federal debt swelled.

The magnitude of the financial and economic meltdown was on the scale of a depression. In fact, the initial stock-market losses were actually greater than those that had occurred immediately after the crash of 1929. But in 2008, the United States was many times wealthier than it was in 1930, and this prevented an even more devastating conclusion from taking place.

When I say we were much richer in 2008 than in 1930, I mean it as an understatement. In 1930, average household income in the United States was about $11,000 (in 2008 dollars).[3] In 2008, average household income was $52,000, meaning Americans were almost five times wealthier in 2008 than they were in 1930 on a per capita income basis.

But there were also many more Americans in 2008 than in 1930. In 1930, there were 125 million people living in the United States. In 2008, there were about 300 million. If you do the math (5 times the per capita income multiplied by 2.5 times the population), you find that America in 2008 was at least 12.5 times richer than America in 1930.

But that's just income. Add to that the value of everything people owned in 2008—80 million homes; millions of farms; hundreds of thousands of factories; millions of cars and trucks; and millions of other products, such as computers and cell phones, that nobody even dreamed of in 1930—unless perhaps if they wrote science fiction— and you begin to get an idea of how different the world had become.

In 2008, Manhattan had twice the amount of office space that it had in the 1930s. Many American cities, such as Los Angeles, Houston, Phoenix, San Diego, Las Vegas, Tucson, and others, were tiny outposts in the 1930s, but vibrant economic hubs in 2008, with millions of people living and working in them. In the 1930s, there was no Silicon Valley, there was no bio-pharma corridor along the New Jersey Turnpike, and the Third Street area of Cambridge was home to a noxious rubber-processing plant. There were no computers, usable antibiotics, TVs, jet airliners, or freeways in the 1930s. There was no air conditioning. In 1930, life expectancy was fifty-eight for men and sixty-one for women; in 2008, it was seventy-eight for men and eighty-one for women—a twenty-year increase. In 1930, the top-selling car was the $500 Ford Model A, with a 40-horsepower engine and no radio (radios were expensive luxuries and had to be installed separately). In 1930, the largest commercial airliner held seventeen people, supermarkets hadn't been invented, and the Dow was at about 240, whereas the Dow reached 14164 in 2007 before falling to a low of 6547 in 2008. Depending on the year and how you count it, the capital markets were between thirty and seventy times larger in 2008 than in 1930. In 2008, the value of all the stocks traded on the US stock markets was about $15 trillion; in 1930, it was about $81 billion—which would be the same as around $1.02 trillion today— that is, approximately one-fifteenth of today's dollar volume.

Even more important, in 1930 there was no unemployment insurance, no Social Security, no Federal Deposit Insurance Corporation (FDIC) for banks, no Pension Benefit Guaranty Corporation (PBGC) to insure pensions, no Securities and Exchange Commission (SEC) to watch over the markets, and no Medicare or Medicaid. In the much poorer world of 1930, everyone was pretty much on their own.

WHAT IF IT WAS A DEPRESSION?

The financial and economic crises that struck in 2008 led to a rich man's depression. Painful as they are, depressions have powerful cleansing effects. What they do best, if "best" is the right word to use when talking about an economic meltdown accompanied by so much pain and uncertainty, is make private-sector debt vanish so that growth can return. The good news about depressions (keeping in mind that most of the news is bad) is that they wipe away mortgage debt, credit-card debt, automobile debt, and other forms of personal debt, albeit painfully. To a large extent, that's exactly what happened in 2008, when much of our personal debt was wiped away. When that happened, it paved the way for an American economic revival.

The chart in Figure 2.1, from the Federal Reserve in June 2013, shows what I'm talking about. According to the chart, as the United States went into the financial crisis, household debt, which includes consumer loans and mortgages, was equal to about 100 percent of GDP. By mid-2012, it had fallen to 84 percent of GDP, a drop of about 16 percentage points, before rising moderately in mid-2013 to 85 percent of GDP. If we do the math, the magnitude of that change takes shape. With America's GDP at about $15 trillion, a drop of 15 percent means that, one way or another, American households owe about $2.3 trillion *less* than they did in 2009. That's a big number: $2.3

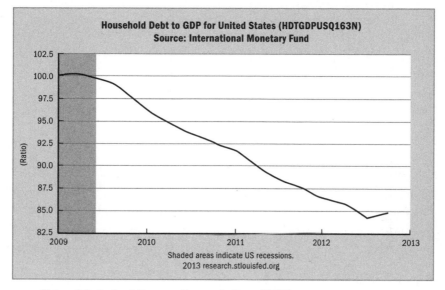

Figure 2.1. Federal Reserve Economic Data (FRED).

trillion is slightly less than the size of the British economy. *The entire British economy!*

Besides showing that personal debt is getting smaller, what the chart and the numbers indicate is that, for the most part, Americans are prudent, thrifty, well-behaved capitalists. They are not loaded up with debt, they are not profligates, and they are not spendthrifts, despite what so much of the media likes to tell us to the contrary.

Another way to look at the debt conundrum is to examine how much of each American's household income goes to pay back debt (see Figure 2.2). When too much income goes to pay back purchases from the past, this limits how much we can spend in the future. Fortunately, that figure, too, is moving in the right direction—*big time.* Just before the financial crisis hit, Americans were spending an exorbitant 14.2 percent of household income to service their debt. In 2013, thanks to falling interest rates and America's new move toward thriftiness, we are spending just 10.3 percent of our incomes to keep the bill collectors at bay. That's quite a bit of progress. Even more important, it means there is room inside America's pocketbooks and wallets to borrow a little more money to make large purchases down the road. When that happens, it will go a long way toward fueling America's resurgence.

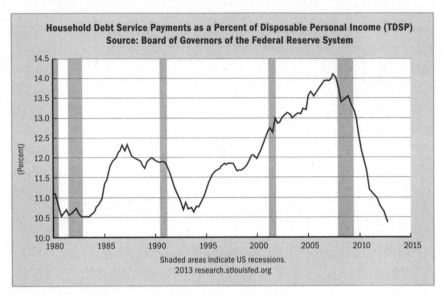

Figure 2.2. Federal Reserve Economic Data (FRED).

This is good news for the economy and for consumers. But it's also good news for the producers of the kinds of goods we make at home. Why is that? Because the age of America's garage full of durable goods—stuff designed to last three to five years or more, such as cars, light trucks, and appliances—is older than at any other time since the end of World War II, when America's manufacturing might was turned toward making armaments, not toasters and roadsters.

In short, our stuff is getting old, and we are going to need new stuff. The average age of America's appliances, as of the end of 2011, was 5.3 years.[4] Cars, at 4.4 years old, were a little younger, on average, but still older than they had been since the 1940s. People will soon be spending to replace all the things that wore out or broke after the financial crisis hit. When that happens, we will feel it throughout the economy.

Just as important, it turns out that we may have been incorrectly counting America's GDP, missing about $500 billion in revenue, a sum equal to the economy of Belgium. The problem has been that economists in Washington and elsewhere have been leaving out some of the most creative parts of the economy—royalties from books, movies, music, and other forms of entertainment as well as educational and research and development activity—when calculating GDP. As a result of this omission, America's GDP figures back to 1929 will be revised to show that we have been richer than we thought.

Consider the facts. Is it profligacy to spend just 10.3 percent of your income to pay off your household debt? If the remaining almost 90 percent goes to paying for everything else, that's not bad.

Not bad at all.

Americans are for the most part a responsible people. The problems that caused the Great Recession were not the problems of *America*, though we all felt their effects. They were the problems of a few *Americans*. They were the problems of a small group of people—at the periphery.

Trust me, I have nothing against low-wage workers, and I don't mean to pick on them, but in normal times, people with incomes below $50,000 would never have qualified for a mortgage on a house costing $232,400, the median price of a house at the time the financial crisis hit. The problem was that low-wage borrowers were in cahoots with unsavory mortgage brokers, who received incentives from banks that sold mortgages to firms like Lehman, who securitized those mortgages. These folks were also in cahoots with ratings agencies that incompetently rated mortgages as AAA, even when they were from borrowers whose earnings were either too low to qualify for a loan or fabricated.

In 2007, 13.5 percent of all loans were subprime—an insanely high level. But not all of those loans went bad. In 2007, there were about 125 million homes in the United States. Collectively, they were worth about $22 trillion, with about a third of them owned outright.[5] The number of mortgages that went bad—about 5 percent—was not an astronomical number, but it translated into an absurdly large amount of money—$800 billion—which is a lot of money to lose. Even worse, since firms like Lehman were leveraged at least 30 to 1, the damage from losing $800 billion was magnified many times over.

THE GENIUS OF TARP

We've all heard about how TARP, the Troubled Asset Relief Program signed into law by President Bush in October 2008, put billions of dollars of debt onto the government's balance sheet. How much money—and for how long—is a matter of debate, since the full authorization, $700 billion, was not spent, and banks and other financial firms that received loans paid back much of what they received.

What TARP and other relief programs did well—*and for which they have been criticized*—was to transfer debt from banks and other private organizations to the federal government. Other programs overseen by the Federal Reserve did the same thing—they transferred private debt from banks, and in some cases homeowners, onto the Federal Reserve's balance sheet.

If the recipients of the government's largesse never pay back these loans, they'll stay on the government books. But that's what they are supposed to do. Governments don't bail out banks, insurance companies, and automobile companies unless all else fails. When they do fail, the point is not to pick a few people and punish them as object lessons for the rest of us. The point is to save the economy as a whole. As the philosophers of utilitarianism used to say, considering how to end up with "the most good for the most people" is the best way to decide what to do.

Economists learned a generation ago that one of the ways you fix economic depressions is to exchange private-sector debt for government debt, not to go in for austerity. When we did that in the aftermath of 2008, we were in effect bailing out dishonest brokers, incompetent rating agencies, borrowers who lied on their applications, and a lot of people on Wall Street—which is a shame, perhaps even a tragedy. But we also bailed out the economy as a whole, and while some may question the morality of the bailout, it was the right thing to do. It's a little like a battlefield surgeon treating a wounded enemy. It's not what the surgeon signed up to do, and it may even be a little repugnant, but it's morally right.

The truth is, even though there's a lot of political noise around putting so much debt on the government's balance sheet, the government has ways to make that debt go away. During the Great Depression, and even in World War II, people worried about our nation's debt. But when peace was restored and the economy began to grow, the debt shrank as a share of GDP. Besides, the best long-term mathematical study showing that too much government debt slows future economic growth, conducted by Harvard economists Carmen Reinhart and Kenneth Rogoff, has been called into question.[6] It seems that a number of errors may have crept into the economic model and distorted its results. When the math errors were corrected and the model rerun by another group of economists, led by Thomas Herndon at the University of Massachusetts at Amherst, it turned out that high levels of government debt had no impact on future growth—none whatsoever.

That's because governments aren't like you or me. Governmental institutions have special privileges that individuals and even businesses aren't entitled to. Governments can create money, change the way banks and markets operate, collect taxes, and even allow for some inflation to make debt shrink as a share of the economy.

And why shouldn't they use this power? Governments are supposed to be there for us. After all, they exist only with the consent of the governed, according to the Declaration of Independence, and as such they are responsible for ensuring life, liberty, and the pursuit of happiness. Therefore, when times are tough, when the economy is about to topple into a free fall, it makes sense for the government to act, even if it means taking on debt or doing other extraordinary things to make sure the economy continues to function and our lives and well-being continue to improve. If you ask me, the purpose of government is not to teach people lessons of moral rectitude. There are other institutions set up to do that. The purpose of government is to keep our economic system operating despite our human failings, not to let the economy collapse and crush us because of those shortcomings.

I make this point because one thing is certain. The problems we faced during the financial crisis were not one-of-a-kind failings. They are hardwired into us. There is no doubt in my mind that despite our best efforts, sometime in the not-too-distant future, when memories grow dim regarding what caused the collapse of 2008, we will repeat our mistakes and it will all come down again.

This is not cynicism, it is fact. In 1933, four years after the stock market collapsed, with the Great Depression working its way through the nation, Congress, in a rare moment of wisdom, enacted the Glass-Steagall Act to preserve the strength of the nation's banking system. It did this by separating basic banking functions from investment banking and brokerage firms.

The ideas behind Glass-Steagall was to make certain that the failure of one part of the financial system would not result in the failure of the entire financial system. It was a good law and it enabled the country to withstand the real-estate and savings and loan crisis of the late 1980s. But in 1998, President Bill Clinton dismantled the Glass-Steagall rules. The world had changed, he argued, and to compete globally, our financial system needed to remove restrictive regulations that kept it from growing bigger. Glass-Steagall, it was said, was relic of a previous era and was no longer needed. In short, the world was very different now.

Different indeed!

WHY IT CAME APART

A fundamental and rarely discussed cause of the crash was oil. To be specific, imported oil. In late 2007, a colleague of mine did a few calculations regarding housing. As we sat in his office going over his figures, the world around us seemed to be shaky, at best. But the numbers proved interesting. In 2008, there were 125 million homes in the United States, with an average price of $232,400, which meant the value of our housing stock was roughly $22 trillion, as already mentioned. By way of comparison, $22 trillion is twice the size of the Chinese economy plus the economy of Japan. Don't ever say the United States isn't big or rich.

The economy seemed to be doing fine in 2007. But then oil prices began rising. Oil had been rising at a steady rate since the beginning of the war in Iraq in 2003, when it sold for about $33 a barrel. By 2007, oil hit $100 a barrel, prompting Arjun Murti, an analyst at Goldman Sachs, to write that oil was in a period of spikes that could be followed by a "superspike," sending it as high as $200 a barrel.[7]

Thankfully, oil prices didn't rise that high. But in July 2008, they hit $145 a barrel, a record. Six weeks later, Lehman collapsed and the world economy went into free fall.

High oil prices act like a tax on the economy because oil is used for so many things. Not only does it go into the fuel tanks of cars, planes, trains, ships, trucks, and buses, affecting the cost of travel and the price of our commutes. The cost of oil also affects the cost of anything that has to be moved from one place to another. And because it is used in plastics, chemicals, fertilizer, pesticides, and even cosmetics, an increase in the price of oil leads to an increase in the price of everything else. Together, food and fuel make up 25 to 35 percent of an average American household's budget, depending on oil prices. The other large household expenditure is housing, which accounts for 34 to 37 percent of a family's budget.

In the period from 2003 to 2008, oil and housing prices were rising. And, while housing prices plateaued in late 2006, mortgage costs continued to rise because of interest rates. Rising food, fuel, and housing costs did real damage to people's budgets, particularly people at the bottom of the income ladder who had taken out subprime mortgages.

The Federal Reserve's survey of consumer expenditures indicated that in 2003, just before the Iraq War, gas sold for $1.72 a gallon. The average American household spent $5,340 on food and $1,333 on gasoline, a total of $6,673. Five years later, in 2008, that same family spent $6,443 on food and $2,715 on gasoline, a total of $9,158. This means that in 2008 the average family spent about $210 more every month on food and fuel than it did in 2003. Despite these increases in the cost of living, incomes were flat, especially at the bottom of the income ladder.[8]

If you wonder why so many people defaulted on their subprime loans, add together the cost of food and fuel with the cost of housing. In 2003, the average household spent $13,432 on housing, according to the Federal Reserve. By 2008, that figure rose to $17,109—an increase of $3,677. If you add it all up, you find that, just to make ends meet, it cost the average American household $6,177 *more* a year to live in 2008 than in 2003, an increase of about $515 a month.[9]

People are rational (more or less). When faced with an increase in the price of fuel, food, and housing, people paid for fuel and food, putting their mortgages on hold. They did it for the following rational reasons: people have to eat, and most people have to drive their cars to get to work. If you don't show up for work, you get fired very quickly, but if you are late with your mortgage payment, it can take a year or more to lose your home. And, besides, people thought that if they continued going to work, sooner or later they would catch up on their mortgage payments. That is, until Lehman collapsed and 800,000 people a month lost their jobs.

If oil prices had stayed low—at 2003–2006 levels—very few people would have gotten behind on their mortgages or lost their homes. If oil prices had stayed low, in my view, the economy would not have collapsed.

So what if energy prices were to remain low into the foreseeable future? What if the United States were energy independent? In fact, what if the United States were to become a major *exporter* of energy—oil and natural gas? That would certainly give the economy a gigantic boost.

That day is near.

TRENDS PUT ON HOLD

Shortly before the economic and financial crises erupted in full, I flew to Paris to deliver a day-long presentation to a group of insurance executives from around the world. My presentation was on where the economy was headed. In my briefcase I had printouts of more than a hundred PowerPoint images that I could use. Of course, that was overkill—and more than sufficient to put the entire city of Paris into a deep sleep. But I like to be prepared in case someone raises an interesting point or asks a question. That's when I can say, "I just happen to have something that relates to that point." For geeks like me, seeing all those charts and tables is like greeting old friends, or showing snapshots of a summer vacation.

I placed those graphs and charts around my hotel room—on the bed, desk, chair, and footstool—and I remember feeling strangely optimistic. I don't think it was delusional, either—or at least no more delusional than the dismal science of economics warrants. But the data told an interesting story. What the data said was that America's renaissance had already begun, especially in manufacturing, and that the winds of change were starting to blow our way. But this was just before the financial and economic crises hit. So where did I go wrong?

The story my PowerPoint illustrations told was the following. In the decade between 1998 and 2008, American exports had doubled. For a mature nation like ours, that is an amazing story. Every month in the 2000s, until the collapse, the United States exported

$150 billion worth of products, such as airplanes, computer chips, wheat and corn, pharmaceuticals, metal-cutting machines, tractors, radar systems, and so on. Some months it exported even more. In addition, the United States exported banking and insurance services, along with consulting, legal, software, engineering, design, and architectural services. On top of that, America exported exotic services such as oil-field services—where American companies with expertise in drilling holes in the ground did just that for clients in places such as Saudi Arabia. In fact, if you wanted to explore for oil, you pretty much had to use an American company to do so. As a result, exports of services were at an all-time high—20 percent of total exports.

In that same decade-long time frame, there was also phenomenal growth in productivity—3.7 percent a year—a blistering pace, again, for a so-called "mature economy." Those gains meant that if the average American worker produced $100 in 1998, in 2008 he or she was producing roughly $145. Moreover, my statistics indicated that from 1981 to 1995, the United States was responsible for 23.1 percent of the world's growth, but by 1996 to 2007, that number increased to 26 percent. That's a remarkable showing for a mature economy like ours. Europe, with a far larger population than ours and a standard of living that was the envy of the world, contributed almost no growth during the same period. Ditto for Japan.[10]

Another important point in my presentation had to do with the topic of manufacturing. Volkswagen was about to break ground on a new plant that would produce 150,000 cars a year at a factory in Chattanooga, Tennessee. Honda was opening its fourth assembly plant in the United States, this one in Greensburg, Indiana. Sanyo, a subsidiary of Japan's giant Panasonic Corporation, was expanding its solar-cell factory in Salem, Oregon. And Iowa had become one of the world's leading manufacturing centers for wind-turbine blades.

Iowa was even attracting European companies that made wind turbines. In 2007, Spain's Acciona Windpower built a plant to make 165-foot-long, ultralight, carbon-fiber composite blades. Carbon fiber is a technology that requires considerable technical expertise to produce correctly, especially when each blade is longer than a sixteen-story building is tall. Who would have thought Iowa would be a world center for that kind of expertise?

Acciona's Iowa plant was only eight miles away from the site where California's Clipper Windpower made its blades. And in 2008, in nearby Newton, Iowa, TPI Composites opened a factory to produce 134-foot-long wind-turbine blades for GE, which held a stake in that company. A little later that year, Denmark's Vestas opened a manufacturing plant to produce 144-foot-long turbine blades, not in Iowa, but nearby in Colorado.

What this shows is that America's manufacturing base was not shrinking so much as changing. Some of it was going from old-fashioned mass production, where metal is stamped into shape, to exotic carbon-fiber composites, which are notoriously difficult to work with. This expertise was a distinct competitive advantage for Boeing, which at the time had five hundred firm, advance orders for its mostly composite 787 Dreamliner, the world's most advanced, most economical, and most successful new airliner. That plane, which now has about a thousand orders, is made from the same stuff as those wind-turbine blades.

The 787 has had its share of problems and delays, such as the tendency of its Japanese-made batteries to catch on fire, which contributed to its late introduction. The reason the plane was delayed for several years was that too many of its 3 million parts—such as its batteries—were outsourced to manufacturers in Europe and Asia, which made the project too difficult to coordinate. As a result, Boeing began moving the work from overseas to suppliers in the United States. The company's experience with outsourcing served as a lesson to other firms, with many of them bringing their factories back to our shores.

Another point in my presentation focused on data from consulting firms showing how other big American manufacturers, in addition to Boeing, were starting to move production back to the United States from China. They were doing so as early as 2008, with one of the main reasons being that prices in China were rising, while access to the Chinese market was limited for foreign firms, even if they manufactured products there.

One study, by the Boston Consulting Group (BCG), indicated that automobile parts manufacturers that moved their operations to China had more trouble selling their components to Chinese car companies than local companies did. China was strangely schizophrenic.

On the one hand, it welcomed investment, because investment put its people to work. On the other hand, indigenous companies considered US plants located inside China to be foreign companies and would not buy their goods. There were, of course, exceptions. But for the most part, that's the way it worked. This rule didn't just apply to automobile parts; it applied to electronics components as well.[11]

In 2008, American companies that had invested in China were facing some harsh realities. They weren't making money there, and in most cases the government required non-Chinese companies to join forces with a Chinese partner. That partner had to have a controlling interest in the venture of at least 51 percent. The Chinese partner thus shared the risks of doing business in China, and contributed a lot of local knowhow, but it also drained away profits. And, on top of that, there was a perennial complaint that Chinese companies very often stole the intellectual property of their American partners, and that the government did nothing about it. China's officials were corrupt and its courts ineffective, something that remains a problem. In China, you can win a case in court—that is, if you are lucky enough to get to court—but that doesn't mean you will get paid the amount the court awarded you. Chinese courts are notorious for looking the other way when a foreigner complains that the loser in a case has not paid the judgment that was ordered.

Other costs were rising in China, too. Shanghai, Beijing, Tianjin, and other industrial cities were experiencing real-estate booms, and the resulting high prices made it more expensive for companies to locate staff and rent office space in China than in *any* major American city. And, because oil prices were high, and cargo ships burn oil, there were additional costs involved in shipping products back to the United States.

But one graph in particular that I showed in Paris proved to be a showstopper (see Figure 2.3). That graph was generated by the consulting firm BCG and was based on available data plus interviews with managers working in China. The figure showed that in 2008, North American manufacturing firms actually had *lower* production costs at home than they did in China. The same was true for firms from Italy and France. When I showed this graph to the people in the room, their surprise was audible. China, for the reasons I just stated, was no longer a bargain. It was a rapidly developing country that was moving its way upward into the middle class. As a result, it was losing its competitiveness vis-à-vis countries like ours, and it was doing this rapidly. I am making this point to show that in 2008, it looked like the trends were headed in our direction.

One reason for the rise in China's cost structure was that its labor costs were increasing, and they were doing it rather rapidly. Low labor costs and a big domestic market were the factors that led American firms to outsource to China in the first place. But from 2000 to 2012, Chinese wages rose 500 percent. That's a very big number.

Labor costs in China are expected to continue their upward trajectory, and the Chinese government understands this. In fact, China's leaders are shifting their emphasis, hoping to move China away from being a global outsourcer to creating a consumer economy—one that will benefit the country's upwardly mobile citizenry. To do anything else would require holding down China's rising wages along with its increasingly middle-class lifestyle.

At the same time that Chinese wages were rising by as much as 18 percent a year,[12] American labor productivity was growing at a surprisingly fast pace between 2000 and 2010. For example, between 2000 and 2007, labor productivity in information services grew at a rate of 5.8 percent, manufacturing grew at a rate of 4.2 percent, and retail grew at about 4 percent—all excellent showings for

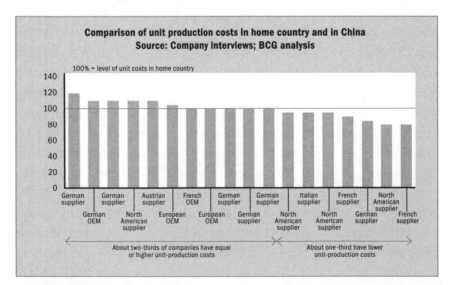

Figure 2.3.

a supposedly "mature" economy.[13] Only mining saw its productivity fall. This meant that although it was more expensive to employ an American worker than a Chinese worker, the extraordinary productivity of the US system meant you needed far fewer workers to make something in the United States than you did in China. The fact was that American factories were more energy efficient, more highly automated, and more productive than their Chinese counterparts in 2008. As a result, the cost of making something in the United States—particularly something high tech—was competitive with the cost of making the same thing in China. And if you compared the cost of making something in these two countries and delivering it to a customer, the United States was cheaper.

Then there was the fact that it was difficult to coordinate complex manufacturing from thousands of miles away—which was Boeing's problem; the time it takes to ship goods from China to the United States; the sometimes uneven quality of Chinese goods; and the hidden risks and costs of China's widespread corruption. It became clear to the people listening to my talk in Paris that for many types of goods, it no longer made sense to outsource production to China.

The situation was similar for India. It was indeed the case that the Indian Institutes of Technology trained a large number of very gifted engineers. The problem was, even though these people were plentiful, they weren't plentiful *enough* to keep up with the growth. For many technical jobs, India simply ran out of talent. Salaries were rising rapidly, and engineers were hopping from job to job, taking advantage of generous signing bonuses offered by nearby competing technology firms. It got so bad that Vineet Nayar, chief executive of HCL, an information technology and engineering firm I worked with, wrote a book called *Employees First, Customers Second*. Aimed at India's mobile job-hopping IT workforce, the book's message was simply this: "if you work for HCL, we'll treat you well."

India's employment problems didn't get better. Not that long after my Paris speech, in early 2010, India's labor costs soared even higher, increasing by 20 percent in that year alone.[14] With labor costs increasing at such a fast rate, a number of American companies had second thoughts about locating there. Some companies—GE, for one—began partial withdrawals from India.

That's not to say these countries will lose all outsourcing. They won't. HCL, for example, has a very innovative engineering center in India that can match the best engineering firms in the world. But in that case, India is competing on knowledge and experience, not price. No one goes to HCL's engineering center because it's a bargain, they go there for its expertise, which is also where American firms excel. In fact, it is where they dominate. In this sector, no one worries that the United States is falling behind. Its formidable expertise will keep it out front.

But other types of services are coming home, albeit in a different form. Increasingly, call centers are automated—try getting someone on the line when you need to speak with someone at Verizon or AT&T. Instead of people, artificial intelligence programs are taking over. Chances are, those programs were designed in America. And for other types of call-center work, Americans—now often working from home, instead of from expensive office space—are taking back the market.

I'm not counting India or China out. China is shifting its policies from an emphasis on export-led growth to an emphasis on building up its domestic economy. Chinese planners know that if China wants to develop further, it can't do so by keeping wages low. And while China focuses on expanding its middle class, India has not made up its mind about which path to take. As a result, India's future remains far less clear than China's, and far less secure.

PUTTING IT TOGETHER

The reason I am going over some of the points I made in a presentation in Paris so long ago is to emphasize that a number of very positive trends were underway in the American economy. I would also like to bring up two ideas that are based on that talk.

First, it should be clear that although the housing and financial sectors were badly damaged as a result of the financial collapse, the rest of the economy muddled along, and the auto industry was transformed.

The automobile industry, moribund for decades and plagued with bad management and expensive union contracts, was revitalized by the bankruptcies of Chrysler, GM, and some suppliers. Bankruptcy gave the companies the opportunity to rewrite labor contracts and re-structure their pension and health-care liabilities. Prior to the crisis, there was actually a clause in GM's contract with the United Auto Workers (UAW) requiring the company to pay assembly workers who had been laid off, even those, in some cases, who were working at other companies. Not only was this overreach by labor, GM couldn't fight it. During the bankruptcy, the rules were rewritten. Pension liabilities shrank (they were transferred from the private sector to the government), and other features of the bailout brought down other types of costs. As a result, the American automobile industry became competitive again, even in the small-car segment of the market.

When I created the graphs and charts for my Paris trip, unemployment in the United States was ridiculously low compared to the rates in other countries. Until the summer of 2008, it was around 5 percent.

But one interesting fact about the unemployment data is rarely reported. Whereas unemployment, in the aggregate, rose to 10 percent following the crisis, that number has always been a bit misleading, because the unemployment was concentrated among young people, especially males under the age of twenty-five without college degrees. For this group, unemployment soared at the height of the crisis. Members of this group have few skills. Traditionally, these people go from high school—many don't graduate—to jobs that require a lot of brawn, but not much brain. In the years prior to the crisis, young people without much education, especially men, found work building homes, roads, and other types of infrastructure projects. When the housing crisis hit, these young men were the first to lose their jobs. As housing recovers—and every indication is that a recovery is now underway—these young men will be going back to work to build new homes—and there will be a lot of homes to build.

The reason for that is simple demographics. As Figure 2.4 indicates, few houses were started between 2008 and 2010 or after that (jagged line). "Housing starts" are not exactly the same thing as "new homes being built"—they differ in what is counted—but if we switch to new homes being built, we find[15] that an estimated 700,000 new homes will be built in 2013, an estimated 900,000 in 2014, and more than 1 million in 2015. People will be making up for lost time.

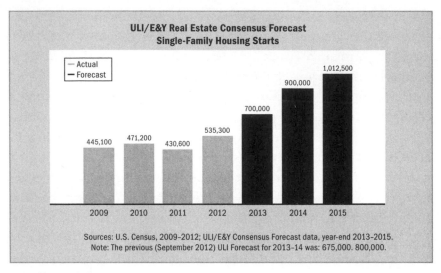

ULI/E&Y Real Estate Consensus Forecast
Single-Family Housing Starts

- Actual
- Forecast

445,100 471,200 430,600 535,300 700,000 900,000 1,012,500

2009 2010 2011 2012 2013 2014 2015

Sources: U.S. Census, 2009–2012; ULI/E&Y Consensus Forecast data, year-end 2013-2015.
Note: The previous (September 2012) ULI Forecast for 2013-14 was: 675,000. 800,000.

Figure 2.4.

And who will build those houses? Journeymen carpenters, plumbers, and electricians, along with an army of the formerly out-of-work young men who (hopefully) will learn a trade. You need skill to lay pipe or string wires. But to dig a ditch, or unload a truck? All you need is a strong back, the ability to listen, and the discipline to show up on time.

Unemployment was also very difficult for young people, those under age thirty, with college degrees but no experience. Of these, many found employment, but not the kind they were hoping for. College-educated men and women worked at stores like the Gap, or as wait staff in restaurants. Lots of young men and women with graduate degrees waited on customers at the Apple store or at Target. For this group, life has not been easy.

To find work, many young educated men and women had to work as unpaid interns—sometimes for protracted periods of time— to get enough experience for a nervous employer to take a gamble on them. But most people don't go to college to work for free, or close to it. They go to get an education, learn about the world, and get sufficient background to begin a career.

But a very promising generation of young Americans—the Millennials, or Generation Y's—seems to have missed a step. In fact, for those who have been idle for the past five or six years, or who have jumped from internship to internship, à la the young people in the TV show *Girls*, that missed step has been long and steep.

The problem I have just described is real. Overall, unemployment has been concentrated in people under age twenty, who had an unemployment rate of about 23 percent in 2012.[16] That same year, people between the ages of twenty and twenty-four had an unemployment rate of 13 percent, and for those between the ages of twenty-five and fifty-four, unemployment was 7 percent. For those above the age of fifty-four, the rate fell steeply, to 5.9 percent, partly as a result of people retiring from workforce, partly because people were getting fed up looking for a job, but mostly because people in the upper age brackets had useful skills honed by decades of experience. For women, the unemployment rate was better than for men early in life, but caught up with men later in life.

As I hinted earlier, unemployment is really a function of age *and* educational attainment. The more education a person has, the less likely he or she is to be unemployed. (This is the information age, after all, which is dominated by so-called knowledge workers.) People with professional degrees—in all age categories—had an average unemployment rate of just 2.1 percent in 2012.[17] People with bachelor's degrees had an unemployment rate of just 4.5 percent, and people with PhDs had an unemployment rate of 2.5 percent. For all ages, people without high-school diplomas had an unemployment rate of 12.4 percent. Add up all the different groups, and you get the overall unemployment rate, which, at the time of this writing in mid-2013, was 7.2 percent.

What these figures show is that the financial crisis did not affect everyone in the same way. Some people suffered while others did not. Those with college degrees or above walked away from the shattered economy relatively unscathed—especially if they were thirty and above. They did not lose their jobs, and their salaries were maintained. They changed jobs, but not as frequently. They remained in demand. True, many of their retirement accounts lost value, and the prices of their homes declined. But, if they did nothing and left their investments alone, chances are the value of those investments recovered to their former levels or rose higher. Housing prices are up again, too, albeit not everywhere.

The unscathed group, made up of Americans thirty-something and above, includes Generation X, older members of Generation Y, and boomers. These people are part of America's very formidable, experienced, highly productive army of engineers, teachers, executives, health-care professionals, lawyers, and so on. They are people who know how to get things done. And, while it is likely they felt fearful during the crisis, and didn't have as much job mobility as before the crisis, they did not lose their jobs.

What all these facts mean is that prior to the financial crisis, America's prospects were good, and during the crisis, the effects on people were variable. Some parts of the economy, and some people, did better than before the crisis, and some held their own. But without a doubt, the people who were hardest hit were those who were the least educated, the youngest, and the least experienced. This was the group that drove up the unemployment rate, while the rest of the country continued much as before. And it is that group—those who are young, unemployed, and without much education—that will soon be called back into action when ground is broken for all those new homes.

TREND LINES

If you look underneath the debris from the past recession, as I have, you will see a number of positive trends that will soon propel the United States forward at what is likely to be an astonishing speed. These trends—which I discuss in the following chapters—are not simply shifts, they are profound transformations. Advances in science and technology, along with massive, newly accessible reserves of cleaner, cheaper energy, large pools of capital, and America's legendary creativity, are not trivial matters. Any one of these attributes can change a country, even a region. But to have all four of them, as the United States does, will give us astonishing power.

Let me elaborate. In the past, countries with any one of these traits have been catapulted into great growth. Saudi Arabia was a desert wasteland until oil was found there in large quantities, and then it suddenly began building modern cities, ports, and an enviable infrastructure. More than a century ago, with high-tech knowhow, Japan began developing its manufacturing and engineering prowess, transforming itself from an agricultural nation into a world power. Switzerland became a global banking center, flush with capital, but before that was chiefly known for its watches, cuckoo clocks, and cheeses. Israel was a country of refugees living in a war zone, fenced in by a global boycott. Its creativity transformed it into a high-tech country with a modern living standard and industries too vital to cordon off.

As my list indicates, any of these four attributes (energy, science and manufacturing expertise, access to capital, and creativity) can transform a country from backwater to powerhouse. So what happens when a country possesses all four of these factors, as America does? And what happens when that country is already the largest and most dynamic economy in the world?

The answer is that we're going to find out. And we will find out soon.

The American economy began to gather speed in 2013. In my view, as people begin to notice that jobs are becoming more plentiful, money is less tight, and home prices are improving, they will become more positive, if not outright optimistic, about the future.

The United States is an immensely important country. It is responsible for much of the world's growth, not only directly, as I have indicated above, but indirectly, too. We may have been the leaders of the revolution in computers, but the whole world benefited from it. As our economic engine revs up, and our pragmatic brand of creativity finds its way into markets around the globe, the rest of today's somewhat preoccupied world will pay attention. People will see what we do, and they will say what they always say about the United States—it never fails to surprise, it never fails to astound, it never fails to amaze.

The positive trends noted above did not end with the events of 2008—they were just put on hold. Thanks to the mastery of people like Federal Reserve Chairman Ben Bernanke—give the guy a little credit please!—that hold has now been lifted. As a result, the sense of optimism I felt in 2008, as I looked through my graphs for the presentation, has returned. The image I have is of a precrisis road that heads toward a bridge. In 2008, the bridge failed, and people had to climb down into a ravine, ford a stream, and then climb up the other side. But all the while, workers were slowly rebuilding the bridge, though bickering all of the time.

The bickering I'm talking about—mindless and sometimes dishonest argument in Washington, coupled with senseless actions, such as failing to raise the debt ceiling—cost us. Growth is slower than it should be, thanks to sequestration, and our credit rating, once the envy of the world, has fallen, all as a result of the partisan bickering I'm referring to. That tumble in our credit rating—from AAA to AA+—is not just embarrassing. Ultimately, it will add to the government's borrowing costs. As those costs rise, taxpayers will have to foot the bill—a bill resulting from Congress's inability to clinch what should have been a routine deal.

Annoying as these actions are, they can't stop what's taking place, only retard it. The forces shaping our future are more powerful than the self-destructive behavior of a few politicians.

In 2013, the bridge I mentioned moved into its final stages of completion. At first, a few people were allowed to walk across it; then, one by one, cars were allowed onto the bridge to cross the ravine. Now, at the time of this writing, workers are removing the remaining barriers, allowing traffic on the new, stronger bridge, a bridge that has been rebuilt.

I'm not saying our problems are over. We will be removing problems from our path for a long time to come. The country remains in debt, budgets are tight, confidence lags, and our politics are a mess. But, soon, even those problems will be brushed aside by the indomitable force of growth. This should happen starting in 2014, as the energy trade deficit begins to decline in a meaningful way. (In 2014, the United States is expected to produce 10 million or more barrels of oil a day, making it the world's largest producer.[18])

That same year, if I am correct, interest rates could begin rising slightly, as Bernanke has suggested, as a response to the country's more robust growth. Taking the country off of life support—as evidenced by rising rates—is likely to provide investors with more confidence in the future of the economy, as long as it doesn't happen too early and too abruptly. Rather than keep their huge reserves of capital in the bank, companies will invest in expanding their businesses. And, since one thing leads to another, in 2014, hiring will move into a more normal range.

With more people working at what they want to do, rather than working either for free, as interns, or in jobs they do not like, America's optimism about the future will return. In 2015, I expect the effects of people working to wend their way through the entire economy, resulting in a more normal housing market and a less jittery stock market.

Along the way, we will see signposts of growth. In 2014, Apple will begin producing some of its best-selling computers here in the United States, most likely in Texas. Volkswagen, Nissan, Toyota, and BMW will be making more of their cars here—employing America's highly motivated, world-class workers. As that happens, people will begin noticing that America's manufacturing is increasing, not declining.

Nothing turns out as you think it will. There will be surprises, negative and positive, that will either accelerate or decelerate the rate of investment into the country, as well as its growth. But one thing is certain. The United States is becoming stronger economically, not weaker, and that is good news for all of us.

CHAPTER THREE

THE UNITED STATES OF CREATIVITY

The people who are unleashing America's second century of leadership, innovation, and growth have several things in common. They are brilliant, creative, and highly motivated, not just to create change, but to transform the world and to do it from their American base. They are not pursuing ideas simply because they are curious—although they are intensely curious. They are pursuing ideas pragmatically. And, although they often have deep associations with America's most important research universities, they are far from ivory-tower idealists. Instead, they see research—including deep, fundamental research into the mysteries of physics, biology, and mathematics—as providing them with the tools they need to make things happen.

The people I've met and interviewed over the past couple of years are but a tiny fraction of the talent that resides here. They are part of America's vast army of geniuses who—as Apple's old advertisement used to say—*think different*. By thinking different, these people will keep America great.

Keep in mind, most of the people I will refer to are unsung—at least for now. But they have been—and will remain—powerful creative forces behind the country's rise. I believe, as the economist Paul Romer has shown, that talent and ideas are the forces that transform society, civilizations, and ultimately the world. If it weren't for the talent and ideas of the people who live in the United States, our farms would be producing at a fraction of their current rates, the oil and gas reserves underneath many parts of the country would remain un-tapped, and the great advances in science, technology, and medicine that American scientists have been responsible for would not have happened.

The American mind is a powerful force. But if you couple that with the bounty that lies on and under our land, the expertise of our scientists, and the knowledge and resources of our technical and commercial leaders, and then add to that our culture of pragmatism, creativity, and attainment, it is clear that we have some very powerful forces working on our behalf.

When I was editor-in-chief of the *Harvard Business Review* in the 1990s, Dan Yankelovich came to visit us on several occasions. Yan-kelovich, now eighty-eight and still going strong, was one of the first, and perhaps the best, survey researchers—a "pollster," to put it in the vernacular. He went to Harvard, where he earned a PhD in psychol-ogy in 1950, then went to the Sorbonne in Paris for further study. He is a man who is at home in many cultures and in many parts of the world as a traveler, as a businessperson, and, most importantly, as a social scientist. Dan is small of stature, a little round, and has huge, inquisitive eyes made bigger by the glasses he wears.

Years ago, Dan and I had a conversation I will never forget. We were discussing the values that so-called Western countries have in common. He had just completed a study on this topic. Dan's conclu-sion was enlightening. He said that Americans and Europeans, for example, had almost identical values with regard to life, relationships, institutions, and what they hold dear. But there was one area where America was truly exceptional. Americans, alone among the people he had surveyed, had a powerful interest in what he called "self-im-provement." Whereas Europeans were pretty much content with their lot in life and with who they were as people, and even with their role in society, Americans were always making an effort to improve them-selves. That might account, as later studies have shown, for why peo-ple in some European countries are a little "happier" than we are. We are antsy, eager to move upward and onward, while they are more content.

But that's who we are—the people who are always on diets, always trying new exercise regimes, who read self-help books and magazines, and take classes at night and online, who do yoga and meditate, and—unlike the rest of the world—embrace all kinds of lifelong learning. And even though a lot of Americans are couch potatoes, sprawled out on the sofa or dozing in their La-Z-Boys, they know they should be doing more. The urge to make ourselves better than we are is national trait.

Americans always want to move up. (And when they move up, they want to move up more.) Americans are the people who start companies because they want to do something better. Americans bring ideas into their companies because they want to improve how things work. They write books and papers filled with their own sometimes highly unorthodox ideas, and they stretch themselves to be better. Americans tend to be at home with the sound of breaking eggs and breaking china and breaking boundaries and records. That uniquely American core value—self-improvement—spills over to make society better. Whereas many countries have a handful of leaders who set the course for the future, America is a country of self-selected leaders who stand up when the time is ripe. What do I mean by that? I mean Americans raise their hands and volunteer to work at night and weekends for the betterment of society. Our school boards are run by volunteers, and so are our museums, churches, synagogues, universities, and community organizations, along with some of our towns and our political parties. Between September 2011 and September 2012, 64.5 million Americans volunteered[1] for something at least once. And although we are not unique in volunteering—some of the Nordic countries also have very high rates of volunteering—our voluntarism does indicate that Americans want to put their knowledge and skills to work.

The point I am making is that while in other countries visions for the future are centralized, in the United States they are fragmented. A new idea can emerge from anyone and from anywhere. People work hard to get ahead, they take courses at night, they read self-help books, and they search online to get tips for getting ahead. And then they apply this knowledge, either through entrepreneurship or by volunteering. We Americans, more than other groups, take our vast intellectual resources and apply them. We do it to make ourselves better and in the process make the world better.

HOW AMERICA THINKS

The propensity for us to make ourselves better by self-study or the pursuit of education throughout our lives is not a new phenomenon in America. Alexis de Toqueville wrote about America's insatiable desire to improve things, rather than leave them alone, in his book *Democracy in America*, published in 1835. The book was based on his travels through the country in 1831.

Self-improvement is a powerful element in the American psyche. But what makes it even more transformative is when we combine it with science, which we have done since the outset. Americans, as long ago as when the country was founded, saw the practical value of science. As is well known, Benjamin Franklin had a life-long interest in the practical application of science and did original scientific work in several fields. Many of the founders, including Thomas Jefferson and George Washington, were learned in the sciences of their day. But what made America truly different was crystallized into words in 1837 by the philosopher Ralph Waldo Emerson, in a speech called "The American Scholar" that he gave in Cambridge, Massachusetts. The speech, which was published first as a pamphlet and then as part of a book of essays by the same name, proved very influential among America's intellectuals and policymakers and has been widely quoted.

Emerson argued that scholars—by which he meant people who work with their minds—should not cut themselves off from the world or from new developments in favor of tradition. They must constantly challenge themselves and their thinking. He warned scholars not to become acolytes and "parrot" what they hear. Instead, he argued, they should welcome new ways of approaching old problems. He also argued for direct observation of nature as a tool for inquiry in addition to the study of past knowledge contained in books.

But Emerson's most important—*and revolutionary*—point was that "scholars" should not distance themselves from what he called "practical men," even though it could seem as if they lived in different worlds—one rough and tumble, the other cloistered and pure. (It was the minister and philosopher Emerson, by the way, who said, "Build a better mousetrap and the world will beat a path to your door," although probably in a slightly more eloquent form.) Separating the so-called ivory tower from the world of making things and of commerce was anathema to Emerson and to his ideas of self-reliance. He argued that scholars must join forces with practical people to see how their ideas played out in what he called "action," in the real world.

Emerson articulated what became a specifically American way of thinking—the inclusion of what he called *action*, and we would call *application*—as an important aspect of scholarship. Back then, scientists used the scientific method of proposing and then testing hypotheses. That's not the same as applying the ideas practically. Testing a hypothesis shows you that similarly charged poles of a magnet repel each other, whereas the practical application of the principle ends up as an electric motor. For most of scientific history, the former was done in an academic lab, while the latter was carried out at a company or in a tinkerer's stable, basement, or garage.

Few scientists, let alone any philosopher other than Emerson, were then advocating anything as radical as narrowing the distance between the academic lab and the commercial company. The academy, in both America's fledging universities and around the world, existed in one self-contained sphere, the world of commerce and reality in another. Emerson changed that way of thinking, influencing the teaching at most universities in the United States as well as the way they were run.

Consider the following, which Emerson wrote in 1837: "Action is with the scholar subordinate, but it is essential. Without it, he is not yet man. Without it, thought can never ripen into truth. Whilst the world hangs before the eye as a cloud of beauty, we cannot even see its beauty. Inaction is cowardice, but there can be no scholar without the heroic mind."[2]

In this passage, Emerson set America on its own separate intellectual course where the application of ideas was not simply necessary, it was a heroic necessity that should be part of a scholar's identity. Emerson argued—and Americans took note—that the "practical man," people with grease stains on their clothing and calluses on their hands, should not simply be considered equals of the intellectual; they should be considered as the intellectual's partner. No other country embraced that view to the extent that Americans have. No other country embraced the notion that the practical man and the scholar, as partners, could generate real improvement—self-improvement, community and social improvement, national improvement, global improvement.

Emerson's speech and the article that followed achieved tremendous influence. The printed version was widely read and distributed. Oliver Wendell Holmes, who was appointed to the US Supreme Court in 1902 by President Theodore Roosevelt, and who was one of the most influential thinkers of his time, called Emerson's essay "a declaration of intellectual independence."[3]

We cannot underestimate the importance of this uniquely American way of thinking. Other countries, even today, continue to separate the world of university research from the world of commerce. And, although this attitude may be breaking down in some parts of the world, it does continue to persist.

THE AMERICAN SCHOLAR IN ACTION

Jay Schnitzer is the kind of person I think of as embodying the American scholar's marriage of science and practicality. He is an "only in America" type. He grew up in Springfield, Massachusetts, was an Eagle Scout, resembles a better-looking version of the comedian Eugene Levy, and is built like a linebacker on a football team. He's something of a strong, silent type, but with a wry sense of humor. And he's also very, very smart and extremely focused.

Jay has a PhD in chemical engineering from MIT and an MD from Harvard Medical School. He's one of the top pediatric trauma surgeons in the world, having performed surgeries in the midst of crises in the Gaza Strip, as well as in Boston, where he lives. He's both a burn specialist and a cardiac specialist and a world authority on each.

Schnitzer was a professor at Harvard Medical School before he went into business in 2008. Not just any business, but the renowned Boston Scientific, long considered one of the world's most innovative companies. It makes pacemakers and devices that manage heart rhythms, open blocked arteries, manage pain, and peer inside the body to diagnose disease. The company also pioneered implantable devices that deliver medicines over long periods, as well as implantable defibrillators that restart stopped hearts in high-risk patients. Boston Scientific has 24,000 employees and 15 manufacturing sites.

One of the company's two founders, John Abele, was an early proponent of "open innovation," the practice through which a company is open to ideas from the outside. Pursuing open innovation sounds a lot simpler than it is. For one thing, it requires confidence, since it means you must open yourself to both ideas and criticism from outsiders. In addition, it requires courage, because some of those outsiders might take your ideas and use them for their own benefit. More than anything, it requires the ability to listen and collaborate, traits that sound easy but are difficult in practice. To be an open innovator, you need to let yourself and your colleagues be challenged, and you need to pay attention to what competitors are doing and involve stakeholders in your research (in the case of Boston Scientific, this would be patients, health-care professionals, and customers). As if this is not enough, open innovation also requires taking risks, since people on the outside who suggest new ideas might not always be there to buy the product once it is developed and released.

Boston Scientific had engaged in open innovation since first opening its doors in 1979, and it even expanded the practice by inviting customers to meet with members of its research staff and to spend time in the company's labs. Back then, opening up the laboratory to outsiders, even when those outsiders were customers, was considered radical. The thinking was that companies needed to keep their intellectual property—their catalog of concepts, ideas, formulas, practices, and processes—secret and protected from outsiders.

But Abele didn't buy that notion. He himself was an outsider of sorts. He was neither a doctor nor an engineer. He had studied at Amherst, a liberal arts college. Abele believed that if you open up your laboratories to your customers and let them walk around and talk to your researchers, they will contribute ideas that your own team might never have considered. And those ideas will be valuable, not just because they are often good ideas, but because your customers are more likely to buy products they helped develop.

Boston Scientific grew rapidly through the talents of its own researchers, but it also grew by listening to what outsiders thought. In thirty-four years, it went from a startup with a tiny laboratory located in a Boston suburb to a global research and manufacturing powerhouse. Open innovation was one of the reasons the company was so successful.

And where does Schnitzer come in? He was the doctor-sur-geon-chemical-engineer who was Boston Scientific's chief medical officer. This job built upon his experience at Massachusetts General Hospital, where he oversaw the integration of medicine with technology. At Boston Scientific, he oversaw four of the company's most important divisions and was involved in everything from concept to product development to post-market-introduction analysis. He was one of the company's many bridges between academic research and the practical world. It was a big job.

But not big enough.

From Boston Scientific, Schnitzer went to work as head of research at the Defense Advanced Research Projects Agency, DARPA. If you're not familiar with DARPA, consider this: it was established in 1958, a year after the Soviet Union launched Sputnik, the first artificial satellite to orbit the earth. It was charged with the task of never allowing the United States to be surprised by a technological innovation from another country. Protecting us from surprise was a big part of Schnitzer's job.

Creating a technology- and science-based institution to keep America from being surprised by another nation's innovations may seem, at first, like a very different task from what Emerson had in mind when he wrote that the worlds of action and scholarship should be coupled, not separated. And Americans were by no means the first to use science and technology to gain military advantage. The ancient Romans had their "mechanics," what we would call engineers, and used them to their advantage. Leonardo da Vinci, the Renaissance artist and intellectual explorer, devised weapons based on what he knew about the science of his day, though they were so advanced for their time it is doubtful any of them worked.

What's different about America's approach is simply that DARPA—and the military in general—do not have many of their own researchers. The Army Corps of Engineers is dedicated to civil engineering projects, not high-tech science. And while there are a lot of uniformed personnel with PhDs, most of them liaise with outside researchers rather than conduct research on their own.

The utility of DARPA, located in Arlington, Virginia, is that it provides a framework for working directly with the nation's leading scientists at universities, think tanks, and research labs without hiring them full time. Some departments at the nearby Pentagon do the same. The beauty of the model is that this enables researchers to spend time on an advanced defense project without separating from the larger research community. DARPA contracts with the best scientists in the country, whose work is to continuously improve our systems. In fact, very few technical people work directly for DARPA for more than a few years.

The launch of Sputnik was traumatic for the United States. The communist Soviet Union and the United States were nuclear-armed rivals locked in the Cold War. Both had massive militaries, and they were rivals not just with each other but for the loyalty of their allies in Western and Eastern Europe. They were also rivals for the friendship of dozens of so-called nonaligned countries around the world, including such places as India, Indonesia, Malaysia, and Brazil. The main worry was that the rivalry between the Soviets and the Americans could turn into a real war, and that technological developments such as Sputnik gave the Soviets the advantage. But there was another worry as well. It was that the nonaligned countries, which accounted for the majority of the world's population, might think the Soviet Union was more technologically advanced than the United States. That perception might cause these countries to side with the Soviets in times of strife.

So when the Soviet Union launched Sputnik, a gleaming 185-pound metallic ball with a radio transmitter inside, America and its allies were shaken. Although both countries had talked about venturing into space, no one in the American scientific or military establishment had thought the Soviet Union would get there first.

It's not that the United States hadn't tried to launch a satellite into orbit. It had made many attempts, all resulting in failure. Rockets blew up on the launching pad, or exploded midflight. There was always a lot of fanfare before a launch, followed by depression and fear in its aftermath. Finally, in 1958, a year after Sputnik, the United States put a satellite into orbit. It weighed just 30 pounds.

But while Americans were celebrating their achievement, the Soviets continued with advances well beyond Sputnik. Shortly before America's first successful satellite launch, the Russians launched a dog, Laika, into orbit inside Sputnik II, a much heavier satellite than the original. Laika's vital signs were monitored during the flight. Gathering information about how Laika was faring physically, as a rocket propelled her into space and then into orbit, was a sure sign that the Soviets were gathering data they could use to safely send men into space.

The Soviets continued to outpace the United States in space with one development after another. Another shocker came in 1961, when the Soviets put cosmonaut Yuri Gagarin into orbit and then returned him safely to earth. The United States did not send a man into orbit until the following year, when astronaut Alan Shepard did a sub-orbital trip through space.

The US-Soviet rivalry was bitter and intense. Both countries built significant capabilities in nuclear weapons, making people nervous in both countries. Seeing the way the Soviet Union was advancing in its space program made Americans fearful. They worried in political forums and in the media that the United States had lost its advantage technologically and militarily.

All of this prompted President Dwight D. Eisenhower to set up the Advanced Research Project Agency, or ARPA, inside the Department of Defense. Renamed DARPA in 1972, the agency's purpose was to prevent surprise, "to make sure the United States maintained technological preeminence," as Schnitzer put it, particularly for the military.

DARPA is an essential element in maintaining America's creativity and leadership. Although other countries have large, government-sponsored research programs, none of those programs are designed to prevent the countries that established them from being surprised by a development taking place elsewhere. Russian president Vladimir Putin announced in 2012 that Russia would launch a DARPA lookalike, but the real DARPA has a fifty-four-year head start and a well-developed methodology for getting impossible things done. Descriptions of that methodology can be found in dozens of places on the web as well as in books.[4] But it's one thing to understand how DARPA works, and another to apply this knowledge in practice.

The significance of DARPA is twofold. First, it supports research that aims to create hitherto impossible things. DARPA is not interested in doing research and development that's easy; it is interested in work that is as close to the edge as possible. That policy sends a powerful message to the country's technical community. Second, DARPA is a research and development agency, but it is also a powerful symbol to many technical people that they have permission—wherever they may be—to push past the limits of our understanding. If an agency inside the US Defense Department can come up with breakthroughs, why can't they?

For an agency like DARPA to attract inventors who want to work with it, and for it to have symbolic power, it must have accomplishments. As it happens, it does. DARPA's track record, right from the start, has been astonishing. It began developing the F-1 rocket engine during its first year. The F-1 is the largest, most powerful liquid-fueled rocket engine ever built, with more than 1.5 million pounds of thrust. When the National Aeronautics and Space Administration (NASA) was formed, it took five F-1 engines, called them "Saturn," strapped them together, and used them to send men to the moon.

DARPA's long list of successes also includes ARPANET, which became the Internet; the U-2 spy plane; global positioning systems (GPS); unmanned aerial vehicles, also known as "drones"; stealth technology; and other advanced projects, such as autonomous flying devices that are the size of hummingbirds, and have flight maneuverability equal to the real thing. DARPA was also a pioneer in developing artificial intelligence.

The development of GPS is especially interesting as an example of America's technological and creativity leadership edge. Although the technology dates back to the 1970s, it continues to evolve with the help of DARPA.

In 2004, DARPA initiated the "Grand Challenge," with the objective of having teams compete to build the first vehicle to travel autonomously—that is, without a driver—along a 150-mile route through the desert. DARPA offered a prize of $1 million, then upped the reward to $2 million, which a team from Stanford University won in 2005.

What's interesting is that by offering a prize, DARPA not only leveraged its money (more than a dozen competing teams collectively spent tens of millions of dollars trying to win), but also excited tinkerers and entrepreneurs throughout the country, creating interesting capabilities. As a result of the 2004 and 2005 competitions—and their successful outcome—DARPA has conducted additional competitions. In June 2013, DARPA selected fifteen out of eighteen teams to compete in a "Spectrum Challenge." The goal is to see which team can advance the use of radio frequencies so that cell-phone and other networks can accommodate more voice and data volume while still letting important communications through. The winner will create ways to use the radio spectrum more efficiently during times of emergency. And the winner is also likely to create billions of dollars of value as companies adopt techniques for sending more data and voice communication through the air.

Another DARPA competition, announced in December 2012, is the "Robotic Challenge," where teams will compete to develop robots that can go into war zones and disaster areas on their own power, navigate through different types of debris and dangerous conditions, and rescue people who have been wounded or injured and stranded in those areas.

Still another competition, called the "FANG Challenge," was in January 2013. Here the goal is to create new types of amphibious vehicles to land troops on distant shores. (FANG is DARPA's acronym for the Fast Adaptable Next Generation Ground Vehicle.)

And in 2009, DARPA conducted another interesting experiment. It hid ten red weather balloons in ten different locations around the country, then announced that the person or group that located all of ten of them would win $40,000. It was called, naturally, the "Red Balloon Challenge." Fifty-eight teams competed from around the world. Some used satellite data, others used iPhones and social media, and some used spamming techniques to throw competitors off by planting false information, in the hopes of gaining more time for the hunt.

DARPA expected that it would take the winner several days to locate the balloons. It's a big country—3.8 million square miles—and even if the balloons were painted red, they were only a few feet across and could float, at best, only about a hundred feet in the air.

So how long did it take the winning team to find the ten balloons? A team from MIT found all of them in just under seven hours.

They did it by using various social media and a very simple technique. They offered their own prizes—up to $2,000—to anyone who correctly identified the location of a balloon. They also said that the remaining funds from the prize money would be given to charity.

Although MIT's strategy sounds simple, it was based on what is called the Query Incentive Network model of Jon Kleinberg at Cornell University and Prabhakar Raghavan at Stanford, who is also vice president of engineering at Google. The model, which uses mathematics to predict behavior based on incentives, taught DARPA valuable lessons about how to use social networks, such as LinkedIn or Facebook, to mobilize people.

Yet another challenge competition, the "Urban Challenge," one of DARPA's most famous, took place in 2007. It required teams to make driverless vehicles that could navigate a sixty-mile "urban" course laid out on the empty runways of an abandoned airport. The course was filled with traffic, obstacles, and other manned and unmanned vehicles. The challengers included large car companies, technology vendors, and components makers, most of them linked to engineering schools. The $2 million prize was won by a team from Carnegie Mellon University.

Think about the power of DARPA. Google, GM, Volkswagen, Ford, Nissan, Toyota, and most other vehicle companies are now racing to build autonomous vehicles. The market is expected to be huge for autonomous vehicles, including cars, buses, taxis, and delivery and long-distance trucks as well as road graders, earth movers, and other types of equipment. All of these would be guided by GPS, radar, laser, artificial vision, and other types of sensing and positioning technology, which will be developed, at least in part, by DARPA.

Autonomous vehicles are expected to be safer than human-controlled vehicles, because they can react more quickly than humans to changing conditions. Because of the accuracy and speed of the sensors, these vehicles will be able to travel closer together, in clumps, minimizing traffic congestion and increasing fuel efficiency. California and Nevada have made autonomous vehicles legal as long as there is a driver onboard with controls he or she can use if necessary.

One can imagine military scenarios where autonomous vehicles are critical—especially for delivering supplies or evacuating the wounded. But the real markets are the commercial ones. "DARPA takes no royalties," Schnitzer said. There was a subtext to his remark: though DARPA's primary mission is military, if it can contribute to the economic well-being of the country, that's part of its job, too.

SMALL BUDGET, BIG RESULTS

What's even more astonishing is how much DARPA has accomplished with so little—its budget is $3.2 billion, roughly 1/215th of the US defense budget. But even more interesting, DARPA only has 120 program managers, who are "geniuses in their fields," according to Schnitzer. What's even more interesting is that these "program managers are limited to four-year terms," said Schnitzer, whose own term ended in 2013. Moving people in and out of DARPA is one of the ways in which "the culture is kept fresh," he said.

Schnitzer then said something even more interesting: "I get evaluated by how many times I failed. Too many successes means I wasn't far enough out on edge." DARPA doesn't need to solve easy problems, or problems companies typically would be able to solve on their own. Its reason for being is to solve problems no one else can.

DARPA's recipe for success is a case example of how American firms in general stay successful. They take chances, have a mobile workforce, are not humiliated when a project fails, and, when it is legal (there are anticompetitiveness laws), even cooperate. They also try to do it all with a small, efficient workforce.

DARPA is quintessentially American because it relies on competition. And although, for all kinds of reasons, some researchers may not want to work on defense projects, they are not surprised when they get a call. As Emerson urged, American scholars should embrace, not fear or disapprove of, the world of commerce and action. As a result, at DARPA, teams fight it out to win a prize, which—almost by definition—means that America gets more than one approach to solving each problem.

Our companies are the same way. They compete with each other vigorously to gain even the slightest technical advantage. There is no better example of how America operates than in the computer and operating system wars of the past few decades. At the beginning of that war, there were just a few companies: Apple, Radio Shack, Osborne, Microsoft (which developed an operating system for IBM), and a host of other long-gone brands, each using different technology, chips, and operating systems.

In the 1980s, for example, I used a Radio Shack TRS-80 computer with its own operating system, called TRS-DOS, which wasn't compatible with any other system. That old beast was built around a chip made by Zilog called the Z80. Another competitor, the Commodore 64, used a chip made by MOS Technology. In the competitive slugfest that ensued, two standards emerged—Microsoft's and Apple's—and hundreds of interesting companies failed. Competition is nasty stuff. But it resulted in a robust, highly competitive industry.

Even so, the long-term dominance of Apple and Microsoft is far from assured. Google and a host of other mobile solutions providers are eating away Apple's and Microsoft's businesses. Shielding Microsoft or Apple from competition would guarantee stasis, however, since you cannot beat the competition without innovating.

The truth is that our brand of capitalism, which generally allows for the Schumpeterian forces of creative destruction to make companies obsolete, is brutal, disruptive, and messy. Companies go out of business in exactly the same way that teams lose a DARPA challenge. But each time a company fails or becomes moribund, we learn something, just as DARPA does when a team loses one of its challenges. Success may be sweet, but failure is a powerful teacher, one that can't be ignored.

Whereas we embrace creative destruction, albeit one softened with Social Security, Medicare, and other safety nets, including the Obama Affordable Health Care Act, most other countries lean toward cuddlier systems that allow companies to slack off and still survive. In China, and even in parts of Europe, for example, companies are owned or controlled by the government in a way that prevents them from failing.

In China, a great many companies in a host of sectors, including resources, shipping, energy, electricity, telecommunications, life insurance, vehicle manufacturing, steel production, shipbuilding, and railroads, are owned partially or wholly by the government. The Chinese government even owns companies in the tobacco, beer, and travel sectors. Companies owned by governments aren't usually very efficient. They are more about job creation than about developing cutting-edge technology. They only have one important shareholder, and that shareholder has access to resources and policies that can keep the company afloat even if it's a market laggard.

France and other countries in Europe also have a number of big companies that are owned or controlled by the government. Sometimes the government only owns a single share—so on paper the company is public—but that share has a majority or near-majority of votes.

My point is, America's brand of capitalism isn't always easy, but it results in companies that are capable of surviving enormous tribulations and constant upheavals. When they can no longer survive the competitive fray, companies fail, but other companies with new ideas take their place. That's the way DARPA operates, and it was the way Schnitzer was evaluated.

Of course, no system is pure. GM, Chrysler, many of our banks, and the big insurance company AIG were saved from extinction by the actions of the Treasury Department and the Federal Reserve after the 2008 crisis.

Russia's DARPA clone has a very narrow focus—hypersonic airplanes and enhanced automation—whereas DARPA's goals are big, bold, and all-encompassing. As Schnitzer explained it, "my job is to create the future. Not to understand it or forecast it, but create it."

Far from being cloistered, DARPA's 120 program officers and their support staff are engaged with the world, as exemplified by the competitions. They are influenced by the latest academic research and also by science fiction, music, art, literature, and even movies. (DARPA has a lot in common with the Broad Institute at MIT, with its full-time artist in residence.)

Even more importantly, DARPA is not a cushy government job that someone can keep for life, given the four-year maximum tenure of DARPA's technical employees. After that, the employee has to find another job or go back to the university, think tank, or company where he or she was employed before. This constant movement of people in and out of DARPA is not that much different from the way companies operate. People are hired, then fired. Or they relocate for other reasons. They learn something, then they take what they learned elsewhere. Employees at American companies change jobs often, spreading ideas everywhere they go.

America is really good at DARPA-like thinking in part because our system allows for bad ideas and outmoded institutions to go extinct. Many people consider our form of capitalism to be uncaring. After all, companies fail all the time, which puts people out of work. And, though no one likes to be unemployed, the need to stay on one's toes can be healthy. As Samuel Johnson, the eighteenth-century British critic, said, "nothing focuses the mind like a hanging." Or, we might add, like the threat of being fired or losing market share.

I'm not saying that getting fired is good because it toughens people up, or keeps them focused on their work, or keeps them nimble. There are plenty of Americans who are good at what they do and who lose their jobs anyway. No one likes that. And job mobility in America is about much more than just getting fired.

What's different about Americans is that, unlike Europeans, for example, we are willing to pack up the car and move to another city to get a job. In the twenty-seven countries of the European Union, only about 0.5 percent of the labor force moves each year within the country for work, and only 0.25 percent moves to another European country for work. In the United States, each year, 2.5 percent of the workforce consists of people who decide to put their things into a moving van to go to a new job.[5] What's remarkable is that Europeans don't move even though some parts of the European Union—Spain, for instance—have an unemployment rate for young people of around 50 percent.

The reason Europeans stay put is not because of labor laws. If you are an EU citizen, you can pretty much work anywhere in the European Union. They don't move because of family attachments and culture, and in some cases language.

Americans have families, too, but they are willing to move away from them to pursue more fulfilling work. Because European distances are smaller, an Italian can move to Germany or France and still drive home to Milan for the weekend. That's not the case for a New Yorker who finds work in Seattle or even Chicago. And yet, we do it.

I mentioned above that Dan Yankelovich talked about self-improvement, which I expressed in terms of lifelong education. What

I didn't say was that one reason why we are so interested in self-improvement is that if we stand still, we're likely to find ourselves unemployed. The simple fact is, if Americans don't get moving, they can be frozen out of the job market for a long, long time, with only paltry unemployment benefits, whereas in Europe, because of its labor laws, the benefits are not only more generous, but once you find work, it's not that easy to be fired, although this varies by country.

With our edge, it doesn't seem likely that other countries will surpass us anytime soon. For example, at a recent meeting focused on alternative energy, a venture capital colleague of mine said he had just come back from looking at companies and going to conferences in Europe and China. In those places, "people are impatiently waiting for the next new idea to emerge from America so they can run with it. They recognize the United States as the world's center of creativity." That investor made a fair statement. With so much of the world's innovation engine situated in the United States, many companies around the world simply steal what we have developed. If they are a little more ethical, they might simply adapt what we do for their use, and if they are outright honest, they will pay for the right to use our technology. Whatever they choose, they are making money off of what we do. Huawei, the big Chinese telecommunications and electronics manufacturing company, is alleged to have stolen many of its ideas from Cisco. That leaves Cisco with three choices: fight it out in court—which it has been doing; capitulate by ceding certain markets to Huawei—the road to long-term decline; and/or continue to out-innovate Huawei—the only viable solution, in my opinion.

CREATIVITY

Though he was a philosopher and a minister, Emerson was also the person who said, probably in a sermon, "Do not go where the path may lead, go where there is no path and leave a trail." This phrase, combined with his advice to "build a better mousetrap," are about creativity and practicality. They are not about what we call innovation.

In my view, innovation has become a hollow term, since what people today usually mean by it is that they are trying to harness some new ideas to drive profits to the bottom line. Or they might mean that they are trying to maximize the share of revenue or profits coming from new products. Or, and this is the worst of what they mean by innovation, "incremental change on a continuous basis."

Fair enough. But isn't innovation what companies should be doing anyway? Isn't it their job to create new products, improve the bottom line, and make continuous improvements? And, if that's the case, why call it innovation? It sure sounds like business-as-usual to me. For example, isn't it business-as-usual for Intel to come with up faster, more powerful chips every year, just like Apple is supposed to dazzle us every few months with new consumer gadgets? And aren't GM, Ford, Chrysler, and all the other automakers supposed to come up with exciting new products and concepts? Aren't they supposed to give us newer, better, safer, cooler technology every year? Innovation, as the term is now being used, is just the entry point. If companies are not constantly putting new ideas into the marketplace in pursuit of revenue and profits, they fail. Innovation is the entry point—not the goal.

Real innovation—what I prefer to call "creativity"—is bigger than that. It's game changing. The first computer chip, the first big box store, the first edition of Microsoft Office, were innovative breakthroughs. But years later, are companies still innovating when they put more transistors on the chip, find a better way to organize the aisles at Home Depot, or add a few features to Excel or Word? Hardly. America is successful not only because it changes the world—what Schnitzer described as DARPA's main job—but because it is also constantly surprising the world.

What's real innovation? I'll give you some examples.

Real innovation would have been Microsoft starting Google. It could have, since the skills and technology needed to create a Google-level innovation are not that different from the technology Microsoft owns. Instead, Microsoft focused on incremental updates of its operating system. It avoided taking a big risk. And, when it introduced Bing, as a competitor to Google, it did so too late in the game. Ditto with the introduction of its smartphone software, since Apple and Google were already far ahead. Innovation needs to be brash—a quality Microsoft used to embody.

Real innovation would have been Sony Music starting iTunes, or something like it, to sell its music. After all, it bought music and movie production companies. But Sony failed to find a way to link these assets to its hardware in the way that Apple linked its iPod, iPad, and iPhones to its online content store. With its own movie studios and recording companies, and with one of the largest electronics businesses in the world, one would have thought that Sony, not Apple, would have gotten there first. But instead of doing so, Sony let its innovation muscles flag. The company that created the Walkman could have created the iPod and everything that followed in its wake.

Real innovation would have been Ford or GM introducing the Tesla—which is not just a new car, but a new system, which includes charging stations and battery swapping stations. Tesla is to cars what iTunes, iPods, and iPads are to music and movies—a new and highly integrated way to sell and control a set of products that have been around forever. But Ford and GM stuck with the tried and true, refining their hybrid technology rather than taking leaps into tomorrow.

Real innovation would be Lockheed secretly starting SpaceX, which is a startup manufacturer of rockets, at its skunk works. SpaceX uses technology Lockheed is familiar with, but is more reliable, less expensive, and more advanced. As a result, Lockheed has fallen behind.

Real innovation would have been Barnes & Noble starting Amazon. That would have been powerful—and possible. B&N's stores could have been its warehouses, and its clerks could have fulfilled online orders to ensure fast shipping rates at low cost. If B&N were first to develop an online store, it might even have been the first company to innovate with an e-book reader. And, rather than declining, B&N could have stayed on top.

Real innovation is not incremental. It's transformative. The good news is that in each of my examples—and there are many more—a competitor that lost its edge has been (or is being) replaced by a new American firm. It's not that Microsoft will disappear tomorrow, but its lead and luster are gone. Innovation is not for the faint of heart; it's for risk takers who want to transform industries and ways of doing business.

That aspect of the term "innovation"—the radical, transformative aspect—has been watered down, which is why I like the term "creativity." Companies that embrace the kind of creativity I am talking about will be around to fight another day. Companies that fail to do so will be replaced.

A CHEETAH MADE OF METAL

In October 2012, I helped organize an event focused on innovation in the biosciences. Jay Schnitzer gave a keynote speech and showed a few videos, one featuring a "mechanical cheetah" about the size of a large dog, Like the real thing, it had four legs, each of which was made with two-piece metallic joints and a set of sensors resembling a head. It also had a see-through body filled with computers, motors, cables, and pneumatic lines. This contraption had the same physical motions that a cheetah has when it walks, creeps, and runs. It was awesome.

When the video started, the mechanical cheetah was standing on a treadmill that gradually increased its speed. As it did, the cheetah's stride lengthened and its pace quickened. After a minute or two, the cheetah was running at 28 miles per hour. Schnitzer told the group that since the video was made, the cheetah's speed had gotten up to 35 miles per hour. Watching the mechanical cheetah run was mesmerizing.

The amount of computing power inside this dog-sized device is staggering, but that's not all. The device is built to sense the speed of the treadmill, adjust the speed of all of its parts, and calibrate its balance. It has to be aware of where each of its mechanical feet lands on the moving belt. It also has to keep itself running straight.

While these requirements may at first seem simple, they are actually enormously complex. The complexity arises from the fact that the cheetah is as autonomous as the DARPA robotic cars. The computer is designed to respond to its environment the same way a real animal does. No one stands at a dial adjusting the mechanical cat's speed to keep it from flying off the treadmill. This type of real-time sensing and moving requires elaborate programming and machinery.

Rather than build up a giant staff of designers and researchers, only to watch as their knowledge and skills go out of date, DARPA acts more like a curator. Rather than design the robot, it lays out specifications for what it wants the robot to do. Then it goes to various companies and asks if they would be willing to build the cheetah or whatever new project is in the works. Boston Dynamics, a firm spun out of MIT's Robotics Lab and located in Waltham, Massachusetts, an old clock-making town a few miles from Boston, jumped at the chance. In a way, Boston Dynamics is an example of the kind of creative company Sony and Microsoft used to be.

Boston Dynamics makes other things, too, in the area surrounding Boston that is known, in the geekier parts world, as the "robotics cluster," because of all of the robotics startups and mature companies that are based there.

Boston Dynamics also made a much larger, albeit slower, four-legged robot for DARPA that is right out of one of George Lucas's *Star Wars* films. The robot is called Big Dog—but in my opinion it should have been called Big Mule, or Big Donkey, because that's what it resembles. Big Dog can carry as much as four hundred pounds. It has four legs, each with three joints, and feet that look like donkey hooves. It has a range of twenty miles before it needs to refuel (it has a gasoline engine), and it's as awesome as the cheetah. No one else, anywhere else in the world, has built anything resembling Big Dog.

Figure 3.1. Two Big Dog robots developed by Boston Dynamics. These robots can be programmed to follow a person over any type of terrain at walking speeds of four miles per hour. They are gasoline powered. Defense Advanced Research Projects Agency.

Big Dog has a head that contains laser range finders, radar, computer vision, and other types of sensors, and, even stranger, it responds to voice commands. It is designed to follow a group of soldiers as they trudge through a variety of terrains, from woods with dense brush and undergrowth to sandy deserts, mud, and even snow. These are environments where legs and feet are far superior to wheels or tracks.

Watching videos of Big Dog walking through the woods, following a group of people and carrying weights to simulate supplies, I realized that the machine shows how far American robotics research has advanced. But what is most interesting is how Big Dog can navigate its way across a parking lot, even when technicians push hard on one of its sides in an attempt to tip it over. When pushed, Big Dog instantly reacts with the same fancy footwork that any real four-legged animal would to regain its balance. The same is true when technicians push Big Dog as it is trying to gingerly make its way across an ice-covered parking lot. On the ice, the robot struggles to right itself and continue on its journey. As Big Dog struggles to keep its footing, it looks like a real animal struggling. Though it's only a machine, you feel for it as it tries to regain its balance and then succeeds.

Boston Dynamics also makes a robot called Petman that looks and walks like a human—it has two arms, two legs, and human proportions. Petman can step over piles of logs and navigate on its own. Like the cheetah, however, Petman has no head (what is it about this company and heads?). Another version of the robot, called Atlas, climbs stairs and can even jump—which is awfully strange to watch.

Boston Dynamics makes other types of robots. But what differentiates this company from other robotics companies around the world is not just that Boston Dynamics' robots are autonomous, and not just that they are able to follow a soldier or a worker around on different types of terrain, but that they are self-balancing.

The technology needed for Big Dog to recover from a technician's push, especially on ice, or that enables Petman or Atlas to walk over piles of logs, or jump, is unique in the world. No other robotics company has been able to duplicate these feats. It is only a matter of time before derivatives of these devices make their way into commercial use. With locational and sensing technology—GPS and its derivatives—these robots are truly autonomous.

When these robots are completely autonomous, which is where America's robotic technology is headed, they will be able to do all sorts of things, from carrying your bags to your hotel room to carrying all your creature comforts when you go camping. These robots could replace people in dangerous jobs, such as mining and jobs requiring work underneath the sea. Robots might be the next generation of firefighters. It could just be that advanced versions of Petman, and other types of autonomous robots, will place their footprints on Mars before we do.

These devices are quite remarkable, and although the industry is still in its infancy, the signs indicate that it will grow very large. After all, robots are designed to replace people, and people are everywhere. That's not to say that people won't find things to do, or that robots will take over. There will always be work for humans. Someone has to design the robots, after all. But it also suggests that, over time, the nature of work will change as more manufacturing processes and even service jobs are done by robots. For those people who are technically proficient and well educated, there is little to worry about. They will always be needed. But for many people, competition for jobs will not come from unskilled, low-wage workers in some exotic land, but from robots.

The word "cluster" is an economics term that refers to specific geographic areas where expertise develops—Silicon Valley for high-tech industries, for example. They tend to spur creativity, largely because people move from job to job and company to company within a cluster. When people move, they tend to bring new ways of thinking and doing things to each new company, often challenging the status quo and seeding the workplace with new thoughts. This tendency makes companies within a cluster very exciting places to work.

▼▼▼▼

Boston Dynamics is only one of many companies in the robot cluster around Boston. (There are more robot companies located in other parts of the country, but the Boston area has the greatest concentration of these firms.) The company was started by Marc Raibert, a professor of engineering and robotic science at MIT, who before that worked at Carnegie Mellon University. Raibert, an elected member of the

National Academy of Engineering, one of the engineering profession's highest honors, swapped the academic life for the commercial world.

It may seem that I am shilling for MIT, since so many of the people so far mentioned have ties to that university. The point, though, is that MIT, along with Stanford and Carnegie Mellon and Berkeley and others, have few peers in the rest of the world. It's not that other countries lack great research universities. What America has, though—great universities combined with an academic culture that does not penalize, ostracize, or look down on a professor who leaves academia to start or work at a company—is unique. My guess is that if Marc Raibert called up MIT and asked to come back to work in his old department, he would be welcomed.

But perhaps, even more importantly, other countries don't have very many professors who want to start companies. It's not part of their cultural makeup. The usual route in other countries, after a student gets a PhD and receives an academic appointment, is that he or she will stay in academia. The chances of that professor entering the commercial world are close to zero.

I'm not saying every American professor of a technical field starts a company. That would be a gross overstatement. And let's be clear. Not every school is MIT, or Stanford or Berkeley. Many American professors are far more interested in academic research than in its commercial application. The point I am making is merely this: whereas in most countries the academic and business worlds are separated by a chasm, that's not the case here. And while professors in many countries are considered tainted, or "sell-outs," that's not how we view it. The ability to exchange ideas between business and academia is simply one of the ways in which we compete.

This in-and-out-of-academia mentality has been a very powerful influence on America and on its rise. MIT, as one of the country's oldest science schools, has one of the longest traditions. But our other top schools are apt to be just as commercially minded.

What's difficult for other countries to emulate is the congenial working relationship American academics have with commercial companies.[6] British or German or French schools may enact policies granting professors leave to exercise their entrepreneurial muscles. But to make that work means those muscles have to be there in the first place, which means professors must have a desire to create companies to make their ideas practical and to improve a portion of the world. In other countries, that's just not the case, at least not yet. As a result, America is not only unique, but it has a special brand of creativity that no other country can match—one that marries academic rigor with the risk-taking functions and discipline of business.

Make no mistake. This unique quality is not genetic. America is, after all, a diverse country. The fact is, academics who come to work in the United States change once they become accustomed to our culture. It does not matter if they are Chinese or Indian or German or French or Russian by birth. What matters is that our culture changes people from introverted "lab rats," as one researcher explained to me, "into full-blown entrepreneurs." Some schools even have programs that foster that transformation. That's why not far from Boston Dynamics you have iRobot, to be discussed below, which makes military bots that disarm improvised explosive devices (IEDs), as well as robotic vacuum cleaners. It also why Hydroid, a maker of underwater robots, is also nearby, and why Medrobotics, which makes robots that perform surgery, is less than an hour's drive away. And, in the areas around Berkeley, Carnegie Mellon, Stanford, and other schools, there are similar clusters to the one around MIT.

ROBOT NATION

Rethink Robotics, a little company in the robot cluster in the greater Boston area around MIT, makes "Baxter," a funny-looking robot that is a game changer. About the size of a man's torso, Baxter has two brawny Schwartzenegger-sized arms that can stretch as wide as nine feet. Baxter's arms are filled with motors and sensors and painted fire-engine red. You can buy a variety of hand-like grabbers that snap onto the ends of the robot's arms. When Baxter is fitted to its gunmetal grey pedestal—sold separately—it is about the size of an average human.

The cool thing about Baxter, aside from the cameras and sensors, is that it has two expressive eyes that look human. These eyes are a part of a display, but they provide visual cues so that people working beside Baxter on an assembly line can know what the robot is doing and where its hands are going to move. And in addition to its visual sensors, the robot uses sonar to shut down when a real human gets too close.

What's new and innovative about Baxter is that it's a robot for the rest of us, that is, small manufacturing companies and mom-and-pop stores. Baxter isn't one of those big, powerful robots that spray-paint cars or perform spot welds on truck bodies. Those robots require an engineer to program them. Instead, Baxter learns by doing, which is novel. You program iBaxter by moving its hands to the spot where you want them to be in a process, and you squeeze the robot's claw-like fingers when it needs to grip something. Manually performing these functions is how Baxter learns.

Baxter is designed so well that it could work next to Lucy and Ethel on that chocolate-wrapping assembly line in the 1952 classic episode of I Love Lucy, where Lucy and Ethel struggle in vain to keep up with a conveyor belt carrying chocolates out from the kitchen. A gruff forewoman in a white uniform and peaked hat explains to the pair that if a single piece of unwrapped chocolate makes it into the boxing room, they will both be fired. To keep their jobs, Lucy and Ethel put unwrapped chocolates into their mouths until their cheeks are full.

Ensuring that all the chocolates are wrapped and boxed is exactly the type of assignment Baxter could help to carry out. And Baxter can be programmed by the people who are supposed to work next to him on the assembly line.

Baxter is cheap—for a robot. He costs $22,000 out of the box— nearly triple the annual pay of a Foxconn worker who assembles Apple's products in China. But unlike a Foxconn worker, you only pay for Baxter once. Even if you outfitted Baxter with a bundle of extras— special grippers, a movable stand, and a drawer-full of software—it would still be cheaper and more reliable than a worker for many types of jobs. And, Baxter is made in the United States.

The first thought people might have is that cheap, Baxter-like robots will put people out of work, especially if they are that cheap to buy and easy to program. Which is true. But the question is, which workers? If lots of Baxter robots are deployed in the United States, resulting in manufacturing jobs returning to our shores, then the people Baxter replaces are not in the United States, but in other countries.

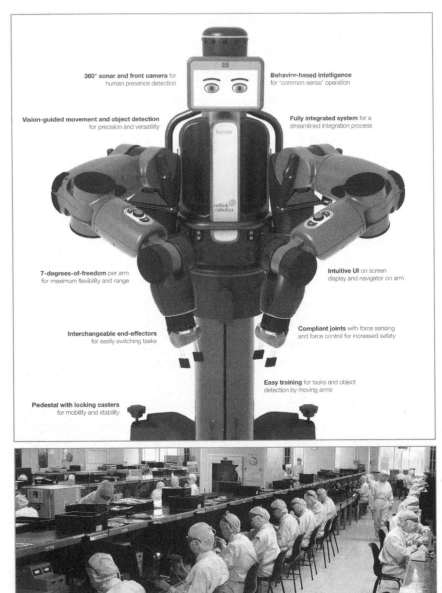

Figure 3.2. Rethink Robotics' "Baxter" versus workers at a Foxconn factory in China. Baxter costs $22,000, is easy to program, and can work three shifts without a break. Each Foxconn worker is paid $8,280 a year, which means it would cost $24,840 for three shifts. Even without Baxter, American factories are more productive than China's. Baxter photo courtesy of Rethink Robotics, Inc. Foxconn factory photo by Jurvetson (flickr).

While that's not great, at least the job loss won't be happening here. True, Baxter is likely to send some American workers packing. But if factories return to America as a result of deploying more robots, those factories will need people to build and maintain the facilities as well as to do a host of related jobs. It will be creative destruction writ large.

Even so, the reason people deploy robots is not to create jobs for truck drivers and insurance workers. It is to increase the efficiency of a factory by automating complex tasks. If that happens as a result of lots of little Baxters stuffing chocolates into boxes on the assembly line, the parent companies will make more money, and that money will make its way through the economy.

I'm not arguing that the future of America will be problem-free. All big shifts in the economy, and most major innovations, are disruptive to the status quo. And, if we're honest, the word "disruptive" in this case really means that some people will win because of these shifts and some will lose. The winners will have better jobs, and the losers might have longer periods when they are unemployed. Still, people are resourceful, and the United States is a very rich country. As a result, it is my contention that it will be easier for us to deal with these disruptions than it will be for, say, China.

I am making that statement because of the differences between China and the United States. In the United States, about 96 percent of the population lives in cities or near them in suburbs, and most of those people have already been absorbed into the economy. We are a middle-class country with a very high average wage level.

But China and many other countries are in a different phase of the development cycle. Half of China's population is urban and the other half rural. Urban residents in China have, on average, around four times the income of rural residents.[7] The reason why the urban Chinese earn so much more than their country cousins is that they work in companies like Foxconn, making products for companies like Apple.

China's goal is to bring more workers into its cities to work in manufacturing jobs. That will position them to earn more money and build the economy. But what happens if China's manufacturing growth rate falls because fewer workers are needed, as a result of the increased use of robots in the countries to which it sells? What happens if auto parts companies in the United States employ Baxter-like robots on the assembly line or in the packing room? Ultimately, in our interconnected world, such a trend is likely to slow down hiring in China, decreasing the rate at which rural Chinese can become urban.

But, even more importantly, for China to stay competitive, it, too, will have to use robots. As a result, in late 2012 Foxconn said that within three years it would purchase 1 million inexpensive robots to replace 1 million people working in its factories.[8] Since that time, Foxconn has taken delivery of only about 10,000 robots, so the project is behind schedule. However, this announcement shows the devastating effect that robots will have on the economies of emerging market countries that compete on the basis of having access to low-wage workers. People assembling goods in factories in emerging countries may be cheap, but robots are always cheaper. And they don't require any benefits.

Don't get me wrong. Robots on the assembly line mean fewer humans building motorcycle frames or lawnmowers—in the United States, too. But my point is that our economy is far more advanced than China's. A majority share of our population already works in service industries, which means we are likely to fare much better than manufacturing-heavy, emerging-market countries when robots enter the workforce in droves.

The robotics industry is still tiny, with about $8.5 billion in revenues in 2012—smaller than most business units at GE. But it is growing rapidly. And, though robots are made in Europe and Japan, the structure of their robotics industries is different from ours, which gives us an advantage.

The companies that make robots in Germany are big firms, such as Siemens. The same is true for Japan. We also have big companies making robots—GE is in that business. But we are also a startup nation with hundreds of small companies started every year. These startups are where the creativity lies, not in the big, entrenched players that make and gradually update robotic welding and painting machines for the auto industry. The machines for that industry, which is the biggest customer for robots, are big, strong, simple, and dumb. They are like the hedgehog, to paraphrase an old Greek poet: they know and do one thing and they do it really well. Next-generation robots are much more like foxes, because they know many things.

By many things, I simply mean that there will always be a need for robots that paint cars. The emerging need, however, is for robots that are autonomous. Autonomous robots use sensors of all types, GPS and other types of locational services, artificial intelligence, and so-called fuzzy logic to move around on their own—like Petman and Big Dog. They even make choices.

Give these robots a destination, and then block their path, and the new robots can find their way to the goal. A dumb robot that paints cars only does exactly what it is programmed to do.

Most of the robotics startups in the United States are making— or attempting to make—autonomous robots of one kind or another, while the big companies stick with their hedgehogs. As a result, there is far more variation in the robotics scene in the United States than in, say, Japan. In addition, there are a lot more robotics companies in the United States than elsewhere. As of November 2012, there were 373 robot makers in the United States, 81 in Japan, 67 in Germany, 41 in Canada, and 40 in France.[9] The rest of the world doesn't make very many robots.

Some of these robotics manufacturing companies are among the most innovative firms we have. Of Fast Company's ten most innovative robotics companies, eight are American, and all but one are small, young companies.[10]

These numbers indicate that the future of the robotic world is likely to be in the United States, which has a robust set of research programs at universities such as MIT, Stanford, Carnegie Mellon, the University of Pennsylvania, and many others. Rethink exemplifies why. The company was started by Rodney Brooks,[11] who conducted research on artificial intelligence, taught at MIT for twenty-six years, and led MIT's robotics research program. One area he focused on as a professor was designing software so robots could be programmed by having someone move their grippers, which is the way Baxter learns, not by sitting at a computer and writing lines of code. It's a prime example of the deep connection between university research and product development.

Even more interesting, Brooks is part of a thriving ecosystem that only exists in America. He was also a founder of iRobot, which makes Roomba for vacuuming floors as well as military robots, such as PackBot, that can enter buildings on their own and stream live video. PackBot was the first robot to enter the damaged nuclear facility at Fukushima, Japan, and to survey the damage. Weighing just 35 pounds, PackBot, when fitted with an arm, is used by the military to disarm bombs. The PackBot comes in several models.

When Brooks started Rethink Robotics, his previous company, iRobot, conceivably could have put roadblocks in his way. After all, he was iRobot's founder and chief technology officer and a member of its board of directors. Presumably, Brooks carried in his head some of iRobot's best ideas and best-kept secrets. Instead of roadblocks, iRobot gave Brooks its blessing. The company's leadership realized that rather than try to stop Brooks, it would be better to let him start a competing company. It did so believing that there was plenty of work to go around and that each new company would further the industry's knowledge. In iRobot's case, it realized that at this stage in the new industry's development, it was important to build an ecosystem that would include designers, engineers, builders, entrepreneurs, and funders.

In all likelihood, iRobot will vigorously compete with Rethink Robotics. The bigger point is that the people running iRobot understand that industries develop and grow when companies compete with each other to survive, even hiring away each other's most talented people. An ecosystem such as this creates survivors that are scrappy and keeps ideas flowing freely. Because America has 373 robotics companies, there is likely to be a vigorous flow of ideas and a constant flow of people among the companies. In the process, some companies will grow, others will die, and new companies will be formed.

Contrast this with the automobile industry, where three domestic firms compete (now two, since Fiat bought Chrysler). In addition, there are a handful of transplanted companies from around the world that operate in the United States. Over time, the so-called Big Three became ossified. Most of the new ideas in that business were coming from companies outside of Detroit. In fact, the automobile industry, for much of its life, has been hostile to new ideas and slow to innovate. Unless it was forced to by legislation, Detroit didn't change.

This reluctance to change almost killed Detroit. Ford did not suffer as much as GM and Chrysler, because Ford had the foresight to put together a cache of capital in advance of the 2008 financial crisis. GM and Chrysler failed and had to be rescued.

Partly they were brought down by their own insularity. They continued to make most of their money off of big, gas-guzzling SUVs, even as oil prices hit $145 a barrel. And because people hired by one company rarely moved to another in these companies, they had no visibility into how the competition operated.

The auto-industry story is a familiar one. But it shows that less competition, coupled with high levels of insularity, is a formula for contraction, not growth. The best-performing companies are those that keep their doors and windows open to the way the world is shifting.

Which is why I believe that iRobot and Rethink Robotics provide us with great examples. I'm no follower of the novelist Ayn Rand, but I do believe that competition produces better results for everyone, especially if it is accompanied by a mobile workforce and the free flow of ideas.

REFINING OUR THINKING

There is more than one type of what might be called "practical creativity," or, as most prefer to call it, "innovation," along the lines of Emerson's statements about building better mousetraps and taking unfamiliar paths. According to Clayton Christensen, a professor at Harvard Business School, there are two types of innovations—those that "empower people" by giving them new products or services, and those that replace old products or services with new ones that are better or more efficient. The first type of innovation is powered by breakthroughs, the second by incremental change.

Henry Ford's Model T was the first type of innovation. It empowered people by opening up access to transportation in the form of a mass-produced, simple, cheap, efficient, and durable car. Ford created not just an automobile, but an industry. Everything that came before the Model T was expensive, hand-built, and one of a kind.

When Ford introduced the Model A, it was the second type of innovation—a better product replacing something that already existed, namely, the Model T. The Model A was a closed-cab car with a modern, simple-to-use transmission, a more powerful motor, and windows to keep out the rain.

Dell is a good example of efficiency, the second type of innovation. Dell didn't invent, or even make, its own chips, software, wires, connectors, circuit boards, or memory. It didn't even make cases to house its machines.

What Dell did really well was create a process for snapping together off-the-shelf parts made by other people. But it didn't even do that until a customer placed an order. The company's innovation was simply its method of making computers it had already sold. Once an order was placed, the machine would be assembled, placed in a box, given to a shipping company, and delivered. Dell was superefficient, and its efficiencies gave it a cost advantage over its rivals. Dell's innovations focused on its business model.

The first type of practical creativity, creating new products, is rare and difficult, and few nations excel at it. Building the Model T, the first airplane, putting the first men on the moon, starting Amazon, the first iTunes store, Facebook—these were all new activities that created new markets or new sectors in existing markets. However, over the past one hundred years, the United States has taken the lead with this type of innovation and pulled farther ahead. China and India may one day follow suit, and Europe may regain its luster, but for now, America is the only superpower of this type of innovation.

This type of creativity is hard. It's the area where DARPA plays such an important role, and which explains why Schnitzer said he got evaluated by how many failures he had. Too many successes means DARPA took too few chances.

But in addition to DARPA there are a lot of organizations, businesses, companies, private labs, and startups of all kinds pushing the first type of innovation. Some of these are financial organizations, such as venture capital firms. Others are advisory, including consulting firms that do research for hire. Others are like MBI, a Michigan-based nonprofit that helps fledgling industrial biotech firms commercialize their products and develop their processes to commercial scale. And then there are "angel investors," people of means who like to invest, often as a group, in startups.

But to get a sense of America's soaring levels of creativity, consider Robert Langer, a chemical engineer and professor at—*yes*—MIT. Langer, who has a lab with about 60 postdoctoral and graduate researchers, has been granted 811 patents[12] based on his ideas and creativity. Polaris Ventures Partners, a venture capital firm headquartered in Cambridge, Massachusetts, invested $220 million in 18 of Langer's companies that develop molecules and devices for medical use. Some of those devices automatically release prescribed doses of medicine into tissues to treat brain cancer. Others measure blood sugar from infinitesimally tiny drops of blood. Each of these companies is at the leading edge, and each of them, if they succeed, will start new industries or sectors within existing industries.

THE IMPORTANCE OF ACCESS

I look at creativity from the perspective of mathematician and inventor R. Buckminster Fuller, whom I was lucky enough to get to know before he passed away in 1983 at the age of eighty-seven. Fuller was about five-foot-six, wore big, black eyeglasses with very thick lenses, and spoke with a New England cadence. He never finished college. In fact, he was thrown out of Harvard. Yet he went on to write dozens of books and to devise and patent many fascinating creations, including the geodesic dome, manufactured houses, three-wheeled cars, and intricate architectural structures. He also developed a new type of geometry that didn't require *pi*, and wrote philosophy as well as poetry—although his poetry is an acquired taste.

Fuller once said something I still think about. He called my attention to the lightweight fasteners used in airplanes. These fasteners, he explained, were made to exacting design standards from special alloys. They needed to withstand stresses five or six times as powerful as the fiercest hurricanes, so that in rough weather and storms and during takeoffs and landings they stayed in one piece.

The proper way to think about these lowly fasteners, he said, was to realize they were products that had been in development for at least 5,000 years, beginning with whatever our ancestors used to keeps rafts and sailing ships from coming apart in the open sea, then progressing over time to the era of trains, oceangoing vessels, and then to the airplanes of today.

Fuller's point was that engineers don't wake up one day and design a part from scratch. In almost every case, they base their work on ideas developed, tested, and perfected by others over long periods of time. No matter who gets the credit, every invention, from Fuller's point of view, is a group effort involving people around the world and over long spans of time.

It doesn't matter if an engineer or tinkerer is scratching a design on stone, using paper and pencil, or running some type of computer-aided design program. Invention is a group process. Britain's De Havilland Comet, the world's first passenger jet (it took to the skies in 1949), was a beautifully designed plane with one of the first sweptwing designs. The problem was, these planes, which had four jet engines hidden inside the wings, crashed on takeoff and broke apart in the skies. One reason was the design of the windows. A second was metal fatigue, which weakened the airplane's metal components a little at a time.

These two issues, metal fatigue and window design, became important topics of discussion and research among aircraft designers, engineers, metallurgists, and maintenance experts around the world. Articles, papers, and books were published about these issues. Teams at different design, research, and testing facilities in the United States, Canada, Europe, and Asia shared ideas, and in a short span of time, about a year, these problems were resolved. Modifications were made to existing Comet aircraft, and new versions of the plane were designed. The point is, airplanes from all of the world's aircraft manufacturers employed insights gained from the Comet's failure.

What I'm trying to illustrate is that ideas move around the world quickly when it comes to invention, and that the pace of that movement has intensified. Whereas in 3,500 BCE it might have taken centuries or more for the "latest" bronze-forging technology to make it from ancient Sumer to what is now China, today, when the Federal Aviation Administration (FAA) wants an airplane part redesigned, such as happened with the Boeing 787, or wants a maintenance procedure changed, it goes up on the FAA's website and stays there until the directive is either superseded by a newer one or canceled. Because of this practice, engineers have access to the latest thinking in their industry almost instantly.

People around the world have simultaneous access to the world's storehouse of technical information and data. Russian aerospace engineers can find out anything their American or Canadian counterparts know without spying, just by going on the web or looking at conference proceedings. For that matter, the technology behind Boston Dynamics' Big Dog is starting to show up on the web, and the intricacies of GPS are now in the public domain.

So the question is, if everyone has access to the same databases of information and tools, why has the United States done so well while other countries have struggled? Or, to put it differently, if the technology behind Big Dog is available on the web, why was it designed outside of Boston and not in Shanghai?

The reason, I believe, is that we are an intensely curious people, and are willing to quickly adopt, adapt, borrow, or perfect ideas that emerged elsewhere. Why else do we constantly remind ourselves that we must look outside our own companies and national borders for ideas?

The United States is an inclusive nation, with people of many different backgrounds working together and sharing customs and ideas. But it is also an inclusive nation for ideas. We are open to new ideas, and as a result, our minds and methods are constantly changing. Which, in my view, is a very good thing.[13]

CREATIVE ADAPTATION

Let me give you an idea of what I mean by adaptation. In the 1980s, when Japanese manufacturing processes were among the most advanced in the world, hundreds of articles and books were written about the Japanese challenge. Many focused on the just-in-time production process as a fundamental element of Japan's success. Just in time (JIT) was a process for delivering component parts to factories when they were needed, thus eliminating the need for maintaining large, expensive parts inventories and warehouses.

It makes sense that JIT emerged in Japan, a country where real estate is scarce and expensive. Toyota, one of the developers of the process, saw no benefit in building expensive warehouses if it didn't need to, or stockpiling windshields, wheels, or gears. Instead, it integrated its suppliers into its production processes so windshields and the other components would arrive at the factory just in time to be placed on the cars working their way through the assembly line.

But it didn't take long—less than a decade—for this quintessential Japanese process to become a fundamental part of the American production process. In the United States, a much larger country than Japan, JIT production went well beyond the original concept. By the early 1990s, trucking, transportation, and shipping companies—Yellow, UPS, FedEx, and others—set up their own massive regional distribution centers where parts could be shipped, kept for an hour or two, and then moved to the factory when they were needed. In a short span of time, this Japanese process became Americanized as shipping and transportation companies transformed themselves from truck operators to logistics handling companies built around just-in-time deliveries. An idea hatched in Japan was perfected in the United States.

Let me give you an example of how we do just-in-time deliveries. This is what was described to me by a senior vice president of a $45-billion-a-year supermarket chain:

> If you go into the back of one of our supermarkets, you'll find it's empty. We don't store anything back there anymore. The entire store is dedicated to sales. We also don't have any warehouses anymore. Instead, in Northern California, we have two distribution facilities for that part of the state. Each facility has two buildings, each of which is about 1 million square feet in size. These are long, narrow buildings. One of them is for refrigerated and frozen foods, the other is for regular food.
>
> Each of these long, narrow buildings has one side with about forty blue doors—loading bays. These are for deliveries. All day long, big tractor-trailer trucks drive into our lot, check in, and are told to back up to one of the blue doors. As soon as they do, people on forklifts unload the trucks. Within a few minutes the forklift operators empty the truck and place the contents in various areas of the distribution center for loading.

On the other side of this long, skinny building are forty red doors—bays—for our own tractor-trailer trucks. Our trucks back up to the red doors, and from the moment our trailer doors are opened, the forklift operators begin loading the trailer with the food the stores ordered on the truck's route. As the trucks are being loaded, one of our tank trucks drives in between the bays and fills our trucks with diesel fuel. If you were in the distribution center, you would be amazed at the activity, at how fast the forklifts buzz along fully loaded. It's amazing they never crash into each other.

It only takes a few minutes from the time a supplier's trucks are unloaded, the contents sorted, and then loaded onto our trucks. Sometimes the drivers don't even turn off their engines. We call this hot-seat driving, because as soon as a driver finishes his shift, he jumps out of his truck, and another driver jumps in and takes over while the seat's still warm.

All of this works like an Indy 500 pit crew. Delivery trucks unloaded, our trucks loaded, our trucks refueled, and put back onto the road. It's like a beehive, and it never stops, day and night. That's how we sell billions of dollars of food a year without keeping—and paying for—any inventory at all. I'm still amazed by what I see.

In the United States, we took a Japanese idea and injected it with steroids.

Transmuting—and sometimes even perfecting—ideas developed elsewhere is fundamental to the way America does business. And, while we chide ourselves unduly regarding what we believe to be a slow rate of change, the fact is that no other country changes more rapidly than we do—nor is any other country as open to new ideas.

These are generalizations, to be sure. But they carry more than a modicum of truth. The JIT concept is just one example of how this openness to new ideas plays out in real life. I could cite many others.

But there is an even more important side of American openness that often gets short shrift. It is, of course, all well and good that we are open to ideas. More important, though, is our openness in our communities to new people, along with their ideas. This kind of openness is what truly gives us the power to grow, and it is much more important than the power of concepts like just-in-time deliveries.

It goes without saying that we are not perfect. Prejudice certainly persists. But no country welcomes and accepts newly arrived people or has benefited from that acceptance the way America has. This has given us a tremendous advantage—and a largely hidden one. According to a study by Vivek Wadhwa, a Silicon Valley entrepreneur who is also a professor at New York University, 24 percent of Silicon Valley's startups were launched by foreign-born entrepreneurs, mostly Indian and Chinese, but also Israeli, Russian, French, and others. For example, Intel, the world's most important maker of computer chips, was cofounded by Andrew Grove, a World War II refugee from Hungary. Google's cofounder Sergey Brin is Russian-born. Indian-born Vinod Khosla cofounded Sun Microsystems, and of the four cofounders of PayPal, two were born elsewhere—Max Levchin, who was born in Ukraine, and Elon Musk, who was born in South Africa. The French-born Pierre Omidyar, whose parents were from Iran, founded eBay. Sandisk, a leader in flash memory, was cofounded by Israel-born Eli Harari.

As Figure 3.3 shows, the list of foreign-born entrepreneurs is long. Moreover, in the high-tech sector[14] alone, companies started by foreign-born entrepreneurs between 1995 and 2005 generated $52 billion in revenues in 2005, employing some 450,000 people.

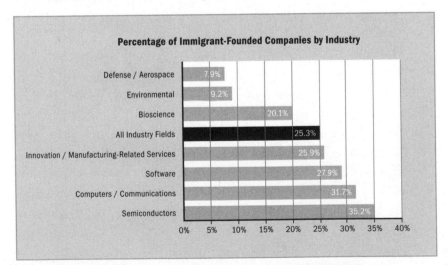

Percentage of Immigrant-Founded Companies by Industry

Industry	Percentage
Defense / Aerospace	7.9%
Environmental	9.2%
Bioscience	20.1%
All Industry Fields	25.3%
Innovation / Manufacturing-Related Services	25.9%
Software	27.9%
Computers / Communications	31.7%
Semiconductors	35.2%

Figure 3.3. Ewing Marion Kauffman Foundation and Vivek Wadhwa.

And yet, aside from Israel, the countries where these entrepreneurs were born are not entrepreneurial at all. Indian business is dominated by handful of old—in some cases ancient—merchant families that have quietly exerted their control over the economy for generations. China's economy has startups, but many of these startups, like the computer company Lenovo, exist because the government decided they should. In other words, it tends to be government policy, not entrepreneurial zeal, that is responsible for China's new companies.

Both China and India are difficult places to do business, in part because they are both bureaucratic and corrupt. But when Chinese and Indian students or businesspeople come to the United States, they are liberated. Many of them become entrepreneurs, creating billions of dollars of wealth for themselves and for the United States.

ONLY IN AMERICA—RADICAL INCLUSION

Edward Boyden is no ordinary thirty-three-year-old. He's a bearded and bespectacled, some would say diminutive, brain researcher who grew up in Dallas and did his undergraduate, graduate, and doctoral work at MIT in fields that at first glance seem far apart—physics, engineering, and biology. His master's thesis at MIT was about building a tabletop quantum computer.

Quantum computers work on the subatomic level—actually, I should say are *supposed* to work, since the first ones are only now coming into existence. A Canadian company, D-Wave, makes a machine that supposedly operates on the subatomic level. I say "supposedly" because there is some debate as to whether D-Wave's machines really work on the quantum level or are simply very fast computers. (Two American companies, Google and Lockheed Martin, bought D-Wave machines and are convinced they work on the quantum level.)

Down there in the subatomic basement where quantum mechanics operates, things are really small, really weird, and really fast. Particles seemingly go in and out of existence based on the rules of statistical probability, not logic. In that strange realm, particles and subparticles, once joined, operate as if they are always joined, even when they are separated. Do something to one particle, and the one to which it was once joined responds at the same time. That makes it appear as if particles can communicate with each other outside of the limits of distance, speed, and time.

The goal of making a quantum computer is to make machines orders of magnitude faster and more powerful than machines based on transistors etched on chips. But all that is beside the point, since tabletop quantum computers were an interest of Boyden's early on in his career, when he was a young graduate student. Boyden moved on and switched to biology for his PhD, and his work is now in the young field of synthetic neurobiology, which brings together the biology of the brain and engineering. Boyden is developing tools and processes for mapping and controlling neurological circuits in the brain. Some of the circuits he is interested in controlling are ones that produce epileptic seizures. What Boyden wants to do is develop tools that turn off the circuits that turn on seizures, so that seizures will never happen.

Boyden has research labs at MIT's McGovern Institute for Brain Research as well as at the Media Lab, which is also at MIT. Among his accomplishments—besides winning every prestigious award granted to a scientist under forty—was the fact that MIT gave him his first research lab before he was thirty years old, something almost unprecedented. In addition to his work at the lab, Boyden has also been busy starting companies.

It is not just his intense, almost hyperattentive intelligence that gives Boyden his edge. In addition, there is Boyden's openness to putting people with diverse technical backgrounds on the same team. Boyden can often see how research in one field can help to solve problems in a completely different field, and he views this ability as one of his strengths. Making these connections requires an unusually broad understanding of highly technical subjects. And, in his case, it includes an ability to get people with different technical backgrounds to work together in unfamiliar areas and in different ways.

▼▼▼▼

Boyden's project—how to stop seizures before they start—involves research with mice. He began by removing certain genes from a type of algae that is sensitive to light. He inserted those genes into specially modified viruses a million times smaller than the width of a human hair. The viruses were then injected into mice that were prone to having seizures.

Once inside the mouse's tiny body, the viruses travel through the blood, make their way through what is called the "blood-brain barrier," and then lodge themselves in the areas of the mouse's brain that produce seizures.

Remember that the viruses that just infected the mouse are carrying genes from algae that are sensitive to light. The reason this is important is that a tiny light has been inserted into the skull of the mouse, and this light is connected to the brain circuit that produces the seizure. When the sensor detects the onset of a seizure, the tiny light switches on inside the mouse's skull; the light, in turn, excites the algae gene, causing it to produce a substance that switches off the brain circuit responsible for seizures.

By bringing together the neurobiology of the brain, the genetics of algae, and an engineered mechanism that switches a light on and off, Boyden has created something that never existed in nature. A new, human-engineered brain feedback loop.

And, I repeat, the dude is just thirty-three.

Genetically engineering viruses and using them to donate genes to other animals is state-of-the-art research. But what really makes Boyden's approach interesting—and quintessentially American—is that he is willing to take risks. This is the same trait that makes MIT such a creative institution.

One thing Boyden did that I doubt would be tried anywhere else in the world is that he picked an engineer to work on this research whose last project had been building an automated ski rack for cars. The rack can pick up and place skis onto the rack by itself. In most universities in most other countries, choosing such a person for the research team would not only be considered, well, weird, but would be forbidden. In fact, it is so out of the mainstream that researchers somewhere else in the world probably would never think of it, or of building such an odd team in general.

The engineer in question did not have a biomedical engineering background; nor was he a physician. He became part of the team because Boyden understood that he could contribute in an important way. Boyden told me, "I tried to figure out the movements that were necessary to insert the light correctly into a mouse, heard about this engineer, realized the moves he used on the ski rack were similar, and brought him to the lab. It worked really well. Everyone on the team likes him and worked well with him."

To be honest, no one knows if Boyden's work on epilepsy will pay off. It's too early to tell, and a lot of things could go wrong. But Boyden's disregard for established academic disciplines is unusual anywhere but the United States. In most countries, Boyden would need approval to bring an engineer without biomedical experience onto his team, and it's unlikely permission would be granted.

But that's the way MIT works. Yes, it has hundreds of traditional PhDs wandering around its labs and research centers doing wonderful things. But it also has people with few of the traditional credentials—sometimes without any of them. MIT calls these extremely gifted people "instructors," and the university pays them well to teach MIT courses. In some cases, it lets them start their own programs and institutes—another heresy.

But MIT recognizes that the world is not the way it once was, and that there are gifted, albeit iconoclastic people who have a lot to offer the world. In fact, one of Boyden's bosses, Joichi Ito, the director of MIT's Media Lab, where technological, biological, and other types of research takes place, does not, as noted earlier, even have a college degree. Think about how unusual it is that MIT, one of the world's best universities, hired someone to run one of its most important and visible labs who dropped out of college. True, Ito had started Internet companies in the United States and Japan, had written books about technology, and also worked as a disk jockey in nightclubs in Japan and the United States, and had led a "guild" of people who played the online game World of Warcraft. But he does not have a bachelor's degree, let alone a doctorate, the currency of the academic realm. Hiring someone like Ito for that type of position is unusual even in the United States—but it is an impossibility elsewhere. Can you imagine an Oxford don who had dropped out of, well, Oxford, so he didn't even have a bachelor's degree? Or a professor at France's École Polytechnique, or Japan's University of Tokyo, who never finished college? Neither can I.

The point is, in a world dominated by academic institutions with fixed traditions, and with set-in-stone protocols and bureaucratic procedures, where status is determined by where you work (and your level), there remain places in the United States that are willing to give a break to a smart kid with lots of good ideas and what used to be called "moxie." And, if Ito works out, and pushes forward the Media Lab's reputation for innovation, you can be sure that institutions in other countries will attempt to do the same.

This is important. High-level research organizations and institutions in other countries would be far less likely to let a gifted young researcher like Ed Boyden build his kind of lab with people possessing such counter-to-conventional-wisdom credentials. Even more remarkable, it is very unlikely that a prestigious research university elsewhere would put someone without a college degree in charge of one of its most visible and important research centers. In other countries, those who were setting up research teams would approach their disciplines and their institutions far more conservatively, with tremendous reverence for tradition. (Ito also has no real management experience. In fact, when asked about his experience managing groups, he said he learned most of what he knows from leading the guild of people playing World of Warcraft.)

This kind of radical thinking is part of what has made MIT into one of the most important and creative scientific and technological institutions in the world. It has enabled MIT to spawn hundreds of startup companies in the area surrounding its campus and around the world. And, paradoxically, it has made the school one of the toughest in the world for students to get into.

MIT is not alone. The United States is filled with institutions that pursue their own paths and that respect—but do not revere—academic traditions.

DEEP CREATIVITY

Andrew Hessel is a self-described hacker, but not the kind who breaks into corporate information systems or into the Pentagon's computers to steal launch codes. Instead, Hessel hacks life. He's a lanky Canadian who moved to the United States for graduate school and has been intoxicated by our innovative air ever since. Hessel did his master's degree at the University of Illinois at Urbana—a supercomputer site—and then moved into its PhD program.

But he never got his doctorate. Instead, Hessel, an intense, original thinker, was recruited by Amgen, one of the pioneers of genetic engineering and the world's largest biotech firm. Among Amgen's original genetically engineered drugs is Epogen, which stimulates red-blood-cell production and is used to treat anemia. Since Epogen, Amgen has developed a long list of bioengineered products.

While working to develop Amgen's information technology capabilities, Hessel had an idea. Why not use an inkjet printer, which sprays tiny bits of ink onto paper, to create new types of genetically modified viruses?

In short, his idea was to use printers to spray tiny droplets of proteins onto glass slides. These viruses could be used as vectors, viruses that carry additional genes into cells and "infect" those cells with the new genes in order to cure a person of a genetically caused disease.

According to Hessel, Amgen wasn't interested in his idea. So he took it public and started what could be called an "open genetics" movement, somewhat akin to the open software movement that gave rise to Linux, a free computer operating system, or Mozilla, which makes the Firefox browser. It also has much in common with Wikipedia, the open encyclopedia project. Rather than calling it "open software," Hessel calls his project "open wetware." And, rather than APL, CL, JavaScript, or any one of the hundreds of other programming languages, Hessel's programming language is DNA.

Hessel is a synthetic biologist. He is part of a group of scientists—and yes, hackers—whose aim is to design and construct new life forms or to change existing ones. Hopefully, they will stick to doing these things in the interests of humanity and the public good.

This may sound scary—and it is!—but it is also at the absolute cutting edge of research. And, because so many synthetic biologists are essentially freelancers, Hessel started a group to bring them together as collaborators. It is called the Pink Army Cooperative, and at present it has about six hundred members who are busy hacking the genetic code. "Pink" is a reference to breast-cancer awareness and the cooperative's interest in finding a cure for that disease.

The materials to hack the genetic code are readily available. And, as long you are not doing anything that appears to be destructive, you can buy the chemicals you need to hack DNA on the Internet.

A great deal of the work done so far in synthetic biology is similar to what Edward Boyden is doing at MIT when he inserts light-sensitive genes into the brains of mice. Making viruses that can respond to photons is something that geneticists are interested in for a number of reasons. Photons are energy—coming to us primarily from the sun—and biological systems are adept at harvesting that energy. Green plants turn sunlight, carbon dioxide, water, and various chemicals into food. If green plants can consume sunlight to live, then can't we? Well, maybe someday.

In fact, among the synthetic biology cognoscenti, there is a large community of people whose aim is to do useful things, such as create ways of removing carbon dioxide from the atmosphere to stop climate change.

Hessel showed me pictures of a number of synthetic biology labs. Some were pristine operations at august academic institutions and traditional company settings. But others looked like labs hastily set up in college dorm rooms or, worse, like the meth labs you see on TV. This technology could pose problems.

Some of this freelance activity, at least to my mind, borders on scary. Do we really want nineteen-year-old geniuses secretly changing our DNA? Do we want this technology to fall into the hands of terrorist groups? Do we want to have our genes hacked—or the genes of organisms we depend upon hacked—without putting it up to a vote? Or at least regulating it? This type of hacking is potentially far more dangerous than the kind where someone slips a software virus onto someone's hard drive. Hessel's folks are talking about putting real viruses into your genes, and we don't yet know what all the consequences of such changes could be.

The trouble is, says Hessel, we're already a little late. Although people are just hearing about synthetic biology and genetic hackers, the field is progressing on its own. It is doing so without sufficient safeguards, and there is little we can do to stop it.

The United States, of course, is at the forefront of this new and unnerving area of research. The field actually has roots going back decades. And it isn't just freelancers who are pursuing these things, but also some of the top university research labs. To test hypotheses about the expression of genes inside of cells, researcher Michael Elowitz at the California Institute of Technology, or Caltech, for example, created synthetic genetic circuits, made of the chemicals of all life, and inserted them into cells. The trouble was, the cells they were inserted into were from the bacteria *Escherichia coli*, which lives in our intestines and is critical to digestion. He also inserted genes into yeast, which is important in food and drug production.

I'm in no position to judge whether this forefront work is dangerous or not, and I am pretty certain that Elowitz and his colleagues and others at their level are doing their best to uphold high ethical and research standards. But the kids in their dorm rooms who are playing around with genes? Those people, I'm not so sure about.

The point of raising these issues is not to scare anyone. It is to show how far we've come and how much is going on creatively in areas about which most people know very little. As so many scientists say, this period in history, particularly in America, is one of the most fertile periods ever. And, while there are chances for carelessness and abuse, there is also the chance that this research will save lives, increase the food supply, remove pollutants from the oceans, and decrease the amount of carbon dioxide in the air.

INSTITUTIONALIZING EMERSON

DARPA and Boyden and Hessel—and the link between MIT and the Boston-area robotics cluster—are but a few of the recent embodiments of Emerson's push to link science and scholarship with practicality, a linkage that has become an American tradition. Emerson's idea took root early on. Abraham Lincoln, for example, embraced Emerson's idea of marrying practicality with scholarship while he was president. Even with the Civil War raging, Lincoln created institutions based on the concepts Emerson had expressed in "The American Scholar."[15] In 1862, he established the land-grant college system, which led to the creation of dozens of universities that were supported by the government and dedicated to education and research. These schools focused their resources on research into agriculture, the sciences, engineering, and matters pertaining to the military. MIT is a land-grant university, as are Cornell, Rutgers, Kansas State, the University of California at Berkeley, the University of Michigan, and others. All in all, seventy-six colleges and universities were started after Lincoln institutionalized these ideas. No one has ever calculated the value created by these schools, but it would not be unreasonable to estimate that for MIT, Berkeley, and Cornell alone it could easily run to tens of trillions of dollars.

The same year, again in the spirit of Emerson, Lincoln elevated the Department of Agriculture to full-fledged status, although without a seat in the cabinet. The department had a branch dedicated to research, as well as an extension service to educate farmers in the latest seed technology, farming techniques, and science. (The extension program was linked to the land-grant universities.) Lincoln's investment in the agricultural sciences and in the extension programs is a major reason why the United States has been the world's dominant agricultural power for more than a century.

And then, in 1863, Lincoln established the National Academy of Sciences. The only way to get into this prestigious group is through nomination and election by the academy's members, a method assuring that members of the group are of high quality and not appointed for political reasons. The academy has always had a small number of members (about 2,200 at present), yet over the years they have garnered about 200 Nobel Prizes. Earning so many Nobels is just one way in which the United States excels. Even so, the National Academy of Sciences is responsible for only about two-thirds of the 338 Nobel Prizes that Americans have received in the history of the award so far (1901–2012).[16] (By contrast, Britain, which is the second-largest recipient of Nobel Prizes, has won 119 Nobels, while China has won just 8.)

By making science such an important element in our culture more than 150 years ago, Lincoln contributed to America's excellence in science. And by making the National Academy a body that recommends policies, rather than just conducting research, he built on Emerson's ideas of practicality.

Some of that practicality can be seen in the broadening of the National Academy's mission, which began when President Woodrow Wilson asked the academy for assistance in making certain that

America was prepared militarily just before it entered World War I. Programs in engineering and medicine further broadened the National Academy of Science's practical mission.

In 1863, the United States was less than a century old, and yet it had already created a way of thinking and a number of institutions that promoted science—not only to further knowledge, but to get practical results.

▼▼▼▼

Since Emerson's time, our universities have blossomed into the world's best. And, though rankings differ, depending on the organization producing them, American institutions always dominate the tops of these lists. Add to that the country's seventeen major national laboratories and research centers, such as Los Alamos, Sandia, Brookhaven, Argonne, Ames, Lawrence Berkeley, Lawrence Livermore, and others, which do very high-level research, much of it focusing on physics, nuclear energy, and defense-related matters, and you begin to get an idea of why America is so far ahead and will remain so for the foreseeable future. These labs began during World War II under Vannevar Bush as military-only facilities. Over time, however, they began to do civilian work, sometimes under contract, with programs to commercialize their activities so they could be employed by businesses. In some cases, venture capital firms have been invited to set up shop inside the labs, for various amounts of time, to help these science centers commercialize their work.

But in addition, our corporations do some of the most advanced research in the world, sometimes in conjunction with universities. For example, the pioneering mathematician Benoit Mandelbrot, who worked at IBM for thirty-five years and also did stints at Caltech, did work that led to advances in the way digital images are formed and to new ways of figuring out how physical structures, such as crystals (everything from snowflakes to silicon chips), take shape. Similarly, Arno Penzias, a Nobel Prize–winning physicist who discovered microwave remnants from the Big Bang, spent most of his career at AT&T's Bell Labs.

The point I am making is that though there are citizens and people in Congress who dispute evolution, or who are dubious about climate change or stem-cell research, the United States is still the most scientifically oriented country in the world. One measure of that orientation is how much money we spend on science and technology.

Comparing countries in terms of their research and development spending for science is very dicey, and not easy to do. Do you count research undertaken by private companies the same way you count funding for research in public institutions, for example? The private companies themselves get into disputes over this. EADS, the parent company of Airbus, a European company, and America's Boeing are bitter rivals, and they engage in constant arguments over whether one company or the other is getting its research unfairly subsidized by the governments where they operate.

And then there's the efficiency issue. It seems like a dollar spent on research by Apple gets a better payoff than a dollar spent by Lenovo or Microsoft. But the advantage one company has over another, or one country has over another, with regard to return on research expenditures fluctuates. Next year, for example, Microsoft or Lenovo might have a breakthrough, while Apple may not.

Given those caveats, and the difficulty of measurement, one can estimate that in 2012, the United States spent about $436 billion[17] on research, and the next biggest spender, China, spent about $198 billion. Meanwhile, Japan spent about $157 billion. These figures are adjusted for how much a dollar buys in each country.

It's my contention that American research is pretty efficient in how it uses its money, perhaps even more efficient than other countries, judging by the results. But there's no real way to prove it. As a result, we have to rely on measures of brute force spending, and in that category America is clearly the winner, outspending the runner-up by more than two to one. The reason for that is that Americans have a deep and abiding belief in the efficacy of science for solving problems. In fact, we've had that belief for at least 175 years.

CHAPTER FOUR

ABUNDANT, CHEAP ENERGY

In 2011, the International Monetary Fund issued an alarming forecast. It was about the prospect of China overtaking the United States as the world's largest economy, an event the IMF thought would happen by 2016.[1] An Oxford-educated economist, Arvind Subramanian, senior fellow at the Peterson Institute for International Economics in Washington, DC, and former head of the IMF's research department, came to an even more alarming conclusion the same year. In his book *Eclipse: Living in the Shadow of China's Economic Dominance*, Subramanian said that 2016 had arrived ahead of schedule, that is, China had already overtaken the United States economically.[2] Not everyone agreed with Subramanian on this timing, but others did agree with the general idea that China was in the process of surpassing the United States. Jim O'Neill, the British economist who was chairman of Goldman Sachs Asset Management, and who had coined the term "BRIC" to designate the fast-growing countries of Brazil, Russia, India, and China, said China would be number one by 2027.[3] And at the end of 2012, the National Intelligence Council (NIC), the American intelligence community's think tank, said China would be number one in 2030.[4] The NIC report came with an asterisk that I will explain below.

The IMF, Subramanian, O'Neill, and the NIC arrived at their conclusions using different metrics and analytical techniques. But their message was essentially the same. The United States would soon be giving up its leading position in the world economy.

Don't bet on it.

It's not that these forecasts were completely wrong. They all contained astute observations. But they did not contain all of the facts. In my view, the United States is in the early stages of a major transformation that is likely to last for decades. It is on its way to becoming energy independent, which is not the case for either China or India. China's reserves of energy are mostly dirty coal, whereas the United States has abundant reserves of much cleaner natural gas. And, while China has natural gas, its deposits are located in places without water, a critical ingredient in bringing natural gas to the surface. In addition, the asterisk I mentioned in the NIC's report was that America's lurch to energy independence would be a game changer.

The significance of America's vast reserves of natural gas—and newly accessible oil—is being underestimated, and not just by the "America-will-be-eclipsed" school of economics. It is being underestimated by almost everyone.

It's not that there is more energy in the ground than we thought there was. Geologists knew the United States had vast, largely untapped reserves of natural gas and oil in shale rock, tar sands, and at the bottom of depleted wells. It's that American energy technology, specifically the high-pressure hydraulic fracturing of rock—or "fracking"—has advanced to the point that these once unobtainable reserves of energy can now be extracted quickly, easily, and profitably. America's tremendous creativity has triumphed once more. So vast are our reserves of energy that it is likely that we will become a net energy exporting country, something we haven't been since Harry Truman was in the White House. As Figure 4.1 shows, the United States has more exploitable energy reserves than any other country, including Saudi Arabia and Russia.

In a typical year, the United States imports about $335 billion of oil. Half of our trade deficit is a result of these imports. Now, imagine what would happen if those oil imports stopped, and that, instead, this same $335 billion a year remained at home to be invested in our domestic economy. Then, imagine that instead of importing energy, we exported it. Even if the United States exported modest amounts of energy—say, $50 billion or $100 billion a year—it would transform our economy.

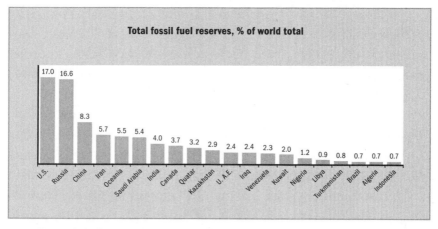

Figure 4.1. Congressional Research Service.

The United States won't become a net energy exporter overnight. But it will happen faster than most people think. One stumbling block for exporting natural gas has been that chemical producers oppose the idea. They use natural gas as a feedstock to make everything from plastics to fertilizers, and hence they do not want natural gas to be exported. They fear that exporting it would cause prices to rise. Like the leaders of any other sector of the economy, the chemical producers are looking out for their own interests, convinced that higher gas prices would shrink their profits. Rather than liquefying natural gas, putting it into specialized ships, and sending it to Germany and other European countries, where it would displace Russian gas (not to mention Russian influence), the chemical companies want to export finished chemicals.

I spoke on a panel in the summer of 2012 in Washington, DC, hosted by Georgetown University and the Milken Institute. The purpose of the panel was to brief Congressional staff members about America's energy future. One of the other panelists was Peter A. Molinaro, a vice president for federal and state government affairs at Dow Chemical. Because the finished chemicals made from natural gas are processed in sophisticated manufacturing plants, he said, they "have eight times the value of raw natural gas." In addition, factories that produce plastics or insecticides from natural gas provide "good jobs for American workers," Molinaro pointed out.

That may be so. Nevertheless, a long-awaited 2012 study by NERA Economic Consulting for the US Department of Energy concluded that the United States has a great deal to gain from exporting natural gas. It also concluded that the impact on natural gas prices from gas exports would be small.[5]

Why small? Because we have so much gas in the ground.

Consider the implications for the United States from exporting this abundant product. At the time of this writing, natural gas costs between $3 and $4 for a million BTUs, a rather archaic measurement of the heat value contained in a fuel (BTU stands for British Thermal Unit). In Europe, the same amount of natural gas costs $14, and in Asia it costs as much as $16 for an equivalent amount.[6]

Natural gas is so abundant, and prices are so low, that, as the legendary eighty-five-year-old Texas energy investor Boone Pickens explained to me, "the number of drilling rigs operating has gone from 1,600 in 2008 to about 400 now." The reason for the cutback in natural gas drilling? "Gas is too damn cheap, and if they keep drilling they'll make it cheaper," said Pickens. "People are waiting for prices to rise before they drill."

That's a wonderful predicament to be in. Natural gas producers have taken 1,200 rigs out of production because of low prices, hoping that if supply dwindles, prices will rise once more. But the moment those prices do rise, companies will put their wells back into production and prices will once again fall.

The problem, according to Pickens, isn't supply, it's demand. We need to find uses for natural gas that go beyond heating our homes and making fertilizer. "I have no problem with exporting natural gas. I don't think you should tell a company what it can and cannot do with the gas it owns," said Pickens.

Luckily, there are many uses for natural gas that can have dramatic, positive consequences for the country. It can be used as feedstock for making plastics, cosmetics, and some pharmaceuticals. It can be converted into ethanol, which can be burned in vehicles, as well as diesel fuel and jet fuel. Natural gas can also be used in fuel cells to produce electricity on a large scale for stores, supermarkets, and shopping malls. And, of course, it can be compressed and used as fuel for cars, or liquefied and used as fuel in long-distance trucks.

THE IMPACT OF NATURAL GAS

As I mentioned, Dow Chemical's Peter Molinaro and I both participated in a session on Capitol Hill to brief members of Congress and their staffs on energy issues. I moderated the panel a few feet from the rotunda, with about forty congressional staffers in the room.

As we discussed America's energy future and took questions about what it all means, and—more importantly—what types of policies should be put in place, Molinaro took out a piece of paper.

The paper was a spreadsheet listing eighty-nine new manufacturing projects that had either broken ground or were about to break ground as a result of our bounty of cheap natural gas (see Table 4.1). Most of these factories had something to do with chemicals, but the range of companies was wide. A number of them would be making machinery, such as a Caterpillar tractor and excavator plant that was originally planned for Mexico, but now would be located in Georgia. Four companies would be making tires. Two companies announced plans to make steel in Louisiana; another announced it would build a glass plant. Two other companies said they would build plants to turn natural gas into diesel fuel.

Dow itself would soon start construction on new factories in Texas and Louisiana, where natural gas is abundant. Some of the plants that are either planned or underway were at first destined for other parts of the world—the Middle East, especially. But now, due to America's cheap and abundant natural gas, those investments are going to be within our shores, not overseas. Even better, since the list was prepared, more new plants have been announced. As Table 4.1 indicates, the projects that are planned or underway are impressive and reflect investments from some very large firms.

The numbers were impressive. Investments in the factories on Molinaro's list were worth $65 billion. And the list, which was current as of the summer of 2012, keeps growing as awareness of America's energy bonanza increases.

The best way to grasp the impact of natural gas is to look at the size of the market corresponding to the countries that signed the North American Free Trade Agreement. The United States, Canada, and Mexico make up the richest market in the world. With about 450 million

Table 4.1. Industry to Invest $65 Billion in Manufacturing Renaissance

	Company	Location	Date Online	Project Type
	Chemicals and Fertilizer			
1	Dow	St. Charles, LA	2012	Ethylene Restart
2	Dow	Freeport, TX	2017	New Ethylene
3	Westlake	Lake Charles, LA	2012	Ethylene Expansion
4	Williams Olefins	Geismar, LA	2013	Ethylene Expansion
5	INEOS	Chocolate Bayou, TX	2013	Ethylene Debottleneck
6	LyondellBasell	Laporte, TX	2014	Ethylene Expansion
7	Westlake	Lake Charles, LA	2014	Ethylene Expansion
8	Williams Olefins	Geismar, LA	2014	Ethylene Expansion
9	Aither Chemicals	WV or PA or OH	2016	New Ethylene
10	Exxon Mobil	Baytown, TX	2016	New Ethylene
11	Chevron Phillips	Baytown, TX	2017	New Ethylene
12	Formosa	Point Comfort, TX	2017	New Ethylene
13	Braskem	WV	2017	New Ethylene
14	Sasol	Lake Charles, LA	2018	New Ethylene
15	Shell	PA	2018	New Ethylene
16	Eastman	Longview, TX	2012	Ethylene/Polypropylene Expansion
17	Indorama	Under consideration	2018	New Ethylene
18	LyondellBasell	Channleview, TX	NA	Ethylene Expansion
19	Sabic	Under consideration	NA	New Ethylene
20	Occidental	Ingleside, TX	NA	New Ethylene
21	Renewable Manufacturing	Northeast	2016	New Ethylene
22	PTT Global Chemical	Under consideration	NA	New Ethylene
23	Orascom Construction	Beaumont, TX	2011	Ammonia Restart
24	Orascom Construction	Beaumont, TX	2012	Methanol Restart
25	Potash Corp	Geismar, LA	2013	Ammonia Restart
26	Potash Corp	Augusta, GA	2013	Ammonia Expansion
27	Rentech Nitrogen	East Dubuque, IL	2013	Ammonia Expansion
28	Austin Powder	Mosheim, TN	2014	Ammonia Expansion
29	LyondellBasell	Channelview, TX	2014	Methanol Restart
30	Methanex	Geismar, LA	2015	Methanol Migration
31	CF Industries	Donaldsonville, LA	NA	Ammonia Expansion
32	Incitec Pivot	Under consideration	NA	Ammonia Migration
33	Koch Fertilizer	Various	NA	Ammonia Expansion
34	LSB Industries	Pryor, OK	NA	Ammonia Restart
35	Dyno Nobel	Waggaman, LA	2015	New Ammonia
36	Dow	Freeport, TX	2015	New Propylene
37	Dow	Freeport, TX	2018	New Propylene

Table 4.1. *(continued)*

	Company	Location	Date Online	Project Type
38	Eastman	Under consideration	2015	New Propylene
39	Formosa	Point Comfort, LA	2016	New Propylene
40	LyondellBasell	Channelview, TX	2014	New Propylene
41	Mitsui	OH	2012	Propylene Expansion
42	Enterprise	Mont Belvieu, TX	2013	Propylene Expansion
43	Exxon Mobil	Baytown, TX	2016	2 New Polyethylenes
44	Chevron Phillips	Old Ocean, TX	2017	2 New Polyethylenes
45	Eastman	Longview, TX	2012	EthylHexanol Expansion
46	Chevron Phillips	Baytown, TX	2014	New Hexene
47	Huntsman Chemical	McIntosh, AL	NA	Epoxy Expansion
48	INEOS	Gulf Coast	NA	Ethylene oxide
49	Kuraray	Pasadena, CA	2014	EVOH Expansion
50	LANXNESS	Orange, TX	NA	Nd-PBR
51	Lubrizol	Calvert City, KY	NA	Specialty Chemicals Expansion
52	Honeywell Specialty Materials	Mobile, AL	2012	Adsorbents; Catalysts
53	Westlake	Geismar, LA	2013	New Chlor-Alkali
54	Dow-Mitsui JV	Freeport, TX	2013	New Chlor Alkali
55	Molycorp	Mountain Pass, CA	NA	New Chlor-Alkali and rare earth metals mining
56	Formosa	Point Comfort, TX	2012	Chlorine/Caustic Soda
57	Formosa	Point Comfort, TX	2012	Ethylene Dichloride
58	Shintech	Plaquemine, LA	2012	VCM
59	Shintech	Plaquemine, LA	2012	Chlorine/Caustic Soda
60	Shintech	Plaquemine, LA	2012	PVC
61	Occidental	Jacksonville, TN	2013	Chlorine and Caustic Soda
62	Dow Agrosciences	Freeport, TX	NA	Herbicide

Steel

63	ArcelorMittal	Cleveland, OH	2012	Expansion
64	Carpenter Technology	Reading, PA	NA	New
65	Carpenter Technology	Limestone County, AL	2013	New
66	Coilplus	NC	2014	Expansion
67	Essar Steel	Nashwauk, MN	2015	New
68	Gerdau	St. Paul, MN	2014	New
69	Gerdau	Navasota, TX	2011	Expansion
70	Nucor	Blytheville, AR	2014	Expansion
71	Timken	Canton, OH	2014	Expansions
72	United States Steel	Leipsic and Lorain, OH	2012	Expansions

(continues)

Table 4.1. (continued)

	Company	Location	Date Online	Project Type
73	Metal-Matic	Middleton, OH	2012	Expansion
74	Vallourec and Mannesmann	Youngstown, OH	NA	New
75	Welspun	Little Rock, AR	NA	Expansion
76	Nucor Phase 1	St. James Parish, LA	2013	New plant
77	Nucor Phase 2	St. James Parish, LA	2017	Expansion
Tires				
78	Bridgestone	Aiken, SC	2014	New off-road radial tire / expansion passenger / light truck tire
79	Continental	Sumter, SC	2013 start / 2021 full capac.	Passenger and light truck tires
80	Michelin	Anderson, SC	2015	Earthmover tires (OTR)
81	Bridgestone	Bloomington, IL	2013	OTR Tires
Plastics				
82	Huntington Foam	Greenville, MI	NA	Expansion
83	JM Eagle	Sunnyside, WA, and Meadville, PA	NA	Polyethylene expansion
84	Springfield Plastics	Auburn, IL	2012	Polyethylene expansion
85	Kyowa America	Portland, TN	NA	Plastic Injection Molding
Natural Gas to Liquids				
86	Shell	LA or TX	NA	Gas-to-liquids
87	Sasol	LA	NA	Gas-to-liquids
Glass				
88	Sage	Fairbaul, MN	2013	Dynamic; Electrochromic Glass
Machinery				
89	Caterpillar	Athens, GA	NA	Tractors; excavators

"America's Onshore Energy Resources: Creating Jobs, Securing America, and Lowering Prices," Testimony of Paul N. Cicio.

people living in those countries, it is the fourth-largest market in the world by population, behind only China, India, and the twenty-seven countries of the European Union. Businesses from around the world, including our own companies, want to sell into the NAFTA market.

But if a European firm wants to sell more cars in North America from its European factories, where natural gas from Russia costs three and a half times what Americans pay, it has to put those cars onto ships that burn oil at the rate of $100 a barrel. And then, after those goods reach our shores, they still have to travel by truck or train. The same is true for Asian firms wanting to sell products in the NAFTA countries. But if, instead, European and Asian companies built more factories in the United States, in addition to their existing ones, they could take advantage of America's inexpensive supplies of natural gas. They wouldn't have to pay for oil-fired oceangoing ships.

Moreover, Boone Pickens has a plan that he believes will make the United States even more attractive. This plan involves transforming the country's fleet of 2 million long-haul trucks—18-wheelers—so that they will run on natural gas, not diesel. "That would bring down their costs quite a bit," Pickens told me. "Right now diesel's something like $4 a gallon, and on an equivalent basis, natural gas would cost about $2 a gallon." With the average semitrailer using about 10,000 gallons of fuel a year, the savings for each truck operator would be significant.

Converting the nation's fleet of trucks to run on natural gas would have another effect as well. If our 8 million medium- and heavy-weight trucks got natural gas engines to replace their diesel engines, the United States would reduce its imports of oil by more than a third. That's because medium- and heavy-weight trucks consume about 2.5 million barrels of oil a day.[7] Simply switching the long-haul truck fleet to run on natural gas would reduce imports substantially. That doesn't even take into account what would happen if delivery trucks and passenger cars converted to natural gas.

But there is more good news: companies see the opportunity and are working hard to take advantage of it. Cummins, a large American company that manufactures engines—mostly diesel—for trucks, earth movers, and other types of industrial uses, released two new engines in early 2013 that are designed to run on natural gas. These engines, which are produced as part of a joint venture with Westport Innovations, a Canadian firm, are among the first designed for 18-wheelers and other types of long-distance trucks. And although other manufacturers also make natural gas engines, Cummins Westport engines are different because they are new designs that are optimized for natural gas. (For $1,250, you can buy a kit on eBay to convert your eight-cylinder, gasoline-powered car or truck to run on natural gas. You can buy kits on eBay for four- and six-cylinder engines, too, for as little as $395. Taxi and bus fleets have been among the first to use conversion kits to transform their vehicles to run on natural gas.)

It's nice to know that market-driven innovation is taking advantage of the natural gas bonanza on the power plant side. But without a network of natural gas filling stations, even the best, most powerful, and sturdiest engines won't go very far. But here there's good news too. A number of companies are building their own network of filling stations along the country's most-traveled long-haul routes—including a company started by Pickens. And although there have been bills brought before Congress asking for subsidies to put natural gas pumps at truck stops, these filling stations are being built without subsidies.

Converting a big rig to run on liquid or compressed natural gas is expensive—a new, natural gas engine for a big truck costs about $60,000. But if natural gas continues to cost half the price of diesel, it would only take three years to pay for a new engine through fuel savings. Service stations would also need to be upgraded, which would add to the overall costs.

While it may seem difficult to put a new engine in a truck, it's done all the time. All engines wear out and need to be rebuilt or replaced from time to time. In my opinion, switching to natural gas when your engine needs to be replaced anyway is not very difficult. The conversion kits I mentioned that enable gasoline engines to run on natural gas have relatively few parts—there are just ten in the $1,250 kit sold on eBay. Of course, you still need to swap your fuel tanks from diesel or gasoline to natural gas, and add a few feet of high-pressure tubing. But the truth is, none of this is very difficult to do.

Making the engines is not a challenge either. Natural gas and diesel engines are different, but not so different that our existing engine factories would have be replaced. Much of the tooling could remain, and some engines could even be refitted to run on natural gas. Again, these are hardly insurmountable challenges. No new technology needs to be invented, and no new skills have to be taught to our factory workers or mechanics.

It would cost a lot of money to make the shift. But consider the magnitude of the payoff. If we invest in this effort, it will take us a third of the way to energy independence.

▼▼▼▼

Of course, this being America, there's always at least one other way to make such a transition. One would be to convert natural gas directly into diesel fuel for use in existing trucks. Sounds pretty simple—and it is. In Qatar, a large-scale commercial refinery has been converting natural gas into diesel fuel since 2011. In 2012, Royal Dutch Shell, one of the largest energy companies in the world, said it would build a plant in Louisiana or Texas to convert natural gas to diesel. Sasol, a large South African energy and chemical company, said it would build a plant in Louisiana to do the same.

Battelle, a nonprofit research and development organization in Columbus, Ohio, spun out a new company in 2013 to convert natural gas into diesel using new technology. The spinout, Velocys, will produce small-scale systems to convert natural gas to diesel fuel so that fleet operators, such as FedEx, UPS, or Yellow, can make their own diesel fuel from natural gas. Not only would converting natural gas into diesel save money and reduce imported oil, it could proceed quickly. And not only that, but it would also save money for truck operators and logistics companies, since they would not have to modify their vehicles.

If natural gas is converted to diesel, companies that build plants to convert gas to liquids would reap the largest rewards. They would pay $2 equivalent for natural gas, and sell it as diesel for $4 a gallon. How we convert or substitute natural gas for oil will depend on which group moves first and which one has the most money to invest.

Perhaps my reasons for thinking that it will take far longer than people have been estimating for China to become the world's largest economic power are starting to become a little clearer.

IT DIDN'T JUST HAPPEN ON ITS OWN

The US Department of Energy's authoritative Energy Information Agency estimates that the United States now has about a century's supply of natural gas—to get technical, ninety-two years' worth. If the technology improves so we can recover more natural gas from each well, or new fields are found, our bounty, measured in years, could increase. However, it is very difficult to accurately forecast our technological future with any accuracy. Until quite recently, analysts were sure the United States would soon run out of natural gas, and as a result, various companies built thirteen facilities for importing liquefied natural gas. Each of these terminals cost $1 billion or more to build, depending on its size. Plans are now underway to convert some of these facilities for export use.[8]

What's interesting is that as recently as 2004, analysts were still warning that the United States would soon run out of gas and needed to build more import terminals. And then, almost overnight, the technology changed, and the United States was back in business as a natural gas and oil producing country (similar methods can be used to extract either natural gas or oil from shale rock). The reason is fracking. So powerful is fracking technology that natural gas production increased by 50 percent a year from 2007 through the present. That is an unprecedented increase in energy productivity.

The advances in oil and natural gas extraction in the United States didn't happen by accident. They are the result of technological ability. Fracking is a complex technology, but it can be safely done. In fact, in May 2013,[9] a research report funded by the National Science Foundation concluded that, while further study is needed, there is currently no evidence that fracking pollutes groundwater. Moreover, the incidence of problems that would cause pollution, such as seals that fail to keep natural gas from escaping from wells, were relatively rare, occurring in no more than 1 percent to 3 percent of wells.

There are different accounts of how fracking was developed and where—fracking experiments have been tried in a number of countries, including Russia—but there is no doubt about who commercialized the process on a large scale—George Mitchell, the founder of Mitchell Energy.

Mitchell, who died in 2013 at the age of ninety-four, was a fascinating gentleman. He was born in Galveston, Texas, the son of Greek immigrant parents who, he told me long ago, made their living as shrimp fishermen in Galveston Bay. Mitchell, like so many children of immigrants, studied hard. He attended Texas A&M University, and became a petroleum engineer.

In the early 1970s, Mitchell funded a group that was building a computer model designed to show how the world used its resources. The study leaders were a husband-and-wife team, Dennis and Donella Meadows, who taught at MIT. They were part of a group called the Club of Rome that consisted of a hundred scholars and business leaders who were interested in what they called "mankind's predicament." The Club of Rome funded numerous studies about the future of our planet.

The Meadows study was frightening—and largely wrong. It depicted a world with ever-increasing levels of pollution—scientists at NASA had just begun to detect increases in the world's carbon dioxide levels—as well as increasing scarcity. The model suggested that the world would run out of gold by 1983, that it would run out of petroleum in 2003, and that food would soon be in short supply as well. This chilling study was released in a book called *Limits to Growth* that caused a sensation around the world.[10] Several governments, including our own, began taking measures to cope with the scarcities outlined in the book. But it got Mitchell thinking.

I met Mitchell in 1978, when I was a graduate student, at a conference he organized at the Woodlands, a community he developed outside of Houston. He was bald, trim, knowledgeable, and super smart. The Woodlands Conference, as it became known, focused on the environment and issues pertaining to our long-term future. Mitchell invited Dennis and Donella Meadows to the Woodlands along with other members of the Club of Rome to discuss their study and humanity's plight. In his wisdom, Mitchell also invited Herman Kahn, a futurist, mathematician, defense strategist, and computer modeler. Kahn was a founder of the Rand Corporation, a nonprofit think tank whose original purpose was to help the military and other parts of the government set strategy during the Cold War. Over time, Rand branched out to study a broad range of topics, including education, health-care policy, economics, energy, and the environment, in addition to its continued work for the military.

The contrast between the Meadows and Kahn could not be more striking. Kahn was a fast-talking cannonball of a man, as bald as Mitchell but perhaps several times his weight. He said he was there to debate the Meadows' findings and that he did not believe their findings at all.

Whereas the Club of Rome team argued that the world was running out of everything, Kahn said that market forces would prevent that from happening. He argued that the Meadows had forgotten an important tenet of economics—the idea of substitutions. If something vital becomes scarce, human ingenuity will find a way to replace it with something else, he said, as long as the price is right. Because natural fertilizers such as cow manure had been in short supply, for example, scientists had figured out how to make substitutes from oil. When the price of copper became too high for use in people's homes, engineers made wires out of aluminum. Car interiors are made from plastic, not wood, and children go to school wearing jackets made of recycled plastic soda bottles instead of wool.

It was a raucous debate with two distinct perspectives on the future. The Meadows' view was linear, meaning they believed that what was happening today would continue happening tomorrow at a standard rate of growth. If people increased iron use by 1.8 percent a year now, they would do so forever. Markets, however, are not linear, said Kahn. Price determines quantity. As prices rise, some people look for new supplies while others search for cheaper substitutes.

In my view, the debate was won by Kahn and his point was later proved by Mitchell's example. As oil and natural gas prices rose in the 1980s, Mitchell invested millions of dollars of his own money in fracking research. He did so, I'm convinced, not only to make money, but also because he was concerned about America's energy future.

HOW FRACKING WORKS

Fracking is not new. In fact, it is an old idea, first used commercially in the 1940s, although by today's standards, it wasn't very effective, efficient, or safe back then. Boone Pickens told me that he had witnessed fracking being done in Texas in the early 1950s. Modern fracking techniques came into use in the late 1990s, and since that time at least a million wells have been fracked.

To frack for natural gas, companies drill a well, typically about 6,000 feet deep. The vertical portion of the well might pass through drinking water or irrigation aquifers, which are usually a few hundred

Figure 4.2. North American natural gas and shale oil plays. The United States, Canada, and Mexico, combined, have more accessible energy than anywhere else in the world, thanks to new technology. US Energy Information Administration (May 2011).

feet below the surface. To protect the aquifers, the hole, which can be 4 feet in diameter, is lined with one or more steel casings and as much as 10 inches of cement. If the casings and cement are put in correctly, they protect the aquifers from leakage of natural gas or oil.

After the initial vertical drilling, the drill bit and mechanism are changed, and the rig now drills horizontally. The reason for doing this is simple. Gas-bearing rock might only be 50 or 100 feet thick, to pick a number, but it could be several miles long or wide. With horizontal drilling, a well can tap into miles of gas-laden rock. After 10,000 feet or so of horizontal drilling, the horizontal section of the well is encased with pipe and cement. Holes are then made in the casing, and water, sand, chemicals, and solvents are pumped into the well under extreme pressure—as much as 10,000 pounds per square inch (normal air pressure at sea level is 14 pounds per square inch). The highly pressurized fluids crack and keep open fissures in the rock, and this liberates the gas that is trapped there.

If you just drilled a well into shale rock and did not frack it, you wouldn't get any natural gas out of the well. Even so, fracking is controversial. The chemicals are not standardized, so people worry about what they contain. People also worry that despite the 10 inches of concrete and steel, methane—a source of carbon dioxide and the main ingredient in natural gas—might seep into the water supply.

These concerns were far more significant when fracking was still new than they are today, especially in the aftermath of the previously mentioned National Science Foundation study—despite the fact that the study found no evidence of fracking harming groundwater. Big companies such as Chevron, ExxonMobil, and Chesapeake have now replaced small wildcat firms. When they use this technology, the big companies either do the work themselves or use experienced drilling contractors, such as Halliburton or Schlumberger, to drill and frack the wells. Exploring for energy is always a dangerous and difficult prospect—who can forget BP's 2010 platform disaster in the Gulf of Mexico? However, if the procedures are followed carefully, and corners are not cut, fracking technology appears to be safe.

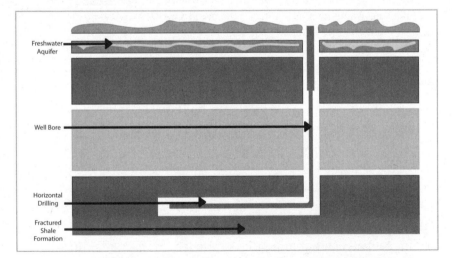

Figure 4.3. Larger, more experienced companies are now doing most of the fracking. These include Chevron and oil-field services companies such as Schlumberger, making it less likely there will be accidental releases of methane. Angelique Robinson.

If a well's life is, say, twenty years, which is a rough average, the fracking process is only a tiny portion of its life. It can easily take a few months to prepare, dig, and encase a well. But despite its complexity, each fracking session (it can be done several times during the life of a well) takes only a few days. If everything goes right after the well is fracked, natural gas will seep out of the shale rock for years.

It's difficult to get at the facts when looking at these wells, but it appears that since the big companies began fracking, the process has become safer and more environmentally sound, with some of the firms even recycling the water they use. As these companies are forced to disclose the contents of their fracking fluids, the data may further dispel concerns. There are a lot of apocryphal stories about people turning on their water and having methane come out, and sometimes even fire. But most of these horror stories, when studied, turn out to be misleading. The reported events are usually not the result of fracking. In some parts of the country, sad to say, the aquifers are already polluted. In other areas, old wells are responsible for the damage, not the nearby newer, safer wells. People are right to be concerned and to want to know the contents of the fluid, however, and they are right to demand recycling.

FRACKING FOR OIL

So far, fracking has been used largely for natural gas, but it can also be used to liberate oil from shale rock. Because oil prices have been high for years, and are expected to go higher, oil exploration companies are finding that they can make a lot of money fracking for oil. Oil produced in this way is coming onto the markets in a big way. In 2005, the United States imported upward of 60 percent of the oil it used. By 2012, that figure had fallen to 42 percent. And it is expected to fall further and faster than people might have imagined.

Texas, of course, still has the nation's largest oil reserves and is the largest producer of oil. But North Dakota, now the nation's second-largest oil-producing state, is obtaining its oil by fracking. In addition, California's much deeper, but richer, Monterey shale-oil deposits are now accessible as a result of technological advancements. Even though Monterey's shale oil is as deep as 16,000 feet below the surface, it can now be recovered profitably.

But there's more. Fracking technology, which currently recovers about 20 percent of the gas or oil in a well, is still improving. According to the NIC's *Global Trends 2030* report, "service companies are developing new 'super fracking' technologies that could dramatically increase recovery rates still further." As a result of these developments, the report said, "energy independence is not unrealistic for the US in as short a period as 10–20 years. Increased oil production and the shale gas revolution could yield such independence." NIC further reported that "US production of shale gas has exploded with a nearly 50 percent annual increase between 2007 and 2011, and natural gas prices in the US have collapsed. The US has sufficient natural gas to meet domestic needs for decades to come, and potentially substantial global exports." Some analysts estimate that recovery rates could go up to 70 percent for each well, a 3.5-fold increase, as a result of superfracking. If that happens, America would not have 92-year supply of energy, but a 322-year supply, perhaps more.[11]

All of this led to an interesting conclusion by the energy analysts at ExxonMobil, the largest publicly owned energy company in the United States. In a 2013 report, Exxon's analysts wrote that if current trends hold, the United States would become a net energy exporter by 2025. This date is similar to forecasts made by the EIA, the NIC, and other organizations.[12]

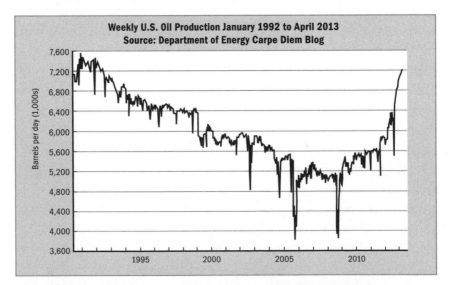

Figure 4.4. Mark Perry's economics blog, Carpe Diem, April 2013.

But that's still not all. By 2025, Exxon said, global demand for energy will increase by 35 percent compared to the present,[13] with demand in the United States and Canada falling as a result of increased energy efficiency. The scenario is pretty clear: the United States is destined to become one of the world's largest—if not *the* world's largest—energy producers *and* exporters.

That puts everything in a new light. Suppose, though I doubt it will happen, China does outpace the United States in GDP by, let's say, 2030—which I don't think will happen. But suppose it does. Since China and the rest of Asia have only limited energy reserves, they will be forced to import ever-increasing quantities of oil and natural gas from Russia, the Middle East, Africa, Venezuela, *and the United States*. China may grow bigger, but as it does, we will grow wealthier.

And when this happens, capital flows are likely to reverse. Instead of America sending money to China to buy the goods produced there, China will be sending money back to the United States to purchase energy, food, and manufactured goods, altering a decades-long trend.

Think about that dramatic turn of events and what it implies. The United States was the world's largest creditor nation from about 1900 to 1960. Then Japan took the lead position, followed by China. During its hegemony as a creditor, the United States built up its capital base and began lending money abroad. It was able to do this because of its exports of energy—coal and oil—and its exports of food and manufactured goods. The United States was the world's breadbasket, its energy source, and its largest source of manufactured goods. As a result, capital rushed to our shores. These conditions are likely to be repeated once again. As Yogi Berra is reported to have said, "it's déjà vu all over again."

Just to put this in perspective, according to the New America Foundation, a think tank in Washington, DC, capital expenditures resulting from shale gas will jump from $33 billion in 2010 to $1.9 trillion by 2035. As a result, over the same twenty-five-year period, the industry will be responsible for 1.6 million jobs and will add nearly $1.5 trillion in federal, state, and local taxes and royalties to cash-strapped governments.[14]

There is no question that the numbers in this forecast are dramatic. But consider the source. The New America Foundation is a young, independent, highly credible think tank with a board of directors that includes energy and economics experts. It is chaired by Eric Schmidt, Google's executive chairman. To have such a credible organization make this forecast is important. Usually, the bias in examining our future tends toward the negative, largely because most forecasters overlook our new ability to extract energy and the potential for that capability to promote growth. In the New America Foundation study, energy is not given short shrift. Instead, it is viewed as an important component in the nation's "comeback" story—something too few analysts take into account. For that reason, the report is called *The Promise of (and Obstacles to) America's Emerging Growth Story*. It attributes the coming growth largely to our newfound access to large quantities of natural gas. And yet, true to form, when this study was released, it barely received any coverage.

ENERGY INDEPENDENCE

Let's assume the projections of ExxonMobil, the National Intelligence Council, and the New America Foundation are correct, and the United States becomes energy independent (or nearly so) in the next dozen years. The implications are profoundly transformational. To begin with, the United States is already one of the most economically competitive nations in the world. By competitive, I mean we are a nation that produces a wide array of highly desirable products and services very efficiently, in an environment that is relatively transparent and friendly to business and investment and that is not subject to political instability. If these organizations are correct, we will be able to do all that with nearly unlimited access to cheap energy.

What the pie chart in Figure 4.5 illustrates is the extent to which business is dependent on natural gas to make plastics, chemicals, and other products and to heat and cool factories and generate electricity. Businesses also increasingly use natural gas in the vehicles they operate, such as delivery trucks. US companies are very large consumers of natural gas, either indirectly or directly consuming roughly 84 percent of all the natural gas produced in the country. The bar graph in Figure 4.5 shows how much less expensive natural gas is in the

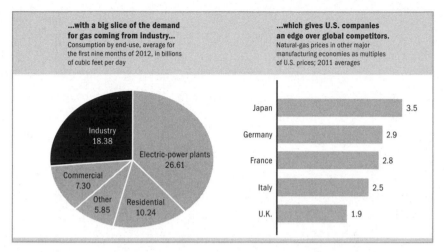

Figure 4.5. Adapted from the *Wall Street Journal*, October 24, 2012.

United States than it is in other countries. Japanese businesses pay three and a half times what American businesses pay for natural gas, and British businesses pay "only" about two times what we pay.

There are two big reasons why natural gas is important. The first is price, which matters because energy is such a large component of our lives. Higher prices mean more expensive goods, services, and even commodities, such as wheat. But since consumers use energy to heat their homes, cook their food, and fuel their cars, the higher the price of energy, the less disposable income people have in their pockets. That is why higher oil prices, to name one form of energy, have such a quick and devastating impact on the economy. When the cost of filling your gasoline tank goes from $50 to $75, and the cost of everything else you buy rises by, say, 8 percent, higher energy prices have the same effect on the economy as a sudden, massive tax hike.

But here is where the United States is lucky. Natural gas is a less expensive energy source than any other type of fuels. It is cheaper than petroleum, coal, nuclear energy, and even renewables such as solar, wind, and biofuels. That provides the American economy with a significant competitive advantage and is the reason why so much new manufacuring capacity is planned for the United States.

The second reason natural gas is important has to do with the costs of national security.

Roger J. Stern teaches and does research as a fellow at Princeton University. In 2010, he published an important paper that received scant attention. I'm actually being generous using the world "scant," because the research paper received no attention. That's a pity. Stern's academic paper was given a fittingly academic title—"United States Cost of Military Force Projection in the Persian Gulf, 1976–2007." The paper was perhaps the first quantitative analysis of the cost to the United States of its decades-long military deployment in the Persian Gulf.[15]

The purpose of those deployments was strategic—to defend the Gulf so that oil could flow from the Middle East to the United States. We did this even though only a relatively small share of our oil comes from the Middle East, compared to Europe and Japan, which get most of their oil from that region. And yet, even though most of our oil comes from elsewhere, protecting shipments of oil from this part of the world falls on our shoulders.

The geography of the Persian Gulf makes its defense difficult. Almost all of the oil exported by Iran, Iraq, Saudi Arabia, the United Arab Emirates, Kuwait, Bahrain, Oman, and Qatar—40 percent of all seaborne oil—passes through the Strait of Hormuz. A small portion of Middle Eastern oil is sent by pipeline to be exported elsewhere.

The Strait of Hormuz is one of the most important waterways in the world. At its narrowist, it is only twenty-one miles wide, with Iran on one side and Oman, Saudi Arabia, and the UAE directly across on the other side.

Since 1990, the United States has maintained at least one nuclear-powered aircraft carrier near the strait at all times, two since the Iraq War. These carriers are big beasts—about 1,400 feet long and loaded up with 120 or so military jets, an unknown number of cruise missiles and other types of missiles, and other weapons systems. These nuclear aircraft carriers could be carrying nuclear weapons as well.

Each of these carriers costs roughly $4.5 billion to build, but when one is deployed, the US Navy needs eight more as backup. At present, the navy has fifteen nuclear carriers. Each one is surrounded by a flotilla of other ships—as many as thirteen, for additional protection. America's carriers are also supported (some say) by a classified number of submarines. It takes 6,000 sailors and other personnel, in addition to those on the nuclear carrier, to fully staff the flotillas that protect our carriers. Thousands more navy pesonnel support the carriers and flotillas from bases around the world. In addition, there are backup crews, and more people who are on leave, or who are being trained. In other words, it takes thousands of troops to patrol the Strait of Hormuz in order to project sufficient power to make certain the strait is always open. And even then, the threats have not gone away.

The United States foots the entire cost of keeping the Strait of Hormuz open and of protecting the oil fields and sea lanes in the Middle East. Even though we provide the world with the benefit of this service, the sheikhs, emirs, presidents, princes, and kings in the region do not give us a break on the price of oil. We pay for the region's defense, and we also pay the market price for the region's oil. In 2003, the price was $33 a barrel, and it was hovering, at the time of this writing, at about $100 a barrel.

That's a really bad deal—one that no rational person would agree to take part in, if it were presented in that way all at once. But it wasn't presented in that way. Our involvement grew over time. And as a result, China, India, France, Britain, and all of the other big consumers of Middle Eastern oil get to sail through the Strait of Hormuz safely, because we pay the entire cost of keeping it open so the oil will keep flowing. Not only that, but China and India continue to purchase Iranian oil in defiance of the United Nations embargo against making such purchases.

True, Saudi Arabia has an air force, and so do the UAE, Qatar, and other countries in the region. That may be. But the United States still pays the lion's share of keeping the Gulf open.

One could argue that the United States has strategic reasons for making such a one-sided deal. As the guardians of the strait, the United States can, at will, determine the world's fate. Putting ourselves at the center of the world's most important sea lane means, at least theoretically, that if, say, China, India, or Pakistan threatened our country, we could shut off their oil. Or, if the Iranians really got belligerent, we could could cut them off from the rest of the world.

True enough. But our presence in the Gulf did not prevent Saddam Hussein from invading Kuwait; nor does it prevent Iran from threatening Israel, or from attempting to build nuclear weapons; nor has our presence in the Gulf stopped Iran from threatening to sink a few ships in the strait and mine the sea lanes to stop the flow of oil to the rest of the world. Every time the Iranians talk about stopping the flow of oil out of the Gulf, the United States sends more minesweepers, salvage ships, and undersea recovery vessels to the area—and the costs rise accordingly.

No one talks about how much our largesse costs, largely because no one pays for it directly. The rational thing to do would be for everyone to pay a fee at the pump to offset the cost of keeping our ships and troops in the Gulf. But that just isn't going to happen. An extra forty or fifty cents per gallon of gas might remind people when they fill up their tanks that the Middle East, *which the world depends upon for its lifeline of oil*, is a very dangerous, unstable, violent, and volatile place.

And so we pay for our massive and continuous presence in the region, and for everything required to keep the fleet functioning and the strait open, through taxes and borrowing. The price tag has been beyond massive. According to Stern's research, in the thirty-one years from 1976 to 2007, the United States spent $7.3 trillion defending the Gulf—almost half the nation's current debt. That $7.3 trillion does not include the billions of dollars spent since 2007 on the surge in Iraq, on arming and training the Iraqis and others in the region, and on moving Pershing missile batteries to Israel. Since Stern wrote his report, the total spent in the Gulf has probably increased to more than $8 trillion—roughly the size of the Chinese economy.

SECURE ENERGY

Becoming energy independent with domestic natural gas and oil will give us the freedom to change our relationship to the Middle East. We might want to do exactly as we are doing—protecting the world's lifeline of oil and picking up the full cost for doing so—for strategic reasons. Or, if we become energy independent, we might want to do a comprehensive review of our policies in the Gulf. That review might yield a different long-term conclusion for the country, strategically and economically. But, at minimum, it would allow us to choose the course we want to pursue not from the standpoint of necessity, or even vulnerability, but from the standpoint of our long-term interests and from a position of greater strength.

Oil is a globally traded commodity, which means that if prices rise or fall in one market, they rise or fall everywhere. However, if we're honest with ourselves, we have to admit that oil is not traded in a real market. Our "friends" at the Organization of the Petroleum Exporting Countries (OPEC) have set production quotas for their member countries in an effort to keep prices at levels that will maintain maximum profitablity throughout the supply chain—a goal that is stated in OPEC's charter. In this way, OPEC's thumb is perpetually pressing down on one end of the balance scale, distorting prices and making a mockery of market forces. The cold, hard economic rules of supply and demand do not operate when the amount of a commodity available for sale is managed by a committee of exporters to achieve a desired price.

Think about what energy independence means. Prices for the world's most important commodity—oil—are not set by market forces. They are set by the continuous manipulation by the handful of countries that makes up OPEC's membership. As a result, because of oil's importance, a great deal of the world economy is distorted. All of this has put the United States in a strange predicament. American service personnel are willing to lay down their lives to defend sea lanes and oil fields. But if they think they are doing it to defend a market system, where the needs of consumers determine prices, they better think again. They are putting themselves in harm's way to defend a system whose prices are rigged.

Kind of makes you feel like a chump.

But it gets even worse. Aside from OPEC's supply-management policies, prices for oil are also set by what can only be called the world's prevailing level of anxiety. When tempers in the Middle East flare, which happens regularly, consumers around the world get the jitters, fearing that production will be interrupted and deliveries slowed or stopped. Traders then scramble to find new supplies, pushing up prices. Tensions in the Middle East direcly affect prices.

When Iran sends a group of rubber speedboats—which cost about $50,000 each—into the waters around the Strait of Hormuz to harass $4.5 billion aircraft carriers, the world gets nervous. Rumors fly, saying that Iran's elite Republican Guard, the members of which man the boats, may be carrying French Exocet missiles, and may be planning to sink a carrier or two and close the strait. Oil prices spike.

Before the embargo, Iran exported about 2.2 million barrels of oil a day. If its cheap speedboats caused sufficient worry among oil importers, enough to raise oil prices by, say, $10 a barrel—a typical rise—Iran made an extra $22 million a day. Oil exporters hungry for cash have big incentives to keep the world on edge.

▼▼▼▼

Most people don't know or perhaps don't care that oil prices are, if not rigged, then at least "managed." But if you don't believe that point, just consider the following.

The United States is the world's largest oil consumer. In 2005, the nation imported a little more than 12 million barrels of oil a day. In 2012, as fracking for oil increased, our imports fell to slightly more than 8 million barrels a day. When the United States changes its oil-importing behavior by so much in such a short time, it is the equivalent of giving the world's oil producers an *extra* 4 million barrels a day to sell. Four million barrels of oil a day is roughly 90 percent of the amount that Japan imports. Japan is the world's third-largest economy.

I mention this equivalency for a reason. If oil were a market-traded commodity, and Japan suddenly stopped importing it, the laws of supply and demand suggest that oil prices would fall dramatically. Four million barrels a day is a lot of oil, and Japan is a very big, very rich country. If the Japanese stopped importing wheat or rice or beef, it would put powerful downward pressures on the prices of those commodities. And yet, from 2005 through 2012, oil prices were relatively stable, hovering at plus-or-minus $100 a barrel, correcting for a few price spikes and valleys and for inflation, despite the fact that the United States is no longer purchasing an amount of oil equal to Japan's total consumption.

How can anyone believe that oil prices are set by the market?

A LOT OF GOOD TO COME

There is a lot of good that will result from America's movement toward energy independence. Not only will it give us time to rethink whether we want to drop another $7.3 trillion in military and civilian expenditures to project American force into the Persian Gulf region, but it will also give us an opportunity to stop sending so much money abroad to pay for oil. Because we are importing 4 million barrels a day less than in 2005, we are already sending about $400 million a day less to our main energy suppliers—Canada, Mexico, Saudi Arabia, Venezuela, Nigeria, Angola, and Iraq.

I don't really mind buying oil from Canada or Mexico. They are friendly countries, signatories to NAFTA, and their economies, not to mention their cultures, are deeply intertwined with ours. They are also our biggest trading partners, buying from us and selling to us. You could say we're the Three Amigos—Très Amis in French Canadian—three busy, highly integrated countries working together, with Mexico growing the fastest, and the United States and Canada the richest.

But it's a different story when it comes to Saudi Arabia. Saudi Arabia is a religiously oriented state and a monarchy that at some point in the future is likely to come undone. It is also a place where women have few rights (at the time of this writing, the country is flirting with the idea of allowing women to ride bicycles, if accompanied by men, and if properly clad). The country's brand of Islam, Wahhabi, is considered by most people to be an ultraconservative—some would say fundamentalist—branch of Sunni. All of which begs the question. With whom would we rather partner? Democratic Canada and Mexico, where women have equal rights, or a fundamentalist monarchy like Saudi Arabia?

The answer seems clear.

As if that weren't enough, Venezuela, under the late President Hugo Chavez, became an ally of Iran's to the point of joining force in a military alliance, with a goal of jointly producing weapons. Venezuela, even under its new president Nicolás Maduro, is openly hostile to the United States and its interests. It would not bother me if we stopped buying oil from Venezuela.

Nor would I mind if we stopped buying oil from Nigeria, which has long been one of the world's most corrupt countries. After decades of oil revenues streaming into Nigeria (the largest share of it from the United States), most people live no better there than they did before the oil began to flow. Even with all that money, Nigeria's life expectancy remains at just fifty-one years old.

Nigeria, the most populous nation in Africa, is in many ways a victim of what economists call the "resource curse," or the "oil curse." In too many countries with oil, most of the oil proceeds are captured by a small group of people at the top. The richest people in Saudi Arabia and in the Gulf countries are those who are part of, or close to, the royal families. In Russia and Nigeria, too, the largest share of oil proceeds stays with the people who have the closest ties to government.

In oil-curse countries, a small group doles out funds to the rest of the country. In some countries, the rulers are generous, providing sufficient resources so that all citizens can lead a middle-class life. One reason they do this is that they feel responsible for the welfare of their fellow citizens and subjects. Another reaon is that they realize they can use money to buy off any opposition that otherwise might form, thereby preventing unrest. And yet another reason is that they want to keep their subjects docile, so that the elite can take the lion's share of the money.

But in Nigeria, the elite are not quite so generous. Nigeria is a rich country for some, but a very poor country for most.

Many oil-rich countries are corrupt, scoring toward the bottom of Transparency International's "Corruption Perceptions Index" rankings.[16] Russia, Saudi Arabia, Iraq, Venezuela, Iran, and even oil-rich Mexico are perceived as corrupt, along with Nigeria. (By contrast, Canada, Norway, the United States, the United Arab Emirates, Qatar, and a few other oil-rich countries are viewed as relatively free of corruption.)

The Nigerian economy is growing, but its per capita GDP is only about $1,555, which makes it number 143 out of 190 countries on this measure, according to World Bank. It is ranked this low despite being the world's twelfth-largest oil producer. Even with its oil, Nigeria has about 24 percent unemployment, with half of its people still living in rural areas. Given those facts, our oil imports can be seen in a new light. Do we really want to be dependent on resource-cursed countries like Nigeria, when we can go our own way?

▼▼▼▼

Not only will energy independence give us the ability to wean ourselves from long-term economic relationships with countries that are volatile, dangerous, corrupt, and/or working against our interests, but it will also put more money into the pockets of Americans.

That's beginning to happen. Because the United States imports 4 million barrels a day less than it did in 2005, at present prices, the arithmetic suggests that $400 million a day *more* is staying within our shores than in 2005. Energy independence means that the United States will be able to keep at home another $300 billion to $400 billion a year that is presently going overseas to purchase oil. Energy independence would cut our trade deficit drastically.

If you cut the trade deficit by half or more, the repercussions are big. To begin with, an awful lot of money that would have gone overseas would stay within our banking system. Giving banks another $300 billion to $400 billion a year to hold would strengthen the banks. And with so much money on deposit, interest rates would most likely remain low, and banks would have incentives to lend.

What I'm saying is that an awful lot of the trade deficit would be converted into low-cost loans—mortgages, consumer debt, and corporate debt. If those loans are made responsibly, they would go a long way toward reviving large sectors of the US economy, such as housing and construction, and toward keeping other credit-dependent sectors, such as car, truck, and airplane manufacturing, strong. An extra $300 billion to $400 billion is equivalent to a company the size of Walmart, which employs 2 million people.

If, in addition to becoming energy independent, the United States becomes a net energy exporter, as ExxonMobil predicts will happen, then the United States is likely to turn the world on its head. As countries such as China, Japan, and Germany buy our energy products and manufactured goods, new money will flood in. And as that happens, the United States might begin a transformation, going from being the world's largest debtor nation to being a creditor nation, its position after the end of World War I and sporadically through the 1960s.

The United States was the world's largest creditor nation in those periods for three reasons. It produced and sold more manufactured goods than any other country, it exported more oil and energy products than any other country, and it exported food. While it is unlikely that we will ever become the world's largest energy exporter, we will become *an* energy exporter. At same time, although we might not *export* as many manufactured goods as China or Germany, we will almost certainly *produce* more goods than anyone else at factories in the United States and around the world, just as we do now. With those two trends in place, history might just repeat itself, thus taking America from debtor nation to creditor nation.

NOT JUST OIL

The possibility that the United States will become the world's largest oil producer by 2020,[17] and either the first-, second-, or third-largest natural gas producer in the world, is not even the entire story.

The United States is already the world's largest producer of biofuels, mostly ethanol. Whereas Brazil gets the credit for transforming its fleet of vehicles from running on gasoline to running on cleaner ethanol, gasoline blends, and even natural gas, the United States produces twice as much ethanol as Brazil—about 13 billion gallons to Brazil's 6.5 billion gallons.[18]

At the beginning of America's foray into ethanol production, the US Department of Agriculture gave ethanol producers big subsidies. These federal subsidies are coming to an end. Even so, the industry has become so good at turning white corn into ethanol that it doesn't need subsidies anymore. "We can make it on our own," said Jeff Broin, founder and chairman of POET, the world's largest producer of ethanol, when he spoke at a panel that I moderated at a conference on the subject. "We don't need subsidies." Broin, who built POET up from a single, family-owned refinery into an ethanol behemoth, didn't always have that point of view. But the situation has changed. Ethanol production is more efficient than it was in the past along the entire supply chain.

POET's refinery technology continues to improve, as do the planting techniques for corn and the seed strains used. When Vice President Al Gore made his famous documentary *An Inconvenient Truth* in 2006, he did not think highly of corn-based ethanol as a fuel. Later, he said that it was a mistake to subsidize ethanol made from corn because it used more energy than it produced.[19] But since that time, American farmers and ethanol distillers have become more efficient.

According to Roger Conway, an agricultural economist with a PhD from George Washington University, who used to run the Department of Agriculture's Office of Energy Policy and New Uses, there is no doubt that Brazilian sugarcane is a better feedstock for making ethanol than American corn. "The only trouble is sugarcane only grows in small areas of the United States," he said. Even so, Conway, who now runs Rosslyn Advisors, a consulting firm specializing in agricultural issues, told me that ethanol production from corn is getting more efficient. "At present, for each energy input, you get 1.7 to 2 energy outputs. That makes it a viable fuel. Not as good a feedstock as sugarcane, but corn has certainly gotten better," he said. "Over time, I think we'll get as much as 4 units of energy for each input of energy. It could even go higher. The seed and planting technology is really improving. Yields are improving at the refineries and with seeds also. And it takes less energy to plant corn using new techniques."

Already, about 10 percent of the fuel we burn in our cars is ethanol. According to Conway, who is known for his shaved head and dapper way of dressing—three-piece suits, pocket watches, and bright, precisely folded silk handkerchiefs—newer cars can burn 20 percent ethanol without any problems, although he acknowledges that not everyone agrees with him.

Right now, a substantial number of cars and trucks manufactured in the United States can run on fuel that is 85 percent ethanol. Almost 10 million vehicles like that are on the road, according to the US Energy Information Administration.[20] These cars and trucks typically have a "flex-fuel" logo on the back. Older cars can be modified to burn 85 percent ethanol with the addition of some simple aftermarket parts costing a few hundred dollars.

Having the capacity to burn ethanol instead of (or along with) gasoline is good for the environment because ethanol releases far fewer carbon dioxide molecules into the air than gasoline—30 to 50 percent fewer, in fact. And ethanol is cheaper. A gallon of E85 (85 percent ethanol and 15 percent gasoline) costs, on average, $3.69 in Los Angeles, at the time of this writing, while regular gasoline costs an average of $4.50 a gallon. Although not all service stations sell E85, there are smartphone apps to help customers locate ones that do.

Food prices, contrary to Gore's analysis, are not really affected very much by the amount of ethanol produced. Ethanol is made from white corn, which—as Conway says—"you need a cow's four stomachs to digest." People typically eat yellow corn almost exclusively, aside from a few local variations. In addition, white and yellow corn are not produced on the same land. White corn is largely grown on marginal land, while yellow corn is grown on prime farmland. "If there is any impact on food prices from using ethanol in our cars, it is minor," Conway told me. He further explained that "at the time of the Mexican tortilla riots in 2007, people said corn-based ethanol had driven up corn prices, which are used to make tortillas. But the fact is, all commodity prices rose that year—across the board, starting with oil. Ethanol was not the reason prices went up. If anything, prices rose because oil prices spiked, and it cost more to plant, harvest, and transport yellow corn."

The United States has the capacity to refine much more ethanol from its corn. But there is one problem. Since ethanol production really took off as a result of government subsidies, exports are not allowed. Now that it is a viable and efficient fuel, that rule no longer makes sense. As soon as the subsidies are dropped, Congress should allow exports of ethanol. The market for this cleaner-burning fuel will then grow. Brazil has already expressed interest in buying American ethanol, and many European countries are likely to buy it as well, since they are required to meet stringent carbon dioxide emissions targets.

What all of this means is that exports of ethanol, along with exports of conventional fuels, could help the trade deficit melt away, since the market for fuels is enormous, measured in trillions of dollars. At one time, the United States owned that market. Texas, Oklahoma, California, and Pennsylvania benefited enormously from their positions in the fuels market. That dominance could be a reality once again, bringing major benefits to the country.

Consider the case of North Dakota, once a sleepy agricultural state plagued by a frigid winter and a sluggish economy. The winter is still long and cold, but when fracking began to take off, so did North Dakota. It's one of the few places where unemployment is negative—there are too few workers and too many jobs. As the North Dakota economy grows, the state faces housing shortages because of

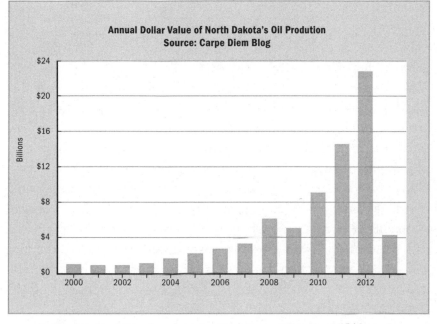

Figure 4.6. Mark Perry's economics blog, Carpe Diem, April 2013.

all the workers coming to take part in the oil shale bonanza. In some cases, it's like the old days of the forty-niners who came to California to pan for gold. Many of the miners of 1849 shared rooms, and some shared beds—one person using a bed during daylight hours, and another at night. In certain parts of North Dakota, that practice has been revived.

As Figure 4.6 shows, North Dakota's riches are soaring. But aside from oil, and some cattle and wheat, the North Dakota economy is far from developed. As a result, when the workers in North Dakota build homes, buy vehicles, take out insurance policies, buy clothes and computers, send their kids to college, or put their money in the bank, that money returns to the rest of the country.

PREDICTION

The logic around our emerging energy picture is pretty straightforward. Since the start of the financial and economic crises, demand for oil in most mature countries has fallen. Meanwhile, it has risen in emerging countries such as China and India. Oil prices have been hovering around $100 a barrel, plus or minus a few dollars, a pretty hefty price.

But as the economic recovery strengthens in the United States, demand for oil will increase, which is likely to cause prices to rise. Will prices rise to $145 or higher, as they did just before the economic and financial collapse? I don't know for certain—no one does, since data is limited. Even so, according to an article in the *Wall Street Journal*,[21] a recent one-day rise in oil prices was "spurred by signs of economic improvement in the world's largest oil consumer." The world's largest oil consumer is, of course, the United States. According to the article, oil prices rose 1.6 percent in one day on the basis of *signs* of economic growth, not growth itself. They rose on expectations.[22]

Do we really want to live in a world where the most important commodity we use rises based on signs of growth, rather than real growth, and on the manipulation of prices by a small group of suppliers? I don't think so.

High oil prices are the reason why we have alternatives to imported oil. When prices are above $60 a barrel over the long term, many different types of energy sources become viable—natural gas; new, unconventional sources of domestic oil; even wind and in some cases solar energy. The high price of fuel has given consumers a reason to buy hybrids and all-electric vehicles. But in order for new energy sources to develop, prices need to stay above that benchmark rate over the long haul. No one will commit billions of dollars of capital to explore for natural gas or nonconventional oil if they believe that oil prices are likely to tumble. Why would they? Their investment in solar fields or in new sources of domestic oil would quickly be lost when imported oil could be used more cheaply.

When oil prices are volatile, for whatever reason, and fluctuate widely, investors in new types of energy—understanding the logic of the market—keep their cash in the bank. They fear losing their money when oil prices drop and they are not able to compete. When oil prices are high and stable, investment in alternatives makes sense. For that reason, our best hope is for imported oil prices to stay high enough to cause people to seek other types of fuels. In the long run, it's better to develop our own sources of energy than to send boatloads of money overseas.

CHAPTER FIVE

MONEY TO BURN

When you have access to capital, the results can be magical. The Capital Access Index studies by my colleagues at the Milken Institute, which were conducted every year for more than a decade, show a clear pattern. When capital is plentiful and prudently lent, and borrowers can obtain it in transparent ways and under good terms, economies grow. In the *2009 Capital Access Index*,[1] the latest available, the authors showed how damaging the financial and housing crises were to the United States and other leading economies. The report indicated that globally, banks posted losses of $685 billion, had to cut 150,000 jobs, and were forced to raise $688 billion to replenish their capital. The authors also found that bond markets froze in a number of countries, which made it very difficult for big companies to borrow the money they needed.

But the report also showed that not all countries fared the same. Because of decades of prudent management, Canada and Hong Kong rose to the top of the list of countries where capital remained plentiful, followed by a somewhat wobbly Britain, and then a well-managed Singapore, with the United States fifth in the lineup.[2]

With the exception of Britain, which tightened its belt following a decision to pursue a policy of austerity (unwise in my opinion), banks in these countries remained strong even though the rest of the world was in crisis. In Canada, Hong Kong, and Singapore, capital remained plentiful, so companies could expand and individuals could buy homes. As a result of good financial management, these countries avoided a housing or mortgage crisis. They did not see housing prices spike, and they continued to prosper during the global recession. Although Singapore's economy contracted in 2009, it was still Asia's fastest-growing country in 2010, growing at a rate of 14.7 percent.

Countries where capital is readily accessible tend to grow the fastest.

This is not to suggest that we should return to the days when mortgages, for example, did not require people to document their employment status or income. That approach got us into lots of trouble. Access to capital simply means that people can raise money to start or expand businesses relatively easily, relatively safely, and without having to pay bribes or be members of a privileged group.

Starting or expanding businesses is what fuels growth and hiring and lays the groundwork for building countries. But it must be done in the most corruption-free way possible. The links between growth, corruption, and access to capital—and a number of other issues— lead to a clear conclusion: all things being equal, countries that have relatively easy access to capital and relatively low levels of corruption, good regulation, well-functioning courts and legal systems, and reliable accounting standards grow faster than countries that do not.[3]

No country is entirely free of corruption. Bribery and other forms of corruption exist everywhere, and the United States is by no means free of it. Every year, people go to jail for giving city contracts to their brothers-in-law or to people who handed them envelopes filled with cash. However, the United States is much cleaner and more law abiding than all but a handful of countries. As a result, in my research, the United States was ranked very near the top with regard to issues relating to its legal system, regulations, access to capital, accounting standards, and corruption and economic and enforcement policies. And, although the United States slipped in the transparency rankings during the financial crisis, it has recovered some of that lost ground.

When sound institutions are added to other factors—including our energy bonanza, our creativity and knowledge base, and our manufacturing capabilities—it is clear that the United States has all of the elements necessary to shift back into a very high rate of growth.

Brazil, Russia, India, and China, while still growing rapidly, though not as rapidly as a few years ago, do not have the institutional capabilities or institutional quality that we do. These countries score poorly especially with regard to corruption, their legal systems, and in some cases their accounting standards. The courts in these countries don't always work, and bribery is rampant. Institutional problems like these exert powerfully negative forces on an economy's future. And although Brazil, Russia, India, and China are rapidly emerging from poverty, their institutional limitations—unless they are fixed—will slow down their growth.

In 2011, I spoke at a small conference in Moscow called the Russia Forum. The forum was attended by many of that country's top government and business leaders. After a long day of talks and meetings, the hosts put on an extravagant formal dinner for many conference participants at a restaurant in an old, pre–Russian Revolution building facing the Kremlin.

I was seated next to a wealthy Russian businessman who had bright gray eyes and a well-trimmed, black moustache. He had been extremely successful developing high-rises and other types of real estate in Moscow. On the other side of the businessman was a talkative German economist in his late sixties who was an expert on corruption and transparency. After too many glasses of vodka—and countless blini covered with caviar—the German asked the Russian businessman about Russia's high levels of corruption.

"How do you do business in a country where almost everyone wants a bribe?" He asked.

The Russian looked at the German economist and adjusted his expensive French tie. He was clearly amused by the German's naïveté. "It's simple," the Russian said. "We pay it."

"Are you ever worried you could get into trouble for doing that?" the German asked.

The Russian's amusement at the first question faded and now he seemed annoyed. "No. It's how we do business here. Everyone pays bribes. It's perfectly normal," he said.

"And do you ever think about the wider impact?" the German asked.

"There is no wider impact," The Russian said. "It's the way business is done." What followed was not exactly a replay of World War II, but it was close as our little area of the lavish table got loud.

Bribes may be normal, yes. But productive, no. It is not productive because only wealthy people can pay bribes sufficient to win contracts. And then, when they win a contract to build a skyscraper, for example, they are no doubt also paying bribes to build it in the cheapest way, using materials that may not be capable of withstanding the strain. They might pay other bribes that enable them to scrimp on insurance or safety measures.

These bribes are hidden costs, but they are costs nevertheless. And although they are not shown on a business's financial reporting, they still must be paid. When corruption is rampant, the best people generally don't win the contracts. Moreover, the cost of doing business is higher than it should be. These hidden costs, and the bad decisions that go along with them, slow down an economy's growth. To grow, you need capital. But you also need transparency.

Fortunately, the United States has both.

ABUNDANT CAPITAL

In April 2012, I addressed a group of thirty Silicon Valley chief financial officers from a variety of companies. Some of those companies made switches for the communications industry, others wrote software that routed people's calls, several made products that kept track of bills, and still others focused on sending data from one person or computer to another. The largest company had about $10 billion a year in revenue from writing and selling software, and the smallest had roughly $400 million per year in revenue from so-called "big data" products that analyzed trends in the way people made purchases at large retail outlets such as Walmart and Sam's Club.

Although the big companies in Silicon Valley, such as Apple, Oracle, HP, and Intel, get all the credit, the valley is made up of hundreds of small- to medium-sized businesses. They make components that go into the products of these and other big companies, or they make products for industry, or write software. For instance, Autodesk (which I will discuss later) makes design, engineering, and manufacturing software that is used by almost every architectural, construction, engineering, and manufacturing company in the world. The company is relatively small, with only $2.21 billion in annual revenue. Still, this company was a pioneer when it was established in 1982, and it remains on the cutting edge.

There are many companies as proficient and successful as Autodesk. I think of them as the unsung heroes of the economy. Salesforce.com is another company like that. Although it has only $3 billion in annual revenue, it is a strong, stable company whose software supports a myriad of other companies around the world and their relationships with their customers.

The companies in the room where I spoke were members of the unsung-heroes group. All of them were growing rapidly and hiring lots of technical people. And, despite a slow economy, these CFOs were optimistic about their companies' growth prospects for the future, especially growth overseas.

▼▼▼

We met in Milpitas, California, at KLA-Tencor, one of those Silicon Valley manufacturing powerhouses you never hear about. But there it was on a campus of its own with several large industrial buildings surrounded by a huge expanse of lush green lawn. The grounds included a gourmet cafeteria and a well-maintained set of volleyball courts. (Engineers need to let off steam every once in a while.) At lunchtime, the volleyball courts were fully occupied, and every seat in the cafeteria was filled. Just glancing around at the technical staff munching sushi and drinking green tea gave me a nice intuitive affirmation that America's technical leadership draws from the best of the best. I could see that this was a diverse group of people whose origins were from everywhere on earth. Race, gender, and family history mattered for naught in this crowd.

I mention the name of KLA-Tencor simply because it provided the space where we met, but there are many such companies. KLA-Tencor makes testing equipment that is used to ensure that the semiconductors we use in our computers, tablets, mobile devices, and almost every other kind of device are made right and work properly. Although the United States accounts for only 4 percent of the world's population, American companies make a third of the world's semiconductors—another indicator that the United States remains an economic and technological superpower. But more importantly,

American companies are dominant at the top end of the market. For example, in July 2013, when China said it had built the world's fastest computer, it also said (perhaps under its breath?) that the brains inside the box were semiconductors made by California's Intel Corporation. And when IBM built the Watson supercomputer, which defeated Brad Rutter and Ken Jennings in the televised game show *Jeopardy*, this veritable rain man of a computer was powered by IBM's Power7 chips, which were developed under a grant from DARPA. It was against this high-tech backdrop of Silicon Valley that I gave my talk about the world's economic predicament.

After finishing my talk, the CFOs and I began a discussion and exchange of ideas. I wanted to get a better understanding of their most pressing issues and listen to what was keeping them up at night so that I could offer solace and solutions. To speak to this group, I had to sign a nondisclosure agreement that prevents me from naming names and listing companies. (We met at KLA-Tencor, but I'm not saying whether anyone from KLA-Tencor was there.) So I switched off my PowerPoint presentation and listened. As we sat in the austere conference room, the talk became interesting—and the CFOs were surprisingly open. Their primary complaint was not what you might think it would be. They did not complain about revenue or profits or about the sluggishness of the economy. They didn't protest interest rates. Their problem was this: *they had too much money sitting idly in the bank*. That's not the worst problem a company can have, but it is a problem. The fact was, these companies were doing so well, and their products were so well suited to the marketplace, that their coffers were full.

All the CFOs said sales had been very strong—and the economic statistics justified their claims. Remember, this was 2012—but despite the financial crisis and the economic downturn, American high-tech companies were relatively unscathed. Companies in the United States and abroad were continuing to upgrade their capabilities in order to compete when growth returned. As a result, the CFOs in the room agreed that their firms were still competitive against their foreign and domestic rivals. They also agreed that they were not worried about losing market share anytime soon. They said that Asian and European firms had been unable to duplicate their products or quality, at least so far. Business was booming and profits were accumulating. They were having some problems finding enough people with the right skills and backgrounds to hire into their workforces. But, for the most part, it was the problem of excess cash that kept them up at night.

These CFOs said their balance sheets were so rich it was making them more than a little bit anxious. They worried that investors might think they had run out of ideas or opportunities—that they had lots of money, but nowhere to spend it. They also worried that investors might look at all that cash and demand special dividends (it was the investors' money, after all). Perhaps a rival company would try to acquire them to get their cash, *perhaps even at a discount*. Having too much cash might affect their stock prices. They were worried about where to put their money, given that interest rates were so low. And they were worried that the government, seeing how much money they had in the bank, might try to tax it. These folks were a worried lot. We all should have such problems!

Why so much money in the bank? According to these CFOs, their boards would not allow them to put their money to work on anything but surefire investments. One of them complained, for example, that his board vetoed every plant expansion plan the CEO and others offered in favor of investing the company's money in a new office building. "Why an office building?" the CFO asked rhetorically. "Because you can't lose money if you build an office building in Silicon Valley." But office buildings are not our business, he sighed. "High tech is our business. We'd do much better if we rented the space we needed and expanded our production."

By putting your money into an office building, you're doing what any fool with good credit can do, everyone at the table agreed. You're breaking ground, pouring concrete, and lifting steel girders. Why in the world would a high-tech firm employing lots of engineers from around the world, who are expert at developing software to keep packets of data flying through the world's telecom networks, want to get into the real-estate business? "Isn't it a better use of the company's time and money to expand production or acquire a related business than to go into a real-estate business? Buying real estate makes no sense to me," said one CFO with his head in his hands. The other CFOs nodded sympathetically.

The group also agreed on another important point: boards of directors are too risk averse; board members don't realize that you can't make money if you don't take at least some chances. To demonstrate the point, one CFO said she had a year's worth of revenue in the bank and no place to put it.

And, just to reiterate: most of these CFOs were from the *smaller* companies—averaging $10 billion or less in annual revenue. But they are not alone. Big companies are also flush with cash, some having tens of billions of dollars sitting in the bank, earning almost nothing. At the time of this writing,[4] Chevron had $43 billion in the bank, Google had $44 billion, Conoco Phillips had $45 billion, Ford Motor Company had $51 billion, Microsoft had $73 billion, Apple had $117 billion, GE had $122 billion, and Berkshire Hathaway, Warren Buffett's company, had $162 billion in cash. That's a lot of money to keep in a money market fund, in short-term bonds, or in bank accounts doing next to nothing.

So how much money are our companies keeping idle? The exact figure is difficult to estimate. Even so, in 2009 American corporations had *at least* $5 trillion in cash, ready to invest. About $1.5 trillion of it was in the United States, and around $3.5 trillion was held overseas. (2009 figures are unfortunately the latest available; it is likely that American companies are now holding less cash because they have begun investing. A good estimate is US corporations are holding $4 trillion in cash.)

And one reason American companies are keeping so much money overseas is because they know if they bring it stateside, the government will tax it. Better a bank account in Singapore, earning 1 percent, than the US taxman's bite.

There is talk in Congress about a tax holiday for corporations so they can bring this money back to the United States. That's a good idea. It's an even better idea to reform the corporate tax rates so that US companies (and individuals working overseas) are not taxed twice—in the country in which they earn their loot and then again in the United States. It's also a good idea to bring down corporate taxes to levels that are more in line with those of other countries. For example, we pay between 15 and 39 percent at the federal level, but, to get the full picture, you have to add in the taxes we pay at the state level—as much as another 12 percent—along with any city taxes. The point is, most countries have a lower corporate tax rate than the United States does. In Canada, for example, the federal rate is just 15 percent and the highest provincial rate is 4.5 percent.[5]

Clearly, the US corporate tax rate is too high. In addition, corporations and individuals shouldn't be taxed in the United States and elsewhere, too.

If companies were taxed less here, they would invest in more people here and most likely would employ more people. In the short term, the government would get less revenue, but in the long term, tax revenue would rise as payrolls and corporate revenues increased. The priority should be to make the United States an easier place to do business, along the lines of Singapore, where taxes can be as low as zero percent at the outset in order to make the country an appealing place for companies to locate. And if money earned overseas were taxed only in the country where it was earned, and not *also* in the United States, there is little doubt that money would come home to be invested within our shores.

No other country has a problem like ours. But, then again, no other country has a business sector as large as ours. Our companies have about $4 trillion that they could invest, with roughly $2.5 trillion held domestically and another $1.5 trillion stashed overseas. I

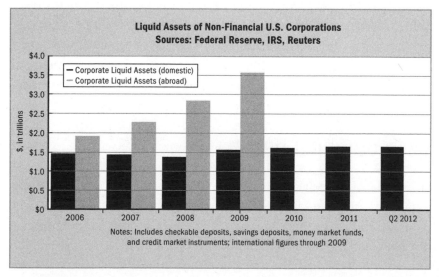

Liquid Assets of Non-Financial U.S. Corporations
Sources: Federal Reserve, IRS, Reuters

Legend:
- Corporate Liquid Assets (domestic)
- Corporate Liquid Assets (abroad)

Y-axis: $, in trillions

Notes: Includes checkable deposits, savings deposits, money market funds, and credit market instruments; international figures through 2009

Figure 5.1.

would give these figures a grade of "C" for reliability, but the lowest credible estimates I've seen still put the total at $3.5 trillion. Either way, we're talking about a lot of loot, an amount somewhere between the size of the Japanese and German economies, the world's third and fourth biggest. That's a lot of money to have stashed on the sidelines.

You might wonder why I care about the cash America's big businesses have on their books. The reason is simple. As the second American Century takes off, it will require investment. You cannot create tomorrow's industries without putting today's money to work. Strengthening the biotech sector, building the robotics industry, conducting research to build chips far faster than the Power7, designing virtual reality classrooms, switching from dirty coal to cleaner natural gas for electricity generation—all of this will take capital. Lots of it.

What does it all mean? It means that corporate America has more than enough capital to invest to extend its lead as the world's largest and most dynamic economy. This is not to say that other countries don't have money to invest. They do. They just don't have as much as we have in the hands of private companies. And here's some even better news. The money that America's companies are holding is likely to grow larger each year as the profits generated by our companies grow.

No one knows exactly how much money it will take to build the future. We do know that fully building America's natural-gas-drilling capacity—its network of pipelines and filling stations and all the other things that are needed to make the country energy independent, and perhaps even a net energy exporter—will take an expenditure of $1.9 trillion[6] between 2010 and 2030—*a twenty-year period*. Corporate America is looking for a productive way to invest what it has in the bank, and it could write a check for that amount today.

RESTRUCTURING DEBT

When the world collapsed in 2008, corporate America did something smart. Big companies used it as an opportunity to restructure their debt. Their decision to do that was farsighted—exactly the opposite of their current reluctance to invest their hoards of cash. Here's what they did.

Corporate bonds, including so-called junk bonds, which companies issue to raise capital, often came with high rates of interest. In the

1990s through the early 2000s, investors buying junk bonds wanted 10, 12, or 15 percent interest, sometimes even more, to counterbalance the risks of lending to these less-than-investment-grade companies. Investment-grade companies—companies that had better credit ratings than the companies that were less-than-investment-grade—paid rates of 6 to 9 percent on their bonds when they needed to borrow money. Since bonds hang around for as long as thirty years before they're paid off, these high-interest-rate obligations ate into corporate profits and made it difficult for both types of companies to expand.

But a funny thing happened in 2008. When the world's economic roof fell in, interest rates fell along with it. At the same time, banks stopped lending.

For big companies, this created an opportunity. They rarely borrowed money from banks anyway. They used investment, commercial, and merchant banks to advise them on transactions and help them sell their bonds—all for a fee—but they didn't borrow money from banks. To raise capital, companies issued bonds and sold them in the world's bond markets.

During the financial crisis, because interest rates fell, companies were able to issue new bonds at, say, 2 percent and use the money they received to buy back their outstanding bonds. The period from 2008 to 2012 was one of the greatest periods of corporate debt restructuring ever. Companies were doing on a huge scale what people were doing on a more modest scale when they did a refinancing of their mortgage debt. The effect was to reduce the amount of interest they paid as well as the amount of interest that accumulated over time. For example, if a company borrowed $100,000 for 10 years at 6 percent, its costs would be $1,110 a month. If the same company refinanced its debt at 2 percent, its costs would be only $920 a month. At 2 percent, you pay $10,416 in interest over the life of the loan, whereas at 6 percent you pay $33,224.

These savings are reflected in Figure 5.2, which shows data on Bank of America Merrill Lynch as compiled by the Federal Reserve. For companies with good credit, interest rates fell from 6 percent, just before the crisis, to a low of 1.5 percent in mid-2012. Companies that restructured their debt watched as their interest expenses fell, which led to an increase in capital, as I noted above, and to increased profits,

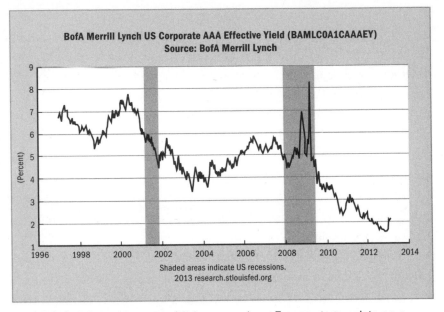

Figure 5.2. Interest rates fell by as much as 7 percentage points as a result of the Great Recession.

even in a sluggish economy. For that reason, although the financial crisis caused a lot of pain and shuttered much of the economy, it did wonders for corporate America's finances, positioning thousands of companies to take advantage of the future.

DEBT TO GDP

Right now, America is in an odd situation. As I mentioned earlier, one tool that governments have for ending depressions is to transfer private debt onto the public's books—which is what we've done. As a consequence, the "rich man's depression" is over, but we have a lot of public debt. That debt is an emotional issue that is at the center of a lot of contentiousness and debate. As a result, rather than treating that debt in the technical fashion it deserves, people have done a lot of finger pointing and expressed a lot of emotion.

Debt is always a difficult issue, but for reasons no one really understands. The economic system is not a product of nature, and it was not divinely inspired. It is the handiwork of humans. Even so, money, economics, and finance are inextricably linked in our psyches. The

Bible and other religious books, for example, are filled with injunctions against charging interest and taking on debt.

I've puzzled over why this is the case. The devil didn't invent debt—we did. And debt is at the heart of our monetary and banking system. It is at the heart of the economy as well.

Ben Bernanke is a debt technician—adept at what he's been doing to right the economy, and with as much training in his field as any surgeon has in hers. And who are we borrowing from anyway, but ourselves? The world would be better off—and our Sunday-morning talk shows would be quieter—if we could learn to focus on debt and the economy as technical issues rather than as measurements of our qualities as human beings.

The fact is, the government took on private debt to prevent the economy from failing, which is something we've learned how to do. The next step is to reduce that debt in as painless a way as possible. And, although I agree with many that Wall Street was exceptionally greedy, the nation's car companies made one wrong decision after another, and too many bankers were, well, idiots, there is no doubt in my mind that we would have been worse off had we let those entities struggle and die. Did we really want to bring the economy to a halt—a real halt, not a metaphorical one—to prove a moral point? Did we really want to watch as unemployment went above 20 percent the way it did during the Great Depression? I don't think so.

Our government's debt is the result of technical programs we used to restore the economy. But it is also the result of earlier schemes to cut taxes while fighting two wars, along with building up the military. Whether you hide what you spend at the department store from yourself or the person you live with, or hide what you spend fighting two wars and building up your army, this type of behavior will catch up with you. And, while you can delay the inevitable using financial, banking, and accounting tricks, at some point the inevitable will happen. You will have to make good on your debts. It's simply arithmetic, and it must be dealt with.

The US government debt totals about $16 trillion, or $52,000 per person—slightly more than what the country earns in a year. Sixteen trillion is a big number. But so what? The world is filled with big numbers.

Think about it this way—and allow me the liberty of using a rather clumsy analogy. Suppose you were a banker and were visited by a creative, go-getting couple—let's call them Mr. and Mrs. America, each earning $52,000 a year (I said it was a clumsy analogy). Both of the Americas had good jobs, lots of energy, a good record of success in business, tattoos of the stars and stripes on their arms, and a tremendous amount of dynamism, enterprise, and chutzpah. If this bright, shiny couple walked into your office looking for a loan to buy and fix up a house, how much would you lend them? Would you lend them the equivalent of their salaries? Twice their salaries? Three times their salaries? Or more?

You would probably lend them at least the amount of their salaries, because they were employed, had a good track record, and seemed to have good prospects for the future. If you lent them $104,000, their combined incomes, you would be pretty certain their incomes would grow faster than their debt payments. Besides, they'd be borrowing $104,000 once, but they would be earning through their jobs a combined $104,000 *every year*. And, because this couple is relatively young (mid-thirties), vivacious, and eager to get ahead, with lots of creative ideas, they have a future. As a result, their credit scores and prospects might qualify them to borrow two, three, or even four times their incomes. And, because Mr. and Mrs. America recently found an abundance of natural gas and oil on their land, and businesses wanted to buy fuels from them and develop factories nearby, you might lend them even more—many times more.

If we extrapolate in a conservative way, we can see that, over the next few decades, this cool couple, the Americas, are likely to see their incomes rise and their debt go up. But because of their prospects, and their reserves of natural gas and oil, their debt is likely to rise at a much slower rate than their income. So if we measure their debt as a share of income, the debt will be shrinking. That's a trend bankers like to see. It means the Americas will be able to pay back their loans.

We've seen this before. In 1996, Sergey Brin and Larry Page, two Stanford PhD students, borrowed as much as they could against their credit cards to start a business called "Back Rub." Then, with their credit cards maxed out, and with interest rates on their debt at about 18 percent, Sergey and Larry must have appeared to their bankers as victims of student excess. After all, Stanford graduate students, like grad students everywhere, rarely have any income. And, though there is no doubt they were both bright young men, neither had any business experience. And what kind of a name was "Back Rub," anyway? But a year later, Brin and Page's prospects looked a little better. They changed the name of their company from Back Rub to Google, moved their operations into a friend's garage, and the rest, as they say, is history.

I'm using Google to illustrate a point. Whereas $10,000 must have seemed like a lot of debt when they were just starting out, once Brin and Page's creativity took root, the significance of that debt faded. Ten thousand dollars is a lot of credit-card debt if your income is $10,000. But it's not a lot if the company you started has more than $50 billion in revenue and you have billions of dollars of the company's stock. That means the important metric is not the size of your debt. It is the size of your debt relative to other factors.

What's important to know is that over time, if revenue grows faster than debt even as interest accumulates, the ratio is likely to come down. That's what is happening in the United States. By contrast, Japan's debt-to-income ratio is 242—and going up—meaning that for every dollar's worth of GDP, Japan has 2.42 dollars of government debt, which is worrisome.

As I noted, beginning in 2008, corporate America began a massive restructuring of its debt. But companies weren't the only entities to seize the economic moment. Government did a restructuring, too. In 2008, interest on ten-year Treasury bills was about 5 percent. Five years later, bonds issued by the Treasury Department are paying less than 2 percent. As a result, in 2008, Treasury Secretary Timothy Geithner began exchanging hundreds of billions of dollars of high-interest-rate debt for debt paying just 1.5 percent. Because of that move, even though the country's government debt is piling up, the government's monthly payments are down. Even more importantly, the amount of money the government pays out in interest as a percentage of GDP is also down, an extremely important (but largely ignored) fact. Why is it ignored? I'm not sure, but my guess is that it's politics. Why focus on what's important—that a declining share of GDP is needed to pay the interest on our loans—when you can bash a political opponent?

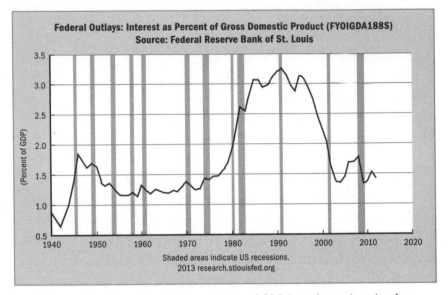

Figure 5.3. Interest outlays as a share of GDP have been dropping for more than two decades, a fact that is largely ignored.

The chart in Figure 5.3, created by the St. Louis Federal Reserve Bank, illustrates this concept and shows why Mr. and Mrs. America are in better shape than one might at first expect. The share of GDP devoted to paying interest on our debt has fallen to levels not seen since Richard Nixon was in the White House. And, although it is true that the country has a lot more debt than it did in 1973, that is not the metric that matters. Warren Buffett and I can both owe the same amount of money on our MasterCards, but I can assure you that if we measured that amount against the amount of money we respectively had in the bank, Buffett would come out ahead.

I like to think about our government's debt this way. When you go to buy a car, the financial institution lending you the money to make the purchase wants to know about your income and debt. That's why we fill out those forms. Lenders are not stupid—at least they haven't been stupid since they precipitated the financial crisis a few years back. They understand, at least for now, that if someone takes on too much debt, he's less likely to pay back the money he borrows. As a consequence, Figure 5.3 could be applied to either countries or individuals. I'm convinced that if you went into your local Chevy dealership and showed the sales manager a chart from your bank indicating that your debt payments had been declining at the same staggering rate as the Fed's chart shows for the country's debt declining, you would drive off the lot in a new car.

GROWTH FIXES EVERYTHING

If the United States were to resume growing the way it did when Bill Clinton was president, at a rate of 3.8 percent a year, no one would be talking about debt. Growth solves a lot of problems and changes our perspective. When Clinton took office, unemployment was 7.4 percent, about the same as the time of this writing. But with the economy growing at 3.8 percent, the unemployment rate tumbled to 3.9 percent, a drop of 3.5 percentage points, which is a big change. Back in the 1990s, economists were marveling at the fact that the United States, for the first time in decades, was at full employment. Anyone who wanted to work could find a job. But it also meant something just as important. When you have full employment, you also have more people paying taxes, which means the government has more resources to pay off its loans.

During the Clinton era, the national debt increased slightly, but the debt-to-GDP ratio plateaued at 60 percent, meaning that for every $1 in GDP, there was $.60 of government debt. By contrast, when World War II drew to a close, the debt-to-GDP ratio was 120 percent, a high for the United States. That same ratio fell to a low of 30 percent when Jimmy Carter was president in the late 1970s.[7] I mention these ratios to illustrate that the country's debt levels change, sometimes rapidly, which means that today's situation is no doubt temporary.

And there is more than a single way to lower the debt-to-GDP ratio. You can cut spending, as Herbert Hoover did; you can increase taxes, the approach of George H. W. Bush; or you can grow, the approach Bill Clinton took.

▼▼▼▼

The Clinton approach is the best and least painful path to take. It favored prudence with regard to spending, it reduced certain entitlement programs (emphasizing Welfare to Work for many who once relied on government payments through the Aid to Families with

Dependent Children [AFDC] program, better known as "welfare," for example), and it reduced spending on the military in the aftermath of the breakup of the Soviet Union. Cutting military spending, which people feared would lead to job losses, actually produced the opposite effect. The benefit from cutting the defense budget was large enough to be given a name—the Peace Dividend.

Shortly after Clinton left office, the 9/11 attacks took place, and we were involved in the costly wars in Iraq and Afghanistan. When Clinton was president, the United States spent about $325 billion annually on defense, excluding the undisclosed cost of the CIA and the other intelligence agencies. By 2011, defense expenditures had more than doubled, rising to more than $645 billion, again excluding the cost of intelligence.

That's a lot of money. These US expenditures are five times greater than those of China, the second-largest military spender in the world, ten times what Russia spends, and twelve times what Britain spends.[8] If you combine US military spending with what we spend on intelligence, the total could be as much as $1 trillion, which is roughly the size of New York State's GDP. Think about that. We spend on defense an amount equal to what everyone in New York, with a population of 20 million people, earns and produces in a year.

Getting the government back to its Clinton-era military and domestic spending levels is no easy task. During Clinton's two terms in office, government spending accounted for an average of 20 percent of the economy, versus 24 percent at the time of this writing. Four percentage points might not seem like a lot, but it is—$600 billion. That's an amount midway between the GDPs of Illinois and Pennsylvania, with each state having roughly 13 million people. Cutting that much from the budget won't be easy.

As I've mentioned, I'm not a worrywart when it comes to deficits. I know there's a lot of opposition to that line of thinking. There are academic economists, think-tank mavens, and lots of pretty faces dotting the economics profession who argue that deficits are a curse. But when the United States borrowed 120 percent of GDP to fight World War II, it didn't exactly pay back that debt the way an individual pays off his or her balance on the MasterCard bill. The American economy simply grew to the point where the sum that was 120 percent of GDP in 1945 became an increasingly smaller share as GDP grew. The same thing is happening now.

I say it's happening for this reason. The American economy is about to get as much as a $400 billion annual infusion from becoming energy independent, and it may get more of an infusion if it decides to export natural gas. In addition, if America returns to a more "normal," faster rate of growth—between 3 and 3.5 percent a year—that will add another $400 billion to $500 billion a year to GDP, compounded. These two figures alone—close to $1 trillion—and more, will be added to our GDP each year. Because of that, without the economists resorting to any tricks of the pen, the nation's debt-to-GDP ratio will begin to shrink. And—here's the really good news—this back-of-the-envelope estimate doesn't take into account what would happen if America's private corporations got a little tax relief and began investing even more heavily in the United States.

GROWTH CHANGES EVERYTHING

When growth happens, things change, often quite rapidly. Typically, greater access to investment capital is the impetus for change, setting off a chain reaction of sorts. Investment begets hiring, hiring begets increased consumption and sales, sales beget profits, profits beget a rise in the stock market, and rising stock markets beget the "wealth effect," which makes people feel confident enough to spend money. All this begetting switches on America's economic engine.

When America gets going, imports rise, offset by exports of American-made goods, such as bioengineered drugs, airliners, testing equipment from KLA-Tencor, jet engines, and commodities like wheat, natural gas, oil, and chemicals. As America imports more, the rest of the world starts to grow as well, which brings the whole begetting process to other countries, which in turn buy more from us. And, as growth returns, the debt-to-GDP ratio falls, and all the bickering over the federal budget goes silent. When the debt-to-GDP ratio shrinks because of growth, people will smile when they recall our tribulations of yesteryear, the way Google's billionaire founders must smile when they remember how they maxed out their credit cards to get their fledgling company off the ground. Growth heals all economic wounds—even those that are self-inflicted. And when there is "big growth," the kind that will underpin the next American Century, the economy will not just heal, it will be transformed.

JUST THE START

America's industrial corporations, such as Apple and Microsoft, are not the only business entities that are flush with cash. At the time of this writing, American banks had deposited, with the Federal Reserve, almost $1.83 trillion in *excess* banking reserves. Banks must hold reserves in case Bill Gates, or another member of the "Forbes 400," walks in one day and demands a billion or two for the upcoming weekend. Since banks lend most of their deposits, a reserve requirement keeps them sufficiently liquid so they can deal with everyday deposits and withdrawals.

But excess reserves? As shown in Figure 5.4, the average long-term total of excess reserves on deposit with the Fed is zero. With that being the case, why would banks lend money to the Fed, and receive only 0.25 percent interest in return, when they can lend that money to customers at market rates?

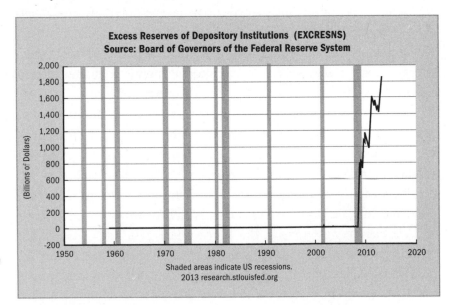

Figure 5.4.

There are a number of possible answers. One might be that banks are less sanguine about the future than I am—their pessimism motivates them to refrain from lending. A second possibility is that, at today's low interest rates, lending money is not worth the risk. Third is that banks are constraining lending to conserve capital in case there are more problems in the housing market. The fourth possibility is that banks are holding extra reserves because they are subject to so-called stress tests by their regulators. Fifth could be that demand for loans is still slow. And finally, the sixth option is that banks are behind the curve.

The answer to the question of why banks have excess reserves is easy: all of the above.

Bankers like to be thought of as relatively balanced people, biased toward the conservative. But, in truth, they are more like a character in an old morality play or John Bunyan's *Pilgrim's Progress*, oscillating between periods of wanton recklessness and excessive behavior followed by periods of deep repentance. During those periods of wantonness, they do stupid things, like they did in the run-up to the mortgage crisis. And when they repent, just try to pry a nickel out of the hand of your local banker. You can't.

After visiting Lehman Brothers, before the financial and mortgage crises hit, I sold my real estate, as I mentioned earlier. Then, in the deepest depths of the financial crisis, I decided it was a good time to buy some real estate, under the theory I mentioned at the beginning of this book—*no one ever made a plugged nickel betting against the USA.* So I went to my bank and asked to take out two new mortgages so I could buy two houses, one on each coast, and take advantage of what seemed like once-in-a-lifetime bargain prices. As I filled out the paperwork, I asked my banker if he was making many loans. "We'll lend you your own money, but that's all," he said. In other words, if you wanted to buy a house for $1,000—assuming you could get one for that—you had to have $1,000 on deposit with the bank from which you were borrowing. That's pretty conservative, a little like wearing a belt and suspenders. Mortgages give banks a claim on the real estate against which they lend; if you can't pay back the loan, they get the real estate. That's the belt. If they want a claim against the money you have on deposit with them as well in order to grant you a loan, that claim is the suspenders. That's awfully conservative, and it's also highly restrictive. Not that many people have the price of a home on deposit at their bank.

So I smiled at my banker as I finished the paperwork and then muttered something under my breath: "You guys broke it, but you're putting the squeeze on us to fix it."

"What was that?" He asked.

"Oh, nothing," I said, smiling, waiting for my loans to be approved.

▼▼▼▼

One of the problems banks have is that large corporations, as noted earlier, no longer use them when they borrow money. Instead, big companies sell their bonds directly to investors. True, they sell those bonds using investment banks, but those are different operations from the neighborhood bank George Bailey ran in the classic 1946 movie *It's a Wonderful Life*. Bailey's bank made loans and issued mortgages to the so-called little guy, the 99 percent, while investment banks mostly bundle mortgages and sell bonds to big companies and the 1 percent. Investment banks don't typically hold loans. Bank CEOs may still strut, but their customer base is made up of midsized and small companies, retail consumers seeking loans to buy a house or car, and credit cards. Even so, banks still control large sums of money.

During the worst of the recession, the country's primary job-creating companies—startups, midsized businesses, and companies that wanted to expand—were starved for cash. They kept their doors open, but America's banks might as well have been closed. With banks behaving so selfishly, the nation's growth engine was stalled.

That's not how the world is supposed to work. Banks exist under federal or state charters and in return are supposed to operate on behalf of the community. That way of doing business is long gone. Sure, they're businesses charged with making profits. But they're in the business of taking prudent risks, not parking their money at the Fed.

Let me give you a personal example of what I mean. I am on the board of directors of a small, entrepreneurial company that provides online tutoring services to high-school students and helps college-bound students prepare for the SAT and ACT exams. It also develops curricula for schools and provides other educational services. The company has about $24 million in revenue, which means it is tiny compared to giants in the education field like Britain's Pearson and New York's McGraw Hill. But the people who work there are young and energetic and filled with enthusiasm and big ideas. They also have a social mission, which they take personally. You have to love what they're doing.

This tiny company employs about 100 people full time, and about 500 people (mostly tutors) part time. Compared to GE, with 305,000 employees; or back-from-the-dead GM, with 212,000 employees; or Walmart, with 2.2 million employees, it's as small as the dot at the end of this sentence. And yet, 100 full-time employees and 500 part-time employees earn a living working at this company and are pinning their futures on its growth.

The jobs these employees have enable them to pay their mortgages or rent, shop for clothes, pay for their children's educations, and make payments on their cars. These 100 full-timers, and 500 part-timers, are the reason lots of others stay employed. The economy works because one hand washes the other.

I mention this because when the company needed to borrow money to grow, in late 2009 and early 2010, there wasn't any available. Not for a company as small as this one. Banks wouldn't lend. Neither would individual investors, unless they received usurious rates of interest *and were also given a share in the company.*

Think about it. You start a company and employ 100 people. You go to your bank and ask for a loan, and they turn you down. So you go to that guy or gal with whom you ride mountain bikes, or to your rich aunt, or to that guy who gave you his card at the cocktail party. When you get to them, you ask for a loan.

But when you pose the question to your cocktail acquaintance, you hear a cartoonish chuckle and watch as he strokes his big, black moustache. Then he tells you he'll charge 14 percent for the loan *and* take 15 percent of the company—the company you built and bleed for. The only thing that guy didn't say is that he'll tie you to the railroad tracks if you can't make the payments.

I'm not making this up. (Okay, I'm making up the parts about the moustache and the railroad tracks.) But without a doubt I can tell you that this scenario has happened to thousands of little companies around the country that collectively employ millions of people. It has put enormous strains on entrepreneurs, has slowed growth, and has diluted ownership in any company that gave up equity for a loan.

Where were the banks? Where indeed.

Had the little educational company been able to borrow money from a bank at market rates, I'm convinced it would have grown much more rapidly than it did. Instead of having to lay off twenty-five employees as it languished, capital starved, it would have hired between fifty and seventy-five employees between 2009 and 2013. It just didn't have enough money to develop its list of programs on the drawing board and to market them, or to train new employees to develop and sell the products.

This isn't an anomaly. It's the state of affairs. As a result, there is a lot of pent-up demand for investment in companies that are the country's engines of employment, small- and medium-sized businesses. Once that investment flows, I have no doubt that jobs will be created.

UNSPENT CASH

Add up the $4 trillion in the coffers of large companies that has *not* been invested or spent, and the $1.6 trillion parked with the Fed, and you would be forgiven for thinking that, well, that's a lot of money. In fact, $5.6 trillion (an amount about the size of Japan's economy) is peanuts compared to where the real money lies, jangling around at the bottom of our purses and pockets, that is, in our investments, in our money-market funds, and in the bank accounts of millions of individuals.

When it comes to capital—which is what so-called professional investors call money—Americans need to wake up to the fact that the pundits are wrong. We are not a pauper nation that is hopelessly in debt. We are, in fact, the richest country the world has ever known.

I sometimes wonder at how ill informed people really are, especially with regard to matters of debt and the fact that the best way to overcome debt—as I've said—is to grow your way out of it, sometimes by borrowing a little money first.

But debt has strange connotations. There are biblical injunctions against lending money and charging interest, and the world has a history of debtors' prisons. Children and adults in previous times (and every once in a while now) were sold into slavery to pay debts.

There is a deeply ingrained notion in many of us that debt is evil. In ancient Hebrew, Sanskrit, Aramaic, and Greek and in present-day German, the words for "debt" and for "sin" are the same. The opposite is true as well. The world "redeemed" means to pay back a debt and to be spiritually liberated or "saved."

The reason for these nagging associations, I believe, goes back to the fact that for most of human history, economies did not grow. People planted wheat or barley, or raised cows, chickens, or pigs, and the productivity of the land did not change. In the days before fertilizers, tractors, and pesticides, an acre of land produced only few bushels of food a year.

In an environment where the output is fixed, debt is very dangerous. If, in 300 BCE, you borrowed 100 shekels from a neighbor, how would you pay him 110 shekels the following year, unless you scrimped and your family ate less bread? And, if the rains were delayed, or there was a drought, you neighbor might simply seize your land, forcing you and your family to live in shame and abject poverty, or even starve.

Our notions about debt—and its sin-like character—were fixed in our psyches in the long period before economies grew.

Consider the following. In medieval England,[9] a typical farm yielded roughly 5 bushels of wheat per acre, with yields on some farms even less. This figure remained constant from 1250 to 1600—a period of 350 years. By contrast, in 2012, the average yield for wheat in the United States was 46.2 bushels an acre, according to the US Department of Agriculture, with some states—Wisconsin, for example—having yields as high as 70 bushels an acre. Between 1948 and 2012, agricultural yields in the United States increased two and a half times, from 17.9 bushels to 46.2 bushels an acre, and productivity grew even more as machines replaced farmers and farmhands in the field.

You can imagine why families of six or eight or more people would steer clear of debt, and even be frightened of it, if their farms yielded just 5 bushels of wheat an acre, about 300 pounds. But if farms are producing 2,772 pounds of wheat per acre and if farm families are made up of four people, or even one to three people, there's no reason to fear debt. Manage debt—yes. But fear it? No.

My point is that our notions about debt were developed during long ages of scarcity, when productivity was flat and economic growth nonexistent. But today, we live in an era of plenty.

We must adjust our psyches to that change.

AMERICA'S DEEP POCKETS

Collectively, Americans had $2.60 trillion[10] in money-market funds in September 2013, $13 trillion in mutual fund investments at the end of 2012,[11] and $19.4 trillion in retirement accounts as of December 2012. There was an additional $1.3 trillion in ETFs, exchange-traded funds, at the end of 2012.[12] Add to that the fact that in fall of 2013, Americans had $7 trillion deposited in their savings accounts (some of this amount is also counted in the money market statistics).[13] The numbers get even bigger if you add in the fact that our stock markets had a collective valuation of roughly $19 trillion at the end of 2012, a number that has increased significantly since then.[14] And then, there are the illiquid assets we own—our houses, cars, and all those

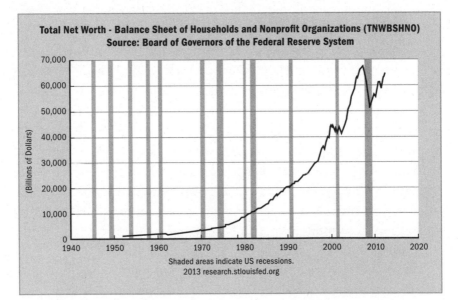

Figure 5.5.

tchotchkes down in the basement, out in the garage, and in those storage lockers.

I don't want to double count the numbers—which is pretty easy to do. So, I will go to a higher authority to add up my figures—the Federal Reserve.

According to the Fed's chart, shown in Figure 5.5, households in the United States collectively had a net worth of $64 trillion[15] in assets as of December 6, 2012. Although this figure is down from a prefinancial-crisis high of $68 trillion, the chart shows that Americans have undergone a significant recovery in overall wealth from the dark days of 2008.

The $64 trillion divides roughly like this: $23 trillion in cash and other highly liquid assets and investments, such as savings and money-market accounts, mutual funds, stocks and bonds, and ETFs; $23 trillion or so in retirement funds (depending on where the stock market is trading); and $18 trillion in housing. That last item— housing—is important because it reflects the positive equity value of our homes, houses, coops, and condominiums, less mortgage debt. As such, it should be comforting to know that the housing market is not a cesspool of negativity. Rather, it has an overall positive value and is growing. In fact, the housing market, even though it was battered, still has a very large positive equity value. Taken together, Americans are worth about nine times what China produces in a year.

If corporate America has $4 trillion in cash, and Americans have about $23 trillion in cash and other liquid assets, excluding their retirement savings, it suggests that there is plenty of money available to invest in the future. Pension funds, which have about $20 trillion in retirement funds in their coffers, also invest in the future. The nation's largest pension fund, CalPERS, the California Public Employees Retirement System, has about $180 billion under management. It uses that money to buy stocks and bonds, but it also places a lot of it with venture capital investors, which invest it in new companies, and private equity firms, which invest it in more mature companies. What that means is that retirement funds do a lot more than sit in the bank. They are actively engaged in fueling the country's growth engine.

So, ask yourself. Is America really broke?

INVESTMENT'S SLOW RECOVERY

With so much money available for investment, one wonders why the country hasn't recovered faster. On the one hand, in many sectors of the country, such as clean energy and natural gas, the United States is investing at the same rate or more than before the financial and economic crises. On the other hand, in some areas, investment has either stopped—as the CFOs I talked to complained to me—or is sluggish, that is, slowly rising, but not yet at pre-crash levels.

Investment has been sluggish because confidence is at a low ebb. People put their money at risk and make investments when they believe the future will be better than the present. They hide their money under the mattress when they fear the future will be worse than the present. Right now, people are still worried.

One reason people are worried is that unemployment remains high, at least when compared to the George H.W. Bush and Bill Clinton years. When a family member or close friend is unemployed, it spreads a sense of fear and dread. But even worse is the negative effect on morale that comes from the inability of political leaders to work together. The chart on "consumer sentiment," shown in Figure 5.6, illustrates my point. It shows that the national mood plummeted in the period of the Great Recession. No surprise there. People were scared about the

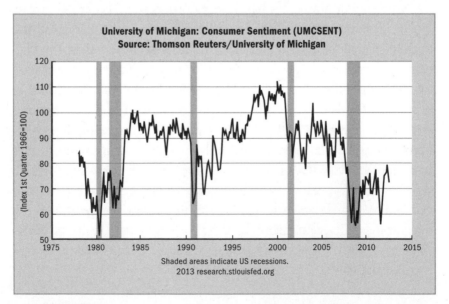

Figure 5.6.

long-term survival of the economy and about whether they would lose their jobs, savings, and homes. People felt worse during the financial crisis than they did in the aftermath of 9/11, according to the chart.

As the economy began to recover, so did our mood—at least somewhat. No one was euphoric, but, beginning in 2010, many felt that the worst was over. Then, in late 2010 and 2011, there was another big dip. There is little doubt about what caused it—politics. As the US election began to unfold, people began to feel that the political system was broken. Commentators and pundits fueled the flames, to be sure. But the nation's politicians did most of the damage themselves. Then, as the chart shows, there was an upturn in how people felt, followed by another fall—which is where it was at the time of this writing—in the run-up to budget sequestration of 2013.

What this shows is that although we all understand there is a cost to behaving badly—drinking and driving, for example—there is also a cost for politicians behaving badly. Trillions of dollars remains idle in the bank, parked with the Fed, or under the average person's mattress. As a result, as my group of high-tech CFOs testified when we met in Silicon Valley, the great V-8 engine of the American economy has not yet been put into gear, largely because of politics.

So when will people start moving all this cash from the sidelines to begin investing once more? A couple of things might precipitate this transition. First, it could happen when hedge funds, or a new breed of 1980s-style corporate raiders, see that they can acquire a company cheaply enough that they can buy a $1 share in a company's bank account for less than a $1 investment. That's likely to scare corporations into pulling their money out of the money market and putting it to work. Second, when the economy starts growing again, companies with a lot of cash will want to put that money to work by expanding. They'll do it by building new plants, investing in other companies, and acquiring rivals. Third—and it's something of a paradox—they'll invest when interest rates rise, because it will seem to them that the Fed has blown the "all-clear" whistle indicating that the bad times are over, thereby renewing people's confidence in the future. At the same time, when rates rise, banks will start lending, because higher returns from those rates will justify the risks of lending money. When these factors come into play, hold onto your hats, because the economy will start to rock.

CHAPTER SIX

AMERICA MAKES THINGS

Before the horrendous economic and financial events of 2008, a trend was unfolding that the Great Recession put on hold but did not derail: the so-called resourcing of American manufacturing. American factories are coming home.

"Resourcing" is a new term that some wonk somewhere came up with to describe something simple. For a myriad of reasons, such as the natural gas bonanza, it now makes more sense for companies to make their products in the United States than elsewhere. But other issues are a lot simpler—wages and productivity.

A German automobile worker makes roughly $67.14 an hour, depending on where the euro is trading against the dollar, which includes benefits, one of which is between twenty-four and thirty-five paid vacation days per year. American automobile workers aren't exactly paupers—they make an average of $33.77[1] an hour including benefits, about what their Japanese counterparts make. An American automobile worker gets, on average, thirteen paid days off a year. But in addition to paying lower wages to their American workers than their German counterparts receive, carmakers based in the United States don't have to ship their cars across the ocean if they want to sell them in Virginia, California, or Ohio.

You could argue that American wages are too low[2] compared to the competition in other countries, given America's phenomenal levels of productivity. But you can't argue that they are too high. When the US automobile industry, with the exception of Ford, went bankrupt, it triggered a reset of labor policies that added huge efficiencies to the production process and brought down labor costs without doing too much damage to existing wages. Labor costs and wages are similar but different. For example, at GM, as a result of a crazy contract GM made with its unions, some production workers were kept on the payroll even though their jobs were eliminated. Workers in this program were paid even if they spent the day at home, at a coffee shop, or in a bar. There must have been a reason for GM to agree to a contract as ridiculous as this one, but it is beyond my capacity to figure it out. Costs like this made it extremely expensive to produce vehicles in the United States and made it difficult to calculate just how much the average automobile worker was paid. Brain-dead labor policies like this ultimately contributed to the industry's collapse. But luckily, those days are gone. As a result, rather than losing money on each car—in 2010, GM, Ford, and Chrysler together lost an average of almost $3,000 a car—Detroit is now making money, an average of about $2,000 a car.[3]

These wage figures comparing American to German workers show why it is increasingly attractive to make things in the United States. But they don't tell the entire story. American quality has gotten much better, and largely without much fanfare. In fact, based on the 2013 J. D. Powers Initial Quality Study,[4] which surveys new car owners and measures the problems they encounter after they take their vehicles home, you could argue that the quality of American cars is now the best in the world. Consider this example. In 2013, GM— once known for shoddy workmanship and uninspired design—won eight J. D. Powers Initial Quality Study awards, more than any other company, foreign or domestic. In fact, in 2013, American companies dominated these awards.

American workers in general are far more productive than workers in Europe or Japan. What's even more surprising to many people is that American factory workers do better still.

Aside from tiny Luxembourg (population 531,000) and energy-rich Norway (population 5 million), the United States is by far the most productive country in the world.[5] In 2010, the average American worker produced $102,903 in value each year, for example, while the average French worker produced only $81,977 a year in value. The average German produced $78,585 in value per year, and the average Japanese worker produced just $68,764 in value per year. The value produced each year by the average worker in a country that was a member of the Organisation of Economic Co-operation and Development (OECD)—that is, one of the thirty-four wealthiest industrial countries in the world—was just $76,697 a year. Clearly, locating a business in the United States, rather than Germany or France, makes sense, since American workers are so much more productive.

If you look only at manufacturing, the differences between countries are even more striking. American workers produced $132,449 a year in added value in 2009, compared to $84,097 in Japan and $76,240 in Germany (see Figure 6.1). The average value added for

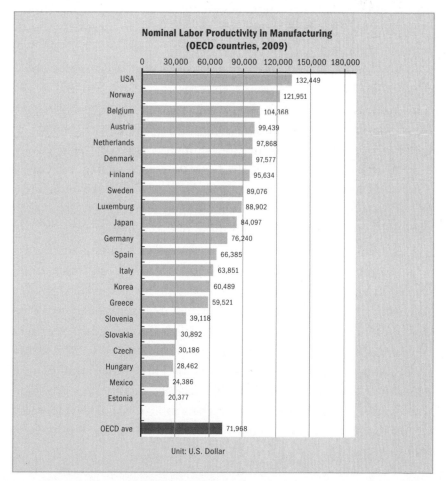

Figure 6.1 Japanese Productivity Center.

manufacturing workers in OECD countries was $71,968. (Workers in countries such as Hungary, Mexico, or Latvia were paid less than American workers but also produced much less value).

The Japanese Productivity Center, which compiled these figures, has a good reputation for doing quality work, and the implications of that work are pretty straightforward. If the average American manufacturing worker produces $62,000 more than his or her counterpart in other countries, it means that companies locating their production facilities in the United States will spend significantly less producing each product and, it stands to reason, make more money on everything they sell. This fact alone goes a long way toward explaining why American companies are bringing their factories back to the United States, and why non-US companies are locating factories in the United States to serve the North American market and to export from America around the world.

In addition, since American workers in general produce about $30,000 more value than their counterparts in the rest of the world, it also stands to reason that companies in non-manufacturing-related businesses would also find the United States an attractive place to locate. Toyota understands this and built and exported 124,000 vehicles from the United States in 2012. BMW does as well and exported roughly 210,000 vehicles made in the United States the same year. Detroit's Big 3 auto companies, which exported very few vehicles in the past, exported more than 1 million of them in 2012.

Success begets success, and it is not difficult to imagine the re-sourcing movement gathering steam, especially as foreign companies choose to locate here. American products are not just cool to look at, thanks in large measure to Apple, but they are also made to very high quality standards. As a result, it is not difficult to imagine companies moving their design and engineering operations to the United States.

As I mentioned earlier, this is already happening in the biotech corridor around MIT, where Novartis, Sanofi, and other non-US companies have located large parts of their research and development operations. Companies in other sectors of the economy are likely to follow that lead.

If you connect the dots, the picture looks interesting. The United States has the world's highest level of productivity and increasingly the highest levels of quality, as well as wage levels that don't break the bank. It has plenty of energy and a massive market. And, if you make products here, you don't need to ship them across thousands of miles of water, in ships that burn oil, to sell to Americans.

All of these changes started before the financial and economic crises of 2008, but the crises put them on hold. In a few instances, however, the 2008 debacle actually cleaned house, which is one reason why American automakers are doing so well. As the financial and economic crises fade into the past, these trends will pick up steam, and as they do, there is little doubt that they will have a profound, positive impact on the economy.

In addition, our workforce is not only competitively priced, it is well trained, disciplined, mobile, and willing to work long hours. Our technology is world class, supported by the world's greatest research institutions, and America has plenty of investment capital available.

Even though the resourcing trend is still in its early days, a lot has been happening. For example, take NCR, a 130-year-old company with a storied history that can be summed up in its original name—National Cash Register Company. It was called this after the product it invented, the first mechanical cash register, which was produced in Dayton, Ohio, where the company was started. NCR soon dominated the market for these machines. In the 1950s, NCR began acquiring companies in the electronics and computer sectors. Cash registers would one day be digital, and would be connected to big databases. NCR led that trend.

In the 1970s, NCR began making automated teller machines—ATMs—and a few years later it began making small computers. In 1991, NCR was acquired by AT&T, which smashed it together with a few other high-tech companies it bought and changed its name. The results were horrendous. But that was to be expected. In the early 1990s, you could say that AT&T's strong suit was destroying the value of the companies it bought—and, in some cases, squeezing the life out of them altogether—which is what AT&T almost immediately tried doing to NCR. By changing NCR's name, AT&T showed it was oblivious to the fact that it was nearly destroying a century's worth of brand equity. Fortunately, AT&T decided to spin out NCR, and in 1996 the newly independent company was doing business as NCR once more. Immediately, it began acquiring high-tech companies, especially those involved in electronic financial transactions.

The point of this long-winded windup is to say that part of the company's renewal involved sending its production of ATMs abroad, first to Scotland, and then to China. It did that in an attempt to bring down costs. But as the trend toward resourcing got underway, NCR took note. It began closing its overseas manufacturing facilities in Scotland, Brazil, and Canada, and then, in 2010, in China.

ATMs, such as the ones made by NCR, are not simply machines that dispense cash from the back of your local 7-Eleven, or from the outside wall of your bank. They are important parts of our highly networked and integrated financial system. They are doorways into a system that moves trillions of dollars around the world each day. Not only is it vital to have the most up-to-date technology in a bank's network of ATMs, it is also important that these machines are robust and secure, for obvious reasons. For one thing, they are subject to the elements of weather and abuse by the people who use them—people bash them when there is some problem, or spill drinks on them while punching in their pin numbers. And then there is the ever-present threat of robbery, not only from the direct assault of patrons, but increasingly from cybercrime (for example, in 2013 there was a coordinated theft of $45 million from ATMs around the world[6]). This augurs well for the companies making ATMs that can stand up to a wide range of physical and cyber assaults. While robustness is important, security is even more essential. Security is not where China excels.

Security and trust are important considerations in where to locate a business. And, although most countries do some snooping, as evidenced by the 2013 disclosures of Edward Snowden about the National Security Agency (NSA), there is a difference between spying on a country for security reasons and spying to steal corporate information. In the case of the NSA's activities—which, as a staunch supporter of the Fourth Amendment to the Constitution, I do not condone—I will at least grant that the purpose, as far as we know, was to ensure national security. That does not mean it was right to countermand the Constitution; it does mean, however, that the breach was at least not done for crass commercial reasons.

That's not the case with China. In early 2013, the Pentagon released the results of a multiyear research study by Mandiant, a computer security consulting company based in Washington, DC. Mandiant reported that there had been a concerted effort by a group within China's People's Liberation Army—Unit 61398—to hack into American computer networks. Among Unit 61398's targets were America's electrical grid, aerospace, defense and high-tech companies, a number of government agencies, *and our financial firms and networks*. If China is undertaking a concerted military effort to hack American companies, agencies, businesses, financial firms, and telecommunications networks in the United States, one can only imagine how they are treating American firms with operations in China.[7]

In April 2013, when I was preparing to lead a panel discussion at the Milken Institute on global risks, we had a phone call with the people who would be on the panel. Among them were General Wesley Clark, former member of Congress Jane Harmon (D-CA), and Larry Zempleman, who runs the Principal Financial Group, a large financial services firm. As we discussed the risks we would talk about, Zempleman said that his firm was currently defending itself against a cyberattack that began that morning—and he agreed to discuss it when we met as a panel. He also said his company was attacked by hackers hundreds of times a year. So far, he said, the company had been successful in repulsing the attacks.

It's one thing to use computers and related tools to protect yourself from attacks by terrorists, or to defend your country against an avowed enemy wishing to destroy you—as it is alleged the United States did in cooperation with Israel with the computer worm Stuxnet, which destroyed a number of Iran's centrifuges before the Iranians discovered the worm in June 2010. But attacking another country's financial system, as China is alleged to have done against us on numerous occasions? Or targeting individual companies in order to steal trade and technical secrets, as it is also alleged to have done? There is no moral argument to justify that kind of breach.

NCR's decision to move its manufacturing from China to Georgia may not be security related. The truth is, I don't know the reason, and it's doubtful that NCR would disclose this as the reason even if it was the case. But given the research I have conducted regarding doing business in China,[8] I would be surprised if a company like NCR did not view operating in China with suspicion. In my own studies, China ranks toward the bottom of the list, in the same league as

Russia, India, and Brazil, when it comes to corruption, transparency, and the rule of law. I say "rule of law"—rather than the laws themselves—because the countries I mentioned in this group typically have wonderfully conceived laws on their books. The question is, are they enforced? And the answer is, it all depends.

In addition, some Chinese firms that make telecommunications equipment—most notably Huawei and ZTE—have been cited by the House Intelligence Committee as posing a threat to our national security. What's both eerie and frightening is that, according to the committee, these companies may even have placed "malicious implants in the components of critical infrastructure, such as power grids or financial networks."[9]

If that's the case, these and perhaps other Chinese firms are selling devices to American companies that can be controlled from abroad to spy on company operations. And if those American companies do business with the government, these devices could potentially offer a backdoor into the Pentagon's computers. Even worse, if the House Intelligence Committee is correct, some parts of our critical electronics infrastructure could be controlled from abroad, at least potentially.

Think of the threat China could pose if its biggest telecommunications and computer firms have already sold products to us that might close down the power grid, or divert money away from where it is supposed to go, if our two countries were enmeshed in some future conflict.

Companies may or may not be leaving China because of the specific security breaches. Even so, China's behavior constitutes a significant risk.

But this is just one of the threats China poses. Over the years, American companies have lost important trade secrets and patent information to Chinese companies. There are many cases alleging in court that Chinese electronics companies stole American innovations and used them to compete against the same American companies from which they stole the technology. Cisco, one of our premier networking companies, has been in court on numerous occasions trying to resolve a dispute with China's Huawei over the unauthorized use of Cisco's technology by Huawei.

This is not to say that American companies are good and Chinese companies are bad. Apple has been involved in fifty lawsuits with South Korea's Samsung over unlawful use of patented material, with Apple winning one of its biggest suits in the American courts, while Samsung won in South Korea. Problems like this are an ongoing part of business. But no one watching the legal war between Apple and Samsung thinks either side was working on behalf of a government.

▼▼▼▼

At roughly the same time that NCR decided to move production back to the United States, the Coleman Company, which makes outdoor equipment, began producing its food and beverage coolers in Illinois instead of China, citing cost and delivery reasons. And the same year, Ford began moving 2,000 jobs back to Michigan from its operations in other countries.

Sleek Audio, which makes high-end headphones, will be making its products in Florida, not Shenzhen, because its Chinese suppliers could not guarantee quality or schedule deliveries precisely enough. GE is in the process of moving the production of "white goods" (washing machines, refrigerators, dishwashers, and stoves, for example) to Kentucky. Whirlpool, one of GE's competitors in the white-goods market, will produce washers and dryers in the United States rather than Mexico. And Caterpillar, despite a history of tough labor negotiations in the United States, will build its newest factory in Texas, not in Asia.

The Dow Chemical Company will be making batteries for hybrid cars in Michigan, rather than South Korea, to be closer to American customers. Mercedes, BMW, and Volkswagen will be expanding their US plants, and Toyota will begin making its Lexus luxury cars in Kentucky, the first time the company will be producing its upper-end vehicles outside of Japan.

Let me be more precise about one of those expansion plans. In 2009, in the depths of the "rich man's depression," BMW spent $1 billion to expand its Spartanburg, North Carolina, plant, which opened in 1994. In 2012, it said it would invest another $1 billion in that facility. BMW built 301,519 vehicles at this plant in 2012 and exported almost 70 percent of them (about $7.4 billion worth of products), many to China. BMW's US plants have been so productive and successful that the company announced in 2013 that it would build a new, smaller SUV, the X4, exclusively in the United States. That is an interesting decision, because it makes Spartanburg BMW's sole global manufacturing center for SUVs as well as a site for manufacturing other BMW vehicles and products. There was a time when executives at BMW—the Bavarian Motor Works—wondered if they could build a car to their exacting standards in areas of Germany outside of the company's home in Bavaria. That has all changed. Increasingly, the United States is a major manufacturing center for BMW, competing favorably with the company's other plants with respect to cost and quality. As a result, a great deal of the company's new investment and production capacity is being focused on the Spartanburg plant.[10]

This is just the beginning.

The United States and China are the world's two largest manufacturing countries, with more or less equal shares of the global manufacturing market, depending on how you measure it. But the United States is becoming a lot more attractive as a place to make things, while China's star is starting to dim.

There are a number of reasons for this change. The average cost of labor in China is increasing rapidly. In 2012, wages in China rose by an average of about 14 percent—a staggering amount.[11] Chinese workers are still inexpensive if you compare them to American workers on an hourly basis. At present, Chinese workers average half of what their American counterparts are paid. But American workers are more than twice as productive as their Chinese counterparts, thanks to our more advanced factories and our more experienced and better-trained workforce. For reasons of math alone, it is obvious why the United States comes out ahead as a place to make things.

Of course, some industries are more sensitive to wage increases than others. The reason, as you might expect, has to do with the amount of labor contained in each product. Shoes, for example, cannot yet be made without human hands. Machines can cut material and fabricate the rubber used to make soles, but there is a lot of trimming, gluing, and sewing that would be difficult for a machine to do, even one such as Baxter, the easy-to-program robot with the smiley face made in the robotics cluster near Boston.

That's not the case with computers. Right now, Foxconn, the big Taiwanese company with huge factories in China and around the world, employs more than 1.23 million Chinese workers, many of them to assemble the iPhone and other Apple products. Despite the low wages Foxconn's workers receive, American companies using advanced robotics devices would be competitive. Robots can snap chips into cell phones faster and more accurately than humans.

Cell-phone manufacturing is likely to leave China for places where labor is more expensive but factories are more automated and closer geographically to the engineers who designed the products. In addition, because automation is expensive—factory robots can cost $50,000 to $500,000, in addition to the cost of the larger, integrated work platform and other technology components—countries with abundant capital at reasonable rates of interest have an advantage. With nearly unlimited amounts of capital, and interest rates at historic lows, and with a well-trained workforce and the world's best university system, America is better positioned than any other country to take advantage of these technological shifts.

The coming robotics revolution doesn't bode well for China, which wants to move hundreds of millions of people from its rural areas to its cities and put them to work in factories. Robots will slow down that migration, because automated factories in the United States and in other advanced countries can outperform many low-wage workers in cost, speed, and quality. In addition, in areas of the economy that do not lend themselves to automation, at least not yet, such as shoe and garment production, there are many countries where human labor is cheaper than in China. As a result, increasingly we are seeing labels on our shoes and clothes which say "Made in Vietnam," or in Congo, Rwanda, or other countries. Moreover, since all but high-end and custom shoe and garment manufacturing left the United States decades ago, America has already adjusted to these changes. Seamstresses, tailors, and other types of garment workers may have dominated New York a hundred years ago, but New York morphed into a city of high finance, the professions, and today even digital media. China has already begun making that kind of workforce transformation, but not on the scale it will ultimately need.

Even though these trends augur well for us, not everyone here will benefit. If a hundred jobs went to China a decade ago, and higher levels of automation mean only fifty jobs come back, not everyone will be pleased. I can just imagine people saying, "So what's so good about fifty new jobs, when we lost a hundred?"

That is the wrong way to look at it. While it is still a problem for the fifty people who are out of work, it's still not a tragedy if only fifty people work at an automated factory. Reopening a defunct production center has broader implications, since it means hiring drivers, buying trucks, and leasing, building, or buying new warehouse space.

Setting up an automated factory involves bringing in engineering consultants to plan the assembly line and work stations. It means hiring construction workers to move walls, pour cement, and expand the roofline, and it means dealing with banks and insuring the premises. It also means hooking up the electricity and making sure the outlets work; refurbishing the heating and air-conditioning systems, along with the water heaters; and stocking the bathrooms with paper products.

On an ongoing basis, the factory will have to be cleaned, the machines will have to be maintained, quality will have to be checked, designs will have to be prototyped and tested, and workers will have to be fed. Bringing back fifty factory jobs to the United States means a lot more than fifty people being employed.

This is what happened in agriculture. In 1900, 41 percent of the US population was employed in agriculture; today it's 1 percent. But these figures are misleading. True, only a tiny fraction of people still work the land. But there are many times more who contribute to the sector, albeit in different ways than in the past. Some people work in factories that build tractors and refrigeration trucks; others work in giant food-processing plants, or research seed varieties, or sell crop insurance, or manufacture pesticides and fertilizers. You can look at the way the agricultural sector has changed and count how many jobs were lost, or you can find out how many new, better-paying jobs were created. The average wage of an agricultural worker is about $21,000, according to the US Department of Agriculture's Economic Research Service.[12] If that worker stops picking corn, walks across the highway, and lands a job in a chemical plant that turns corn into fuel for cars, his average wage jumps to $55,000. True, fewer jobs exist in agriculture today than in 1900, but most of the ones that do exist are far more lucrative than in the past. And, while only 0.7 percent of America's workforce trudges into the fields to grow things, milk the nation's cows, or shake almonds and walnuts off of trees,[13] more than 20 percent of our economy is based around agriculture, agricultural and food products, and related supporting services.[14]

The same goes for manufacturing. As companies move their operations back to the United States, some jobs will be lost. Will the rate be as high as the 50 percent I mentioned above? Not likely. American manufacturing is already the most productive in the world. As a result, one American worker produces multiples more than one Chinese or Italian or German worker. (Although, for reasons I don't quite understand, French workers, who take leisurely lunches accompanied by glasses of wine, work just thirty-seven hours a week, and are entitled to vacations as long as six weeks, are nearly as productive as workers in the United States.) But even if not every job comes back to the United States, a myriad of new jobs will be created to support the plants as they are built or reopened.

HIDDEN COSTS

An economics professor of mine in graduate school once said in class that the more complicated something is—a car, airplane, or computer, for example—the more opportunities you have to make it cheaper. Hence, he said, the need for outsourcing.

If your business is carving wood blocks into sleek duck decoys, which you sell, the only inputs you have are the cost of the wood, varnishes, and paints, the cost of tools, your time, and the space in your garage where you do your work. Depending on where you live, you may have to heat and cool your workspace, and you need to deliver what you make to your customers.

For duck decoy makers, I count only five or six elements that are vital to the process of making and selling the handmade products. But for automobiles, there are a multitude of inputs, each with inputs and costs. If you build cars or trucks, you need steel, rubber, glass, and plastics. You need machine tools, forges, presses, and robots to do the welding and painting. You also need computers, research centers, accountants, marketers, and design labs. And lots more. The cost of each of these, my professor said, could be negotiated down.

That's a lot of negotiating.

Domestic car companies outsource the production of many components, mostly to companies in the United States, Canada, and Mexico. Some parts used in their cars come from factories located in Europe and Asia. Dashboards are usually made by an outsource company that snaps them together to be complete with whatever the dealer ordered—satellite radio, navigation system, digital instrument cluster, leather, oversized display unit, heater and AC controls, vents, and outlets—*whatever.*

Car interiors are typically outsourced, too. Seats need frames, padding, upholstery, electric motors, controls, runners, and seatbelt connections. And don't get me started on engines. They need hundreds of parts. So do transmissions, batteries, gas tanks, computerized controls, serpentine belts, fans, pumps, spark plugs, and so on.

And then you need people. Lots of them. Not just to put the car together, a process that is highly automated. You need people to manage the process, solve problems as they come up, and incorporate those solutions into new versions of the process.

Making something as complex as a car is a daunting task. The automobile company has to design and engineer the car. It will make some of the components, and it will work with hundreds of suppliers around the world to engineer and produce the rest of what goes into the vehicle. Then it has to assemble the product flawlessly and make sure the final result is sexy, performs well, is coveted, and wins a J. D. Powers customer satisfaction award.

And, while the bean counters of yore, and my old economics professor, told the car companies to take the plunge and commit to outsourcing (then negotiate the hell out of their suppliers), they failed to take into account one of the largest costs of all—the cost of transacting all of the business needed to coordinate a complex process like making 7,000 Ford F-150 pickups a week, in each F-150 factory, with no two trucks exactly alike.

Those transaction costs are big. You know all of those business meetings people are always complaining about? The meetings people have to go to in order to discuss *their* part of the business? The meetings that take talented workers away from their *real* jobs? Those meetings are responsible for some of the costs I'm talking about.

Add to that the cost of negotiating thousands of contracts with suppliers. Then, add to that the cost of negotiating the prices of each of the myriad things a car company buys. Consider how much time all of that takes.

I know, Bill Gates and other high-tech visionaries said that the Internet would take us into a world of frictionless transactions, where computers linked to computers would automatically order whatever was needed to make things when the bins were low. That's a "way cool" vision, as we used to say in the 1990s, but it is the smallest part of the cost structure.

True, the guys in undershirts sitting in the parts department thumbing through greasy catalogs to order shock absorbers are long gone. And so are the racy calendars and the phone numbers written on the wall. But that's the inexpensive part of the process. The expensive part is when engineers, executives, lawyers, and other technical people travel to make deals or to make sure everything is running smoothly.

Sending an engineer from Detroit to Cleveland or Toronto to check on whether the axles are correctly made is one thing. Sending that same engineer to Shanghai or South Korea is something else.

Transaction costs like these are part of the cost of making things—cars, computers, toasters, and so on. But, until recently, they were not calculated into the process. They were simply considered "overhead." It is when these so-called overhead costs are eliminated that the cost of a product really drops.

THE TRENDS CONVERGE

One reason manufacturing jobs are coming back to America is that the cost of labor—which frightened American companies into sending work abroad—represents a declining cost for most products. The time it takes to build a car, in general, is decreasing. In 1987, it took 42 hours to build a car, according to consulting firm McKinsey & Co. In 2002, that number fell to 25 hours, thanks to new manufacturing techniques,[15] and the number of hours is continuing to decline.

These figures can be misleading, however. They only include stamping, welding, painting, assembly, and various quality checks. But in addition to the stamping and welding, a car is made of 30,000 parts, a large share of them, as noted above, made by outside suppliers. If you take these parts into account, the amount of human labor that goes into building a car is small—a little more than 22 hours at the best companies. That number has been decreasing for years.

In Henry Ford's day, the first half of the twentieth century, more than half the cost of a car was due to labor. When that was the case, outsourcing to another country made sense. But with just 22 hours of human labor needed at the best factories, even at today's rate of $38 an hour, that's only $836 per vehicle. In a $15,000 Chevy Cruze, that's about 6 percent of the purchase price. But in a $50,000 Cadillac, it's only about 2 percent. Modern, highly productive manufacturing techniques have reduced labor costs to a small share of overall costs.

So what are the real determinants of where to make things? Since metal-stamping presses, welding and paint robots, assembly lines, and real estate are all expensive, capital costs often trump labor costs. Very few companies pay cash when they break ground to build a factory. Usually, they issue debt. With US interest rates low, debt is cheap—cheaper than in decades.

In the first week of March 2013, the federal government borrowed $45 billion on a short-term basis to manage its debt. What kind of interest rate did Uncle Sam have to offer up to get the loot? Less than 1 percent. And, since most commercial interest rates are pegged to the price of government debt, the cost to GM or Ford or Chrysler of borrowing money was at historical lows. It wasn't quite as low as the government's 0.07 percent short-term rate, but it was dirt cheap nevertheless. Interest rates are likely to stay low for a while.

That means that the American capital markets are providing our companies with money that is almost free of charge. To overstate this only slightly, the capital markets (thanks to the Fed) are paying companies to automate their plants. Combine that with the fact that corporations are themselves flush with cash—though reluctant to spend it—and you can see why making things in America is attractive.

Obviously, operating a factory means locating it somewhere. On the one hand, you have Asia—which has some of the most expensive cities in the world. Shanghai housing prices have soared so high, in large part as a result of speculation, that the government is making it against the rules to own more than one apartment. At the same time, the price of office and factory space is also soaring. And, although China is spending more than any other country to develop its infrastructure, including high-speed trains, it still has a long way to go before its roads, its bridges, and the majority of its trains are at Western standards.

India is no different. The price of real estate in Mumbai, Bangalore, and Calcutta is off the charts. US real estate is a bargain by comparison. New York City and Los Angeles, America's priciest places to live, are tied as the twenty-seventh most expensive cities in the world.[16] Tokyo, Osaka, Singapore, Sydney, Melbourne, and Hong Kong, among others, are far more expensive.

▼▼▼▼

While the Great Recession was still raging, I traveled to Detroit and met with a group of individuals from Michigan's investment community, including its then-treasurer, and a number of venture capital investors and entrepreneurs.

A car picked me up at the airport, and as we drove into and then through the city I was amazed at the number of abandoned buildings. I had been to Detroit many times before, but I hadn't really seen the economic damage like I did that day. We passed dozens of brick row houses that must have been elegant places to live back in the day. A great many of these homes were boarded up, and some looked like they had been set on fire.

I looked around and at first felt sorry for my driver. "It's a tough place to live right now, isn't it?" I asked him.

He looked at me through the rearview mirror and smiled. "Not really," he said. "My father and I bought a house a couple of weeks ago for $8,800. We're going to fix it up and sell it. We now own three houses," he said proudly.

Interesting, I thought. On the one hand, there is New Delhi, where a bungalow can cost as much as $10 million or more, and on the other, Detroit, where a row house costs $8,800. (And you can drink the water in Detroit.)

My driver was originally from Lebanon, he told me. And he was thrilled to be in America. He told me he was old enough to remember Lebanon's civil war along with the devastation and death that accompanied it. He also told me that he felt at home in Detroit, that some of his relatives lived there, and that, although there was too much crime, it was nothing like living in a war zone.

I considered what he said as we drove through the city and then out to Dearborn, near Ford's headquarters. Detroit's suburbs were as beautiful as I remembered them. They were lush and green, with many diverse neighborhoods and communities.

It was late when I got to the hotel, a Ritz-Carlton, with a very nice restaurant, luxurious rooms, and a wood-paneled lobby. But when I looked at the rate I was charged, I was amazed—$140 a night, not the $400 to $600 a night typically charged by that hotel chain in New York or Los Angeles. I'm sure I was on some sort of discount plan, but even so, a Ritz-Carlton at $140 a night?

The next morning I was scheduled to make a presentation about the economy to about forty people, mostly investors of one kind or another. Before I make a presentation to a small group like the one in Dearborn, I like to talk to as many attendees as possible to get a sense of who they are and what they are thinking. I always find that getting to know the people to whom I am presenting helps me to create a connection. I adapt the session to address their concerns.

One of the participants, who was responsible for running a pension fund for a small Michigan city, told me there were more than 120,000 engineers in Michigan, many with PhDs, and that Michigan has one of the highest concentrations of scientists of any state. He also reminded me that Michigan has several world-class research universities—the University of Michigan has a research budget in excess of $1.2 billion—and that Detroit has more manufacturing expertise than any other US city.

Another participant, who invested in alternative energy, told me she recently moved into a new home close to Ann Arbor, where the University of Michigan is located. She said it was a large home on ten acres with a stream-fed pond, and because the house was solar-heated, her heating bills were low—important because Michigan is awfully cold in winter. Then she dropped a bombshell—her house cost about $160,000.

I was blown away.

Real estate prices in Detroit and the rest of Michigan have recovered somewhat since that visit. But they are a fraction—*a tiny fraction*—of what it costs to set up shop in much of Asia, Europe, and the emerging world. And, although we chide ourselves on our crumbling infrastructure—*and we should!*—you can still manufacture a part or product in Detroit on Monday and get it to a customer in San Francisco on Tuesday, via air, or on Thursday or Friday, if you send it by truck or rail.

I'm not saying Detroit is our nation's future. But as I visited with these people, who were intelligent, experienced, and articulate, I couldn't help thinking that if I ran Europe's BMW or VW, or a similar Asian company, Detroit would have to be in the mix if I were selecting cities for expansion.

Now, the truth is, the city of Detroit's finances are a mess, and on July 18, 2013, the city filed for bankruptcy, stating that it was unable to repay its debt due to the city's decreasing tax base and shrinking population. The state of Michigan took over the city and began running it even before that. Even so, businesses are beginning to recognize that the city is a bargain. Blue Cross and Blue Shield of Michigan is moving 3,000 employees to downtown Detroit, and Chrysler is moving its marketing department from the suburbs to downtown Detroit. Chrysler is also refurbishing an old urban factory to build Jeep Cherokees, according to reports in the *New York Times*. At the same time, Dan Gilbert, founder of Quicken Loans and the owner of the Cleveland Cavaliers basketball team, has been buying office buildings in the city, some for as little as $5 a square foot. Gilbert, a multi-billionaire, now owns thirty buildings, many in the elegant art-deco style, with a total of 7.6 million square feet, including parking. The reason Gilbert is buying this real estate is that he believes Detroit will stage a comeback—with his help—and when that happens, people will need office space.[17]

▼▼▼▼

There is no Detroit renaissance, at least not yet. But the wind is blowing in Detroit's direction because of two powerful forces—capabilities and cost. Detroit embodies both of them, and the world is noticing. Since 2010, roughly a hundred German industrial firms, and dozens of Asian companies, have built manufacturing plants in Michigan and in other similarly inexpensive parts of the country with highly trained workers, such as Kentucky, Missouri, South Carolina, and Alabama. The United States is a less expensive place to do business than the countries where these companies are based, and it remains the largest single market in the world. That's part of the reason why real investment, as opposed to financial investment, has been above $200 billion in both the United States and China, the world's two largest recipients of outside investment, for the past four years.[18] Considering that the United States has been receiving outside investment for decades, while China is a relative newby, it is remarkable that so much money continues to flow into new investments in our country. In addition, if looked at on a per capita basis, there are far more dollars invested in the United States per person than in China, since China's population is about 1.3 billion and ours is just 313 million.[19]

SPEED TO MARKET

But it's not just labor costs that matter. It's speed. A fridge can roll off of Whirlpool's Michigan assembly line on Tuesday and be delivered to someone's home in Boston by Thursday. There are no customs to clear, very few weather delays along the way, no moisture problems resulting from days at sea, and no one to bribe to make sure the container gets on the ship. A shorter delivery time means less working capital tied up in stock, less insurance to pay from the time the refrigerator is produced to when it's sold, and a much shorter supply chain.

In manufacturing, one thing always leads to another. To make washing machines, you need gaskets, hoses, motors, and controllers. You also need sheet steel, chemicals, and paint, which means that if you make your machines in Cleveland, chances are you'll buy all the odds and ends you need to make those machines from suppliers nearby. And, if those suppliers have stopped making the proper gaskets or hoses, once they see demand pick up they will get back in the game, because that's what capitalism is all about. As the old-time American industrialist Henry J. Kaiser used to say in the 1930s and 1940s when he made cement and built roadways, runways, and docks, "find a need and fill it." That, in a nutshell, is how Adam Smith defined capitalism.

Those needs don't stop with stuff—bending metal and spot-welding steel. There are service businesses that are driven by manufacturing, including insurance, banking, accounting, food service, and so on—all of which illustrates the way one thing leads to another in the manufacturing chain of events.

Economists have long sought to measure what they call the "multiplier effect" of one job on another. How many actual jobs does one worker at the Ford F-150 light-truck factory generate throughout the rest of the economy? To find that out, economists build elaborate "input-output" models. In the case I am describing, you type into the computerized mathematical model the number of employees building cars in Detroit, for example, and the model shoves those numbers through an array of linked equations that smash, smoosh, and crash the numbers together until they spit out an answer.

Economic Modeling Specialists International (EMSI), an economic analysis and consulting firm in Moscow, Idaho, modeled the multiplier effect for a number of employment categories in a number of cities. It's important to mention the areas studied, because, as Enrico Moretti,[20] an economist at the University of California at Berkeley, showed, location is as important in labor economics as it is in real estate. Some cities have higher multipliers for the same job category, largely as a result of differences in wages and rates of growth.

According to EMSI, each worker employed in a Detroit factory building cars generates 5.4 jobs somewhere else in the region, and every worker building light trucks in Detroit creates 11 jobs. Laying asphalt in Detroit has a multiplier of 9.1, and working in a Detroit-area oil refinery has a multiplier of 7.8.[21]

EMSI's analysis is particularly interesting because, after examining the economic and job-creation impact of millions of workers in dozens of fields, it showed that manufacturing jobs in Detroit and similar cities had bigger multipliers than, say, software-publishing jobs in San Jose, California, which had a multiplier of only 4.3, or data-processing and related services, which had a multiplier of just 3.

The equations inside of these intricate economic models work both ways—as all equations do. Because the jobs of 11 workers elsewhere in the economy depend on the technicians building F-150s on the assembly line, if Ford technicians are laid off, employment contracts throughout the area. When the automakers were in trouble, some people argued against bailing them out (Mitt Romney, for example).[22] But if GM and Chrysler had been allowed to go out of business, it would not have been only the hundreds of thousands of people working in those two companies that lost their jobs. Many more—perhaps millions more—would have lost their jobs in that part of the Midwest as well, because their jobs also depended on GM and Chrysler doing well.

That was the point of filmmaker Michael Moore's outrage when he walked through the boarded-up streets of Flint, Michigan, in his documentary film *Roger & Me*, complaining about the loss of a GM plant. He focused on the indirect jobs—the husband and wife who had to close their diner, the newspaper stand that was shuttered because no one stopped by anymore to pick up a paper on their way to work. And, by doing that, he emphasized the remarkable impacts—both positive and negative—that manufacturing has on the economy.

Detroit may be a work in progress, with tremendous potential, a glorious past, and lots of very talented people. But it's only one city in a country with hundreds of cities that have world-class industrial capabilities and costs of living that are among the most reasonable in the world. Cleveland, Cincinnati, Chicago, Columbus, Philadelphia, Denver, Kansas City, Dallas, Houston—the list is long—are all much less expensive places to live and work than most of Europe is, or much of Asia and the rest of the world. Combine our low costs with our capabilities, and investing in the United States makes sense.

MAKING THINGS

Making things is cool, as everyone knows. When a newly finished ship, its welds still warm, slides off the rails and into the water, people smash champagne bottles against the hull, snap pictures, and cheer. And when Boeing or Airbus introduces a new plane, thousands of people stand on the tarmac for hours waiting to see it. When a new skyscraper goes up, the ironworkers hang flags from the cranes, because they are proud of their mechanical chops. Tens of thousands of people go to computer and electronics shows to admire the next new thing, and millions watch programs on TV showing people building hot rods and motorcycles, or sailing the world's biggest ships, or building the largest offshore drilling platforms. There are documentaries that go micro, showing how pencils and cereal and tennis rackets are made. People love building things, and they love watching others do it, too, as the book *Shop Class as Soulcraft*, by Matthew B. Crawford, shows so well.[23]

Making stuff is how we are wired, how we as a species survived against all odds in climates as diverse as permafrost, desert, and rainforest. It's how we brought down (and ate) massive wooly mammoths and protected ourselves against cave bears. Making things is in our DNA.

And besides, who does not have something, some human creation, they love? It might be a smartphone, a camera, a tablet device, a car or computer, or a painting or piece of sculpture. We all have human-produced objects we love.

A friend of mine who studies how the brain works posted two images that were circulating on his Facebook page. One of those images was an ancient hand ax carefully chipped and shaped from stone by our ancestors perhaps 40,000 years ago. It was almond shaped, and you could imagine holding it snugly in your hand as you pounded grain into flour, smashed rocks to make clay, or defended yourself against another creature. Next to the hand ax, on his Facebook page, was an iPhone 5, at the time the newest, coolest smartphone.

The message in that post needed no words. It said that there is an unbroken chain starting with our distant ancestors who picked up rocks and extending through time to smartphone designers in Cupertino, California. It extends as well to the autoworkers in Detroit, the geneticists in Cambridge and San Francisco, and the materials scientists who are starting to work with substances a single atom thick. It extends, that is, from those cavemen wielding a hand ax to the dual-degree scientists testing compounds that they hope will one day cure cancer, reverse brain damage from strokes, or stop aging.

This unbroken chain from the hand ax to the iPhone and beyond is not an abstraction. Rather, it is a statement about who we are.

MAKING STUFF HERE

Back in the day, as an editor at the *New York Times*—just before newspapers entered their decline—I worked on a number of stories about manufacturing in the United States. Back then, outsourcing was still in its infancy, and Americans were worried about how Japan, not China, might one day dominate the global economy. Instead of having their children learn Mandarin, as they do today, parents were eager to have their kids study Japanese.

The same complaints about America that are made today were made back then. Our children were not well enough educated, didn't have the same work ethic as their parents, and were falling behind. When comparing themselves to the Japanese, Americans thought of themselves as lazy, while the Japanese were considered focused and disciplined. Our cities, it was said, were falling apart, while Japanese cities were orderly and gleaming.

Most people writing those stories or repeating the clichés had never been to Japan. On my visits there, I was amazed at how efficient their manufacturing appeared to be, but I was astounded by how unproductive their executives were. Executives stayed in the office for long hours—in many cases doing very little—then went out for elaborate meals, where they drank what seemed like gallons of alcohol. The first half of the following day was spent getting over their hangovers, while the second half was more or less devoted to work.

There's no point in recounting how it ended. We—the lazy Americans—grew like mad in the 1990s, while the focused, disciplined Japanese missed out on a decade of growth. Many of the anti-Japanese alarmists from that era have morphed into anti-Chinese alarmists in this era. For example, every time a Chinese company wants to buy an American one, it raises a ruckus, just like it did years ago. Okay, I can understand not wanting to sell the Chinese one of our oil companies, or a high-tech manufacturing firm. But should we really be worried about the Chinese company Shuanghui purchasing Smithfield Foods? Since when did bacon and smoked hams become a strategic national asset?

In any event, I was sitting in the newsroom working on my story and I wanted to find out about the future of outsourcing. I did some homework, called around, and spoke to all the usual experts, and ended up dialing up a professor at UC Berkeley named John Zysman, codirector of the Berkeley Roundtable on the International Economy (BRIE). I was never quite sure what BRIE was, beyond being an interdisciplinary group of academics who got together to discuss the world economy and each country's place in it.

Even now, so many years later, I vividly recall my conversation with Zysman, along with his prescience. I asked him about outsourcing manufacturing to places like Mexico, since China was not yet on anyone's mind. Zysman said the primary problem with outsourcing was that product designers and engineers at the home office begin losing touch with how products are built. "They are cut out of the feedback loop," he said. "If a US company has a Mexican manufacturer make its TVs, all of the snags in the manufacturing process—*and the learning that results from them*—stay with the Mexican firm. As a result, the Mexican company moves ahead and the American company falls behind." I remember thinking how very wise and insightful this statement was.

Those sentiments—almost verbatim—appeared in a March 2012 *Harvard Business Review* article by Jeffrey Immelt, chairman and CEO of GE. Immelt argued that one of the reasons why GE was renewing its commitment to manufacturing products in the United States, and moving production of refrigerators and other white goods from South Korea to Kentucky, was to keep GE's designers and engineers from losing touch with how their products were made and with the markets where they were sold. He went on to say that "outsourcing that is based only on labor costs is yesterday's model."[24]

I agree with Immelt's point, especially with regard to labor costs, for reasons already specified. I also agree that it's important to keep your designers close to your markets and your engineers close to your factories. How else can companies compete? They can't do it by following the unthinking herd and sending their manufacturing capabilities far from their customer base. It only took twenty years for Zysman's insights to make their way from Berkeley's academic halls to the corporate corridors of GE and other companies, but at least they made the trip.

But it's not just American companies, like GE, that want to be close to the American market. Every company wants to sell its products in the United States. By doing so, a company can easily access the 460 million people residing in the NAFTA countries of the United States, Canada, and Mexico. The NAFTA countries have tremendous appeal. They are rich, and demographically they are younger than people living in Europe, Japan, and soon China. And, in addition, they reside on top of the world's largest concentration of energy reserves.

As shown in Figure 6.2, these attributes are enormously appealing for foreign investment, and they will pay off for the United States and its economy. America's NAFTA neighborhood happens to be one of the best places to do business anywhere. Mexico, even with its drug cartels and corruption, has somehow found a way to grow at an average rate of 5 percent a year. It has also managed to shrink its debt to about 20 percent of GDP, compared to the United States' 102 percent, and to train an increasingly large number of talented engineers. The most

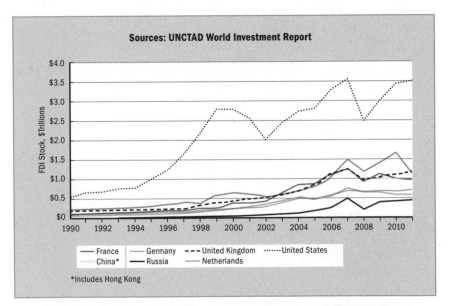

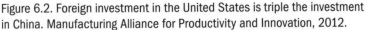

Figure 6.2. Foreign investment in the United States is triple the investment in China. Manufacturing Alliance for Productivity and Innovation, 2012.

radical element in Mexico's dynamic shift in fortunes is President En-
rique Peña Nieto's decision to take steps to make the country's national
oil company, Pemex, at least partially private. Despite its large reserves
of oil and natural gas, Pemex has failed to explore for and locate additional reserves. The government-owned company's corruption is legendary, and its production costs are among the highest in the world.

Prying Pemex out of the hands of the government won't be easy,
even for a president as determined and sophisticated as Peña. Nation-
alizing Mexico's oil wealth was one reason the country's decade-long
revolution, which began in 1910, was fought. In addition, government
ownership and control of the country's oil resources was written into
Mexico's 1917 constitution. Still, even if Pemex is partially denation-
alized, it will lead to more exploration, which will create more wealth
for the country and propel it to faster growth.

For the United States, this is a positive. Developing Mexico's
domestic market means selling more goods south of the border. The
same is true for foreign firms that want to crack the Mexican market.
If you ran a German, Japanese, or Chinese firm, wouldn't the best
(and safest) place to locate your business be the United States? Doesn't
it make more sense to service the Mexican market from Dallas, San
Diego, or Los Angeles than from Tokyo, Shanghai, or Frankfurt?

Yes, it does.

A FACTORY IN EVERY HOUSE

This is not a book about technology per se, but about America's
unrivaled creativity, its manufacturing muscle, and the luck of our
geography—or, more accurately, our geology. It's also a book about
America's awesome storehouse of capital.

But technology does play an important role in bringing the country into its second century of leadership. The greatest leaps forward
since the industrial age began were the result of a unique blend of
technological advances and sufficient money to develop them. Luckily, we have both.

One development that will change things a lot is 3D printing.
There have been news reports about this awesome technology. But let
me explain briefly what it is and why I think it's important.

Three-dimensional printing is in some ways similar to ink-jet printing, something familiar to all of us. Most offices and many homes have at least one ink-jet printer. And if you ever go to a Staples or Office Depot store, you'll find aisles filled with expensive, colored inks made by HP, Lexmark, Canon, and many other companies for these ink-hungry machines.

The secret to these machines is in those ink cartridges that spray ink onto paper or photographic sheets. Silicon chips inside your printer receive instructions from your computer to cause little electric sparks to rapidly heat and vaporize minuscule quantities of ink inside the cartridge, which shoots it out of a tiny nozzle and onto the paper, like a miniature squirt gun. Because this process happens so quickly, and because the spritzes of ink are so tiny, they form images on paper that look seamless to the naked eye, but are actually made up of tiny dots, sometimes with one dot, a yellow one, say, on top of a blue dot, to make green.

In 3D printing, something similar is happening, but instead of laying down layers of ink onto paper, the printer's tiny hot spritzes are of goo—fast-drying epoxy-like plastics that become hard, in some cases, or metal that gets vaporized with heat ("sintered," in the technical lingo) and becomes hard when it cools.

So, in short, these 3D printers lay down one thin layer upon another of plastic resin or sintered metal to make real things based on the instructions the 3D printer gets from a computer running a design program. You can download programs to make things, and you can buy the printers from a number of companies. But perhaps the best known of the companies making these products is MakerBot, located in that hotbed of tech innovation called Brooklyn, New York. MakerBot's products are mostly for hobbyists, but its real advantage in the marketplace comes from what it calls its "Thingiverse," which is MakerBot's library of software designs that tell your printer how to make a lot of different things. In June 2013, MakerBot was bought by Stratasys, a publicly traded industry pioneer which was started in 1989 and is based in Edina, Minnesota.

Starting in late 2012, 3D printing received more than its fair share of media coverage, but not for the right reasons. It's been all over the web, on TV, and in newspapers and magazines. Unfortunately, most of the recent attention around this technology is the result of a few knuckleheads who call themselves Defense Distributed, a non-profit gun advocacy group. Defense Distributed posted design software on MakerBot's Thingiverse website to enable those who own or have access to 3D printers to print what are called "lower receivers" for semiautomatic rifles. Once printed, these receivers can change a semiautomatic assault rifle into one that is fully automatic.

Defense Distributed posted this design shortly after the killing of twenty children and six adults at Sandy Hook Elementary School in Newtown, Connecticut, in December 2012. The goals of this group include not only enabling everyone to make guns using a 3D printer, but making them so they are undetectable by airport scanners when concealed. The group also printed out high-capacity magazines for assault rifles. You see why I call them knuckleheads?

I'm not anti-gun. Far from it. I'm a member of a gun club and I'm a pretty good shot—much to my own amazement. But Distributed Defense shows what we will be forced to contend with because of the democratization of manufacturing, thanks to 3D printing. Give everybody a flexible factory of their own and who knows what they'll make—good and bad, smart and, well, not so smart. And, though I

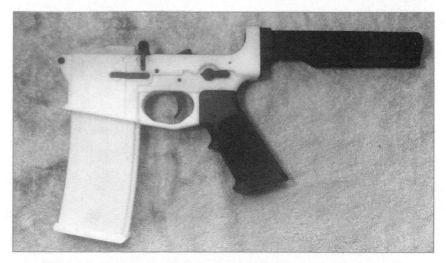

Figure 6.3. The lower receiver, in white, was printed out on a rented 3D printer and turns a semiautomatic assault rifle into a fully automatic assault rifle. The barrel and stock are attached to the receiver. Defense Distributed.

fully expect 3D printing to be overwhelmingly positive, technology always has its side effects.

Anyone who can download software, create a design on a computer, or use a digital 3D scanner can recreate it in 3D. Late-night TV host Jay Leno has a 3D scanner and printer in the garage where he keeps his car collection, so his mechanics can make spare parts for cars no longer in production.

With a 3D printer and scanner, you can make or replicate eyeglass frames, jewelry, false teeth, toys, busts of Einstein, prototypes for manufactured products, replacement parts for things you own, keys, and, sadly, conversion kits to make assault rifles automatic. Some 3D printers are as big as a small refrigerator; others are small enough to fit on a desktop or table.

Given all the publicity, you would think this American-made technology was new—which it's not. What's new is that 3D printing machines are coming down in price and that there are thousands of designs for products you can download from websites. Those designs

Figure 6.4. A leased tabletop-sized 3D printer, like the one above, made by Stratasys in Edina, Minnesota, was used by Defense Distributed to print the receiver of the automatic assault rifle. Stratasys canceled the lease and confiscated the printer when it learned what Defense Distributed was doing with the device. The Intel Free Press.

enable the printer to make real objects. People swap designs, sell them, or give them away.

It's unfortunate that lunatics have drawn attention to the downside of this technology. But technology often gets popularized for uses other than those for which it was originally intended. For example, analysts believe that video recorders became prevalent in the 1980s, followed by DVDs, because so many people wanted them to watch pornography, not opera or ballet. Fringe groups like Defense Distributed might be the ones that popularize 3D printing for the masses.

Actually, getting 3D printing into the news is long overdue. The technology first emerged in the 1980s, with techie names like "selective laser sintering," and "stereo lithography." Whatever you call these machines, software controls what they make. This technology is still in its infancy.

Charles Hull, an American inventor, is credited with creating the 3D printer. He patented the mechanism and started a 3D printer manufacturing company called 3D Systems, which remains an industry leader. In 1988, Hull's company released its first commercial product, called the SLA-250, using the acronym for stereolithography apparatus. After the SLA-250 was created, other companies began producing 3D printers.

The technology is finally gaining traction some three decades after its invention, and it is doing some amazing things. For example, in 2012, LayerWise, a Belgian Company, printed a human jaw made of sintered titanium coated with ceramic. The jaw was successfully implanted in a patient with progressive osteomyelitis to take the place of the original bone. And in 2013, Oxford Performance Materials, based in Connecticut, used 3D printing to print 75 percent of a human skull. The prosthetic was implanted into a patient to take the place of the real one, which had been damaged. The Food and Drug Administration, which regulates medical devices as well as drugs, approved Oxford's material and the 3D printing process. This paves the way for Oxford Performance and others to print individualized replacement bones for people whose real bones have been injured through accidents or disease. And, as I mentioned earlier in this book, Andrew Hessel and members of his Pink Army Cooperative of DNA hackers are already attempting to print DNA nucleotides in an effort to create new types of plants and animals.

▼▼▼▼

Printing out replacement bones and individual nucleotides may sound incredible, but there is still more. Scientists are now in the process of using 3D printing to create new organs. Autodesk, a California maker of computer design and machine control software (the company Andrew Hessel is working for), has teamed up with a small, publicly traded company called Organovo, based in San Diego, to create what they call the NovoGen MMX Bioprinter.

This new machine is not science fiction. It is designed to lay down ultrathin layers of human cells and shape them into living tissue. Organovo's aim, at present, is to create living human tissues that can be used in drug trials, so they won't have to be tested on animals. If Organovo is successful, it has the potential to remove a costly and time-consuming step in developing new drugs.

Printing out tissue is only a start. One aim of the technology is to learn how to print out organs. Instead of ink, plastic, or powdered metal, the NovoGen printer uses what researchers call "bio ink," a mixture of cells (in some cases stem cells) and chemicals.

The implications of this form of 3D printing are vast. Currently, to obtain a heart, a pair of lungs, or a kidney, a person must wait, sometimes for months or even years. Then, when the organ becomes available, the recipient is rushed into surgery as the organ is sent into the operating room packed in ice.

The wait, combined with the suddenness of the surgery, are traumatic enough. But what's even more difficult to contend with is that the organ comes from another person and could be rejected by the recipient's immune system. However, if cells are taken from the recipient herself, cultured, and then used to print an organ, that organ will in all likelihood not be rejected by the immune system. The organ donor and recipient are the same. Researchers at Cornell and various medical centers have successfully printed skin cells to fit precisely into a soldier's wound, and scientists have now grown kidney cells. As these technologies develop, they could be used to successfully treat the types of patients who at present have few good options.

Imagine a world in which organs can be printed and transplanted from a donor to his or her own body. In that world, diseases of the heart, liver, kidneys, and other organs would no longer be lethal.

POSITIVES AND NEGATIVES

On a more mundane level, individuals will no doubt make dangerous objects—swords, knives, and guns—that can be produced by a 3D printer. That's a given. For whatever reason, people do things like that. As soon as a new technology is invented, so is a new type of outlaw. That's why we have cars and car thieves, Internet pioneers and Internet pirates.

For example, suppose you like the silver and gold jewelry designed by Elsa Peretti, which is sold exclusively at Tiffany's. With 3D printing, you could go to a bootleg site, download Peretti's signature designs, and use them to print out perfect copies of the real thing in sintered metal. Or, if the designs were not available, you could simply use a digital camera, photograph the Peretti pendant you liked, and reproduce it. In that way, 3D printing leads to 3D counterfeiting.

Lawsuits will abound as a result. People might print engine or airplane parts, or make counterfeit medical devices like heart valves and artificial titanium hips. These products might look good, but they might not be made of the right materials or be as strong as the original specifications require. What Napster did to songs with the advent of file sharing (and by inference the music industry), 3D printing could do to the world of real things.

But there are many positives as well. As 3D printing evolves, you will be able to print out a dress, or a tuxedo, the morning of the prom. Instead of spending thousands on a wedding dress, you can print one out. If you're creative, you can design and print your clothes, or sell your designs, and try to get yourself on *Project Runway*. The cost of labor for some goods could therefore fall to zero as we start printing those goods at home.

Of course, printing prom dresses or hipster hats, or replacement car parts, will be disruptive. That's what new technology always does. Computers and ink-jet printers reduced the number of typists in the world, from one per executive to a fraction of that. And yet, people adapted. Typists became executive assistants, or, in some cases, executives. And, while it's true that some people lose their jobs when a new technology arrives, and in many cases have to go back to school, the economy always seems to find uses for people. Unemployment in 1980, as the first word processors and printers were making their way into business, stood at 7.1 percent. But once those machines were on people's desks, unemployment fell, averaging just above 5 percent from 1990 to 2007, just before the big recession hit. Not only that, unemployment fell as the workforce expanded as more women and minorities joined it.

My answer to disruptions resulting from new technologies is not simply to say "Don't worry." What I am saying is that, while there are always disruptions that throw the workforce into a mega-version of musical chairs, so far, at the end of each round, most participants have managed to find a spot, especially after enough time has passed and recessions have ended. Jobs are always eliminated, as the statistics show, but they are always created, too. And they are being created now.

Although the thought of so many people having veritable factories in their homes on their desktops might be worrisome, what has to be remembered is that it is potentially a source of enormous power as well. Because this sector is new, we don't yet know what its effects will be on other parts of the economy. Will making replacement parts at home for your coffeemaker or vacuum cleaner have a positive or negative effect on jobs in the rest of the economy? (My guess is it might tilt negative.) But what if you make a prototype at home for an entirely new type of coffeemaker or vacuum cleaner that a big company like GE or Whirlpool wants to manufacture in large quantities? If that happens, my guess is it will have a positive impact on jobs. And isn't that how technology affects the economy anyway? It creates new jobs—stay-at-home coffeemaker designers—and it destroys others.

Think about the evolution of our workforce. In the days leading up to the American Revolution, the Brown Bess was the musket used by the British armed forces. When the Americans lined up to fight the Redcoats in the battles of Lexington and Concord, it was most likely a Brown Bess musket that fired the shot heard 'round the world.

Cottage industry produced those muskets. The Royal Ordnance produced the gun, originally called the Kings Pattern (there were other patterns as well), and kept the original gun in a safe place in London. Gunsmiths who obtained orders from the British Crown to make these guns would come to London, take precise measurements of the Kings Pattern, make drawings, and go back to their cottages and shops to fulfill their orders. This is how the main flintlock musket of Britain's military forces was produced for more than a century, from 1722 until the middle of the nineteenth century.

When there were modifications to the design—the Long Land Pattern, which was used against the American rebels; the Sea Pattern, for the Royal Navy; the India Pattern, for Britain's colonial forces in India, and so forth—Britain's gunsmiths would make their way to London to take measurements of the new variation and make drawings of the gun. Each Brown Bess that was kept in London functioned the way software does now—which explains why they called it a pattern.

Most of the gunsmiths making these guns produced them with members of their family. Sometimes they made the guns in rural areas, with iron furnaces built into their barns, and sometimes they were located in shops in the cities. For much of human history, people worked as families from their homes and farms to produce what they simply called *manufactures*. When these families had shops in town, they usually lived above or next to their shops. This method of making things became prevalent in the New World as well—one example is the Paul Revere House in Boston, which contained Revere's silversmith shop.

Modern mass production, an American invention, came into existence in the early 1800s in Springfield, Massachusetts, when the country needed a supply of guns and other weapons for the American forces fighting the British in the War of 1812. The British were still making their Brown Bess muskets by hand, one at a time, but their American foes began fabricating identical component pieces, batch after batch, and assembling them into identical weapons. When mass production was perfected, it destroyed the old family-run, cottage-industry model, and ultimately, some would argue, destroyed the family itself, at least as an economic unit.

Prior to mass production, people did not go to work, they *lived* at work. After mass production and the rise of factories, when family members first started working outside of the home, they usually had to travel long distances, from rural areas to the cities, to be closer to their workplaces. So the members of the family who began working in the city moved away from home and lived in tenements or board-inghouses. Rather than seeing their families every day, as they toiled together, ate together, and lived together, these factory workers rarely saw their families. Even now, factory workers—and knowledge work-ers, too—usually spend eight hours or more a day at work, commute for another hour or two every day, and have limited time left to spend with their families. (Depending on your circumstances, this may not be a bad thing.)

I bring all this up because 3D printing may alter today's work patterns. When I was growing up in California in the 1960s—at the time the center of the aerospace industry—I worked for my uncle, who sold, repaired, and refurbished high-tech industrial tools and machinery used to make jet engines, civilian and military aircraft, rockets to explore space, and missiles for defense. When I learned how to drive, my uncle gave me the keys to a big, white van and made me a deliveryman.

I recall very clearly my first delivery. My uncle and I put a few boxes of hardened-steel tool bits and precision diamond-tipped cut-ting tools into the back of the van. He gave me the address and told me I was delivering these components to a company near what was then Lockheed's headquarters. By way of background, he told me the company to which I was delivering the parts specialized in shaping hard metals used as wing supports on military jets.

The address was near Burbank airport. But when I found the street and went to the number, I thought I might be lost. Instead of a company, I stopped in front of a typical California tract house. With the motor running, I looked at the address again and then at my map—this was before cell phones and navigation systems. The map showed that I was indeed in the right place.

Still a little dubious, I went to the front door of the rock-roofed, pastel-blue house. A small metal sign near the doorbell said, "Deliver-ies in rear." Maybe I am in the right place, I thought.

I went back to the van, put the boxes on the hand truck, and wheeled my cutting tools to the garage. A little sign on the side door of the garage listed the name of the company on the paper my uncle had given me.

I knocked on the door, opened it, and walked inside. What I saw amazed me. In the middle of the garage was a giant machine, similar to a lathe. It was about five feet wide by seven feet deep and at least five feet tall. There was a plastic door on the machine's housing, and inside that door, I could see what looked like spinning drill bits bathed in a steady stream of water. A man in jeans and a tee-shirt sat at the controls monitoring knobs and dials that were far beyond my comprehension.

A woman sitting at a small desk stood up and walked over to me. "You're Art's nephew?" she asked.

I nodded.

"I'm Dee. My husband, Paul, can't stop right now. He's in the middle of a cutting process with the machine. We've got a big order. You can put the boxes over there," she said.

Dee pointed to an empty spot in the otherwise cluttered garage. When I took the boxes off the hand truck, she went through them to make sure the order was correct.

"Give your uncle Art my best," she said. "We love him. My husband will only do business with him. With Lockheed, Douglas, and Boeing as customers, we need to get our tools fast."

What I learned from my experience was that America's late 1960s aerospace industry—the same industry that put men on the moon—was not that much different from Britain's flintlock musket industry. With aerospace, a few big companies bought products from hundreds of mom-and-pop companies, and made the rest of the parts themselves.

But when computerized machine tools came into existence, most of these tiny machine shops closed up. Hundreds of highly skilled, creative entrepreneurs went out of business.

With the advent of 3D printing, some of this may reverse. It's a long shot, though not impossible, that 3D printing will replace highly automated factories. More likely, 3D printing will be integrated into the production process, with some things—replacement parts for items like vacuum cleaners, dishwashers, and clothes dryers—available for printing at home.

And 3D printing will enable small entrepreneurial shops to open that produce highly creative, one-of-a-kind goods for a variety of clients, industries, and consumers. Some of these items will no doubt be artistic expressions—such as sculptures, clothing, jewelry, movie props, and so on. In fact, one can imagine set designers printing out next-generation versions of the Starship Enterprise, or some Klingon vessel, to use as special effects in an upcoming movie or TV show.

Other items people make at home might be technical. For example, a neurosurgeon I knew when growing up had an extensive machine shop built in his garage. He loved doing surgery, but he also was keenly interested in inventing medical devices to help his patients. On his lathe he made tiny metal devices to relieve pressure inside the skull of a person who had been injured. He patented these devices, licensed them to big medical device companies, and became a very wealthy man.

Instead of going into the garage and cutting metal on a lathe (my neurosurgeon friend worried that an errant shard of metal might hurt his highly trained hands), people like this will be able to use 3D printing, a method that will make the process safer, faster, and—perhaps—easier.

At the same time, engineers could make rapid prototypes of products needed immediately. For example, if 3D printers had been used when the Boeing 787 Dreamliner had problems with its lithium-ion batteries and the cases that housed them in 2013, consulting engineers, working at home or in their offices, could have fabricated a design for the cases, perhaps shortening the length of time the big, new plane had to be grounded. Open up the competition to design a winning solution to the battery problem, and hundreds of engineers and tinkerers might have added their skills to solving the problem.

There are other, more mundane uses for the technology as well. Think of the homeowner who wants a cabinet or bookshelf for his or her cookbooks, or a stand to hold cooking knives.

The point is, 3D printing will change the balance of what is made in factories and what is made at home, at least somewhat. What that change will be, we cannot predict. But as the technology develops, America's manufacturing base will at least in part become democratized. And, just as there are computer hackers, and gene hackers—which is how Andrew Hessel describes himself—there will be *thing*, or *stuff*, or *shape* hackers creating iPhone cases for Samsung phones or Porsche bodies for Volkswagens.

▼▼▼

The technology for 3D printing is gaining momentum, and that momentum is likely to keep growing. Already, there are plans (and of course a TED talk) about building truly massive 3D printers, perhaps long and wide enough to print a house on top of a cement slab or foundation. This type of printer, if it's ever built, might be suspended on a steel frame, and move over the foundation or slab the way TV cameras move on wires suspended above the football field when broadcasting the Super Bowl. This type of massive device would have a printer head instead of a video camera, and it would zip back and forth laying down razor-thin layers of resin. It would then build the house from the bottom up, starting with the slab and ending with the topmost part of the roof. And, because of the way the printing works, it would lay down the plumbing (pipes, sinks, faucets, showers, tubs, and toilets) along with the rest of the house, 1/10,000 of an inch at a time. It would also print the tubes where the wiring would go, in addition to the breakfast nook and, if you want, a plastic-resin couch.

▼▼▼

As I mentioned early in this chapter, the productivity of the American workforce is light-years ahead of most other countries. American workers sitting in front of computer consoles control dozens of machines that together make many of the components, products, and machines we use to make our lives better. And they do it more efficiently than the workers almost anywhere else on earth. For that reason, factories are returning home, and with them, some of the jobs that left our shores in recent decades are returning also.

At the same time, nothing in our country ever stands still. The way we organize production, with parts made around the country and around the world and assembled at a central point, may change. We might print out the box for our next computer to match the drapes, and only order the silicon guts of the machine. We might rent a gigantic MakerBot to lay down our next house one layer at a time, and in a shape as yet undreamt of.

As this happens, many things will change. Our production models may shift, and people themselves might add more value to the items they buy. How big a share will all of this represent in an economy that is at present already close to $16 trillion in size? The answer is, I don't really know. Not yet. But I do know that sometimes it's the relatively simple innovations that change the way we live most profoundly. Mass production, lean production, distributed production—none of these models change what we make so much as they reorganize the way we make it. Every time that happens, these shifts make their way through the economy, forcing some people to adapt, and to do so with pain, while bestowing on others considerable good fortune. Henry Ford didn't invent automobiles, he just changed how we make them, and for that he and his descendants were rewarded handsomely. In my view, we are at the early stages of that happening once more.

Even the foods we eat—and how we make them—could be about to undergo some big changes. I once read a science-fiction story that took place far in the future. In it, there was a device that resembled a refrigerator, only it made the food you wanted from a couple of bottles of chemicals and from the oxygen and nitrogen in the air. I don't remember how the machine worked, but it could have been done by laying down each part of an apple, or tortilla chip, a micro layer at a time until the snack was made (it could have solved the national Twinkie crisis in 2012 when the Hostess parent company filed for bankruptcy). The *Star Trek* shows have something similar—the replicator—though the show never really explains how it works.

I'm not sure if the device described in that science-fiction story will be built during the second American Century or not. But it turns out that researchers in the United States and elsewhere are actually on their way to making such a device, starting with printers that make hamburger using a mix of genetic engineering and new forms of 3D printing. In 2008, People for the Ethical Treatment of Animals (PETA) offered a $1 million prize for anyone who could successfully create "synthetic meat" in an effort to end the slaughter of animals. In addition, the Thiel Foundation made a grant to a biotech startup to use 3D printing technology to produce meat.

At present, the arguments in favor of making some sort of synthetic meat printer or replicator center on animal rights, food-supply issues, and the environment (because large herds of cattle produce large amounts of waste as well as methane, which is harmful to the environment). If these devices are successful and a new source of food is unlocked, I am quite confident that the first units sold will be produced in the United States.

CHAPTER SEVEN

NOT EVERYTHING'S PERFECT

Every silver living seems to have a cloud. And, although I am bullish on America and its prospects, I do have a major concern. As I mentioned at the outset, no country is problem-free.

America is creating jobs, lots of them. It even created jobs during the depths of the financial crisis and the Great Recession. The problem is, are we creating enough workers?

Don't get me wrong. We have plenty of people—men and women, boys and girls. The problem is, too many of them are doing too poorly in school, or are shying away from taking courses in areas of critical importance—the STEM subjects of science, technology, engineering, and math. We need more people educated in these broad subject areas. But if we can't train our own people in these subject areas, then we need to make it easier for people who have these skills to immigrate. We need educated people if the United States is to continue moving ahead.

Here is the sad fact. America is going to be the dominant economic power for a long time. That's because of our vast energy reserves, massive supplies of capital, tremendous manufacturing prowess, and enviable levels of creativity. These forces will propel our country to new heights. But unless our kids do well in school, there will be more workers who look like Baxter the robot, and fewer who are like you and me.

I mentioned earlier that if you take America and graft onto it Saudi Arabia, you have our future. But here's the dirty little secret about Saudi Arabia and the other oil-rich countries in the Gulf. Almost all of the productive labor that makes those countries grow is imported. Teachers, doctors, administrators, investment-fund managers, hotel workers—even tree trimmers—come from somewhere else.

While that might be tolerated in countries with small populations and big resources, it won't work here. Yes, we need a steady stream of talented immigrants to come and invest in the United States, build companies, and stay. That's vital. But we also need our own people to take their places in the workforce. If that doesn't happen, the likely outcome isn't good—a growing disparity between the country's rich and poor—the country's top 1 percent and everyone else.

The statistics bear this out. We've known for a long time that people with college degrees earn roughly twice what people with only high-school degrees earn—$23,520 versus $51,108, on average.[1] People with STEM degrees earn more still, around $100,000 if you have an advanced degree in a STEM subject, versus $72,000[2] if you have an advanced degree in a non-STEM subject such as art, history, literature, philosophy, or another liberal art. The fact is that aside from the occasional genius who is too smart to finish college—people like Mark Zuckerberg, Bill Gates, and Steve Jobs—within the STEM group of graduates lie some of our most creative entrepreneurs.

The forces of economic change are cold and harsh. The logic behind the way economies function doesn't factor in whether people are naughty or nice, or whether they deserve a shot at success. Some highly successful people I've met, people who have accumulated vast sums of money, are warm, wonderful Teddy bears; others are toxic to the touch. The economy doesn't care who you are, it cares what you do. It also doesn't care about where someone came from, or the hardships he or she endured. Fairness is not an economic concept; it is a moral, ethical, religious, and political one. On their own, economies tend not to distribute wealth equally.

Economies create value by producing a continuous parade of innovative goods and services and by doing it ever more efficiently. Efficiencies bring down costs, while creativity and innovation produce the new products and services to sell. To stay ahead, countries need two kinds of people: people who are creative, and people who can make things work (and can make them work better, more efficiently, and at lower cost than the next guy). The problem is that we're not producing enough people in these two categories.

Apple makes iPads and iPhones, which are innovative products, in China because it is more efficient to make them there at present than it is to make them in Cupertino, California. As technology and costs change, that pattern will shift. Making things in China or Vietnam makes sense because labor in those places is cheaper than it is in the United States. But when costs rise in low-wage countries, manufacturers head for the doors.

Perhaps in the future, thanks to robots and automation, tablets and other types of electronic devices will be made in California, not Malaysia or Indonesia. Or, perhaps it will make better economic sense to produce them in Mexico or Turkey or Rwanda. Or someplace in the United States where real estate is not at a premium the same way it is in Cupertino, California, maybe even someplace close by. The point is, every time a company like Apple, in its never-ending quest for efficiency, changes where it makes things, some people win, and others lose.

When expensive American hands, working on assembly lines, were replaced by less expensive hands working somewhere else, we lost. Now, when inexpensive foreign hands are replaced by robotic graspers, and machines with sensors instead of eyes, we win. Or at least some of us win, assuming we have enough well-trained people to design the machines and make them work—which means STEM graduates.

In days gone by, jobs that required hand assembly—bolting wheels onto cars, for example—didn't require much education. When people joined Henry Ford to make Model T's, it hardly mattered whether they were educated at all, or even what language they spoke. What mattered was whether they had the discipline to show up sober and on time and do the same job over and over again each day.

This is an important point, because it shows that when assembly-line manufacturing began, at places like Ford's Victorian-style Piquette Avenue plant, you didn't need a degree to get hired. You just needed hands and some manual dexterity. The same is true now for most of the jobs at Foxconn's gigantic assembly plants in China, where Apple and other companies make so many of their products. People at these massive assembly plants aren't hired for their minds, they're hired for their hands.

That era is over.

As I've already mentioned, that's a worse problem for China than it is for us, given China's stage of development. China has to find work for as many as 250 million people, and these people are largely untrained. The government, in addition, wants to move these people to cities from rural areas. For China, it will be a challenge to find jobs for these people in the era of smart machines. That's a tough problem to solve, and it could slow that country's rate of growth.

In the United States, we've already had to deal with the labor challenges from somewhere else and from automation. We managed that transition pretty well by focusing on services, by using our powers of creativity, and by investing in automation. The shift away from handwork is likely to continue for a long time, and this means we need more people who think for a living and who are adept in the STEM subject areas.

We need to achieve economic efficiencies through the strength of our minds. Consider what this means. Depending on the job it is built to do, a single robot on the assembly line can displace ten to twenty people, or even more, given that it can run three shifts a day without breaks. But what that robot cannot replace, at least for now, are the people who program it, maintain it, insure it, finance it, and, when its life is over, haul it to the scrap heap to be recycled.

In 2000, 1.3 million people were employed in the American automobile industry doing everything from making transmissions and window glass to assembling SUVs. In 2013, only 800,000 people were working in that industry, after recovering from a low of 625,000 in 2008–2009,[3] when GM and Chrysler went bankrupt.

In 2000, 12.7 million vehicles were built in America. It was an extraordinary year, one of our best, in fact. However, forecasts indicate that we will make as many or more vehicles in 2013, and that we will do it with almost 500,000 fewer workers.

We're using fewer workers, but making better products. American-made cars are now the best in the world. And, according to the tough-minded automobile testers at *Consumer Reports*[4] magazine, the Chevrolet Impala is the best sedan of 2014, and the Tesla Model S, an all-electric sedan made in California, is the best car the organization ever tested. But that's not all. The Tesla also scored better than any other car on the safety tests conducted by the National Highway Safety Administration.[5] Tesla is now listed on the NASDAQ exchange.

The Impala, once the butt of so many jokes and a mainstay of police and rental fleets, is a gem. Other American cars are also on the *Consumer Reports* list. In fact, American products dominate it. America's innovation and creativity muscle, combined with gains in efficiency and productivity, are unbeatable. They've made the US auto industry profitable throughout the entire supply chain.

This transformation to a world of smart machines and workers educated in the STEM disciplines is not just affecting the automobile industry, it is affecting *every* industry, which is good news for the country, but bad news if you dropped out of school or only graduated from high school. People who make money attaching wheels to cars by hand are still well paid, but their wages are falling.

Back in the 1990s, when I worked at the *New York Times*, journalists would submit their stories to editors who would edit them online, return them to the journalists with comments and questions, then send back the final result. Everything was electronic—except for one thing.

We journalists worked on the third floor, but on the fourth floor there was what we called the "composing room." This was a relic from the past. It was filled with a couple of dozen aging, unionized typesetters who were trained to melt lead and pour it into molds to form letters, words, and pages, as a generation of printers who were long gone had done before them. The process these people were employed to do had been abandoned years before as word-processing computers and new types of printers took over. And yet, because of the company's unions and their ability to strike, one floor of the building worked the same way it did in my grandfather's day.

The paper's typesetters couldn't be fired and hadn't been retrained. They were mostly surly—and sometimes nasty—since they knew, *we all knew*, they were an artifact from the past. What these people did to stay busy was to take paper out of a big electronic printer, cut it with a razor blade, put sticky wax on the back of each piece, and stick it to extremely thick sheets of paper stock, which were photographed once again. Even in the 1990s, we could have done all these functions by typing in a few codes on our keyboards. (I always wondered if that grand, old newspaper could have fared better if it had taken the money it spent on these processes from the past and invested it in the future.)

I bring this up because it shows that no matter how long people wait around for the so-called "good jobs" to return, they won't return. There will never again be a need for typesetters who specialize in hot lead, and there will no longer be a need for people whose only skill is to bolt wheels onto cars. Those days are long gone.

Earning good wages will require heads, not hands. Even the people who run today's manufacturing machines need to be able to solve problems using math. The problem is, at this moment, we are failing to produce enough of these people.

WE'VE SEEN THIS BEFORE

Let's put it in perspective. We've faced this problem before and solved it. Vannevar Bush, the MIT professor who, during World War II, was the nation's first presidential science adviser, argued that to stay on top, the United States needed to beef up its scientific capabilities as the war came to an end. In July 1945, at the request of President Roosevelt, Bush was the principal author of a report called "Science, the Endless Frontier," which I mentioned in Chapter 1. This report led to the establishment by Congress of the National Science Foundation[6] (Bush called it the National Research Foundation in his report) as a government agency, as well as other science-enhancing agencies.

In the report, Bush noted that during World War II, scientists helped win the war. But he also noted that during the war the United States hardly trained any new scientists and there was a shortage. Instead of going to school, smart young men (they were almost all men, since these were different times) had become soldiers, not scientists. As a result, when the war ended, the United States had far too few scientists to build its future. Bush argued that the United States had to renew its scientific and technical capabilities, beginning by educating young men *and women* in what we now call the STEM subjects. He argued that we had to do this if we wished to continue to lead the world economically. (In World War II, the United States produced more manufactured goods than all of its allies combined.) In words that echoed those of the philosopher Ralph Waldo Emerson from a century earlier, Bush wrote that "there must be a steady stream of new scientific knowledge to turn the wheels of private and public enterprise." And to do that, he wrote, "there must be plenty of men and women trained in science and technology for upon them depend both the creation of new knowledge and its application to practical purposes."[7]

Consider the challenge Bush was addressing. Millions of Americans served in the military in World War II—almost 17 million men and women. And, with the war ending, most of those who were still serving would be taking off their uniforms and returning to civilian life.

Bush wanted to put people back to work after the war, ideally in STEM-intensive disciplines such as engineering and medicine. But that wasn't the only challenge facing the country. As I mentioned in Chapter 5, at the end of the war, the country's debt-to-GDP ratio was 120 percent, about 15 percentage points higher than it is today. In addition, although he wanted to build a modern (for the time), educated, STEM-oriented workforce, only about 40 percent of Americans were high-school graduates when World War II started. Back then, going to college was rare—fewer than 5 percent of Americans were graduating from college at the start of the war.[8] Compare that with the present. About 75 percent of Americans graduated from high school in 2009, and about 27 percent graduated from college. Our job is easier compared to what Bush was up against.

So, what was the result of Bush's efforts, and the country's post–World War II push into the sciences *amid a sea of debt*? More than sixty years of growth, with only a few interruptions, the worst of which occurred in 2008.

As I said, we've solved this problem before.

TOO FEW WORKERS

At present, the United States has too few of the right kinds of workers. Today's unemployment rate of 7.3 percent (6.8 percent for workers over twenty-five years old) is not evenly distributed. College graduates with a few years of experience are in demand.

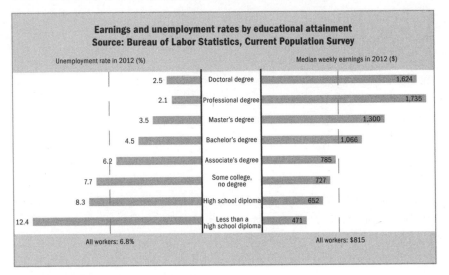

Figure 7.1.

The unemployment rate for this group has held steady at about 4.5 percent and falling, even during the worst of the recession and financial crisis. Given that people take time off, get sick, and move around, a 4.5 percent unemployment rate means that almost everyone in this group who wants a job either has one or can get one. The higher your degree, the better your chances of landing a job. And, if you have a professional degree, say in engineering, employers and recruiters are calling you. As you can see from Figure 7.1, earnings track with education.

Unemployment is really only a problem for those who didn't stay in school, or who just graduated. For people without a high-school diploma, unemployment is 11.3 percent. And for some people without high-school diplomas between the ages of seventeen and twenty-five (depending on the exact age), the unemployment rate is as high as 18 percent.

As the economy recovers, recent graduates will find the job market much more welcoming. That is starting to happen now, although it's not yet in full swing. But what the country really needs are people with STEM degrees—two-year and four-year. That's where we are weak.

Luckily, a number of trends are underway. They are not yet sufficient to solve the problem, but at least they are taking place, which is good news.

Take, for example, Germany's Siemens Corporation. Siemens is Europe's answer to GE, with huge operations in the United States. Like GE, it is a diversified, high-tech manufacturing- and engineering-heavy company that produces everything from energy equipment to medical devices. The United States is Siemens's largest market and home to one of its largest production centers. The company employs 60,000 people in the United States, generates $22 billion in revenue each year (roughly a quarter of the company's total revenue), and annually exports goods worth about $6 billion a year from the United States. Siemens has more than 100 manufacturing sites around the country.[9]

Siemens grasps the enormity of the opportunity in the United States, especially in energy, high-tech items, and medical devices. It would like to employ more American workers, not less. But according to Eric A. Spiegel, president and CEO of Siemens in the United States, there are too few workers trained for the jobs that companies like his need to fill. How many jobs are open right now? Spiegel estimates there are 3 million jobs in the United States that companies cannot fill because they cannot find enough well-trained workers. Three million unfilled jobs is a very big number, and represent the magnitude of the deficit I have been referring to. This number reflects failure on many levels—individual, family, and institutional.

If he were alive, Vannevar Bush, I am convinced, would look at this number dispassionately. He would regard it from an engineering perspective—as a problem to solve. He would look at our skills deficit and ask, How do we bridge the gap? In his day, it was through education. After World War II, the GI bill gave free college tuition to returning soldiers and provided them with cheap mortgages and loans to start businesses. As a result of that bill, 7 million soldiers went to college, many studying scientific subjects. This gave the economy a huge jolt, and it helped the United States keep its lead after World War II ended.

We can't send everybody to college to study STEM subjects. Some students are missing the educational foundation on which to build. Among this group, some can get the foundations they missed, but they need to get educated about the need for a good education. That happened after World War II. After all, 7 million people went to college on the GI bill at a time when only 40 percent of the population had finished high school. Educating people about the need for education can be done. And, once it happens, our network of community college systems can help people get the educational foundation they lack. But these institutions are strained. They need to be expanded— and there are efforts to make that happen, with corporate support. I will focus on this later.

For people who dropped out of high school and lack motivation and interest, or who are unwilling to go back to school, I don't see much hope. The economy and the riches it will be producing will pass them by.

We know the mismatch between skills and jobs needs to be corrected. One answer to that has to do with the 764,000 foreign students who are studying in this country. We need to reach out to them and make it easier for them to stay. Immigrants can be powerful contributors to the country, especially those who are studying here. Foreign students don't take jobs away from Americans. They become Americans when they live and work here. And they also become entrepreneurs. Sometimes, they start businesses that employ a lot of other people.

BRIGHT SPOTS

STEM-based jobs are expected to grow 17 percent between 2008 and 2018, according to the Department of Commerce, versus 9.8 percent for non-STEM jobs.[10] For example, 5 million new jobs are expected to be created in the health-care sector by the end of the decade. If all these health-care jobs were filled by people who are currently unemployed, it would drastically lower the overall jobless rate.

Today, postsecondary schools in America grant STEM degrees to between 14 percent and 19 percent of graduates. But to make up for the shortfall in technical workers that Eric Spiegel referred to, that number would have to increase to 23 percent of all undergraduates, according to research conducted by the McKinsey Global Institute.[11]

Almost every American advantage mentioned in this book depends on the STEM subjects. Without more well-educated PhDs working in the biosciences, that fast-growing part of the economy could stall. Without enough well-trained geologists, seismologists, and 3D visualization experts, fracking for natural gas may not advance. And without well-qualified oil and gas engineers, fracking may not be done safely. In addition, we all know you can't develop robots, or make products like 3D printers, without deep technical knowledge. The cluster of robotics companies that formed around Boston didn't form because the people working in these companies enjoy the snow—although many undoubtedly do. It formed because of MIT and the other schools in the vicinity, and their cadre of technically educated pioneers.

▼▼▼

The changes underway in the economy have not been lost on students. Undergraduate enrollment in engineering schools rose 15 percent between 2007 and 2009.[12] Freshman enrollment in the nation's engineering programs is the highest it's been in the past thirty years.

According to R. Bowen Loftin, president of Texas A&M University, an engineering- and technology-oriented school that keeps track of engineering jobs, "Demand for engineering education at Texas A&M has never been higher."[13] There are already more than 11,000 undergraduate students in Texas A&M's engineering school, but Loftin said his aim is to increase that enrollment to 25,000 by 2025. In addition, between 2009 and 2011, following a plateau, research space at universities for science and engineering increased by 3.5 percent overall. This statistic indicates that even in difficult economic times, universities are investing in the sciences.

One example illustrates this trend. Connecticut, which is the twenty-ninth most populous state, with only 3.5 million residents, is raising $1.5 billion to develop STEM programs at the University of Connecticut, a land-grant college that began as an agricultural school but has been slowly transforming itself into a true research university.

An increase of $1.5 billion on STEM programs is a significant investment for a school with 30,000 students. It shows that American educators are far from complacent. They understand the need to educate and train our students for our high-tech future. In addition, prudent university administrators are continually reevaluating their programs and examining their graduates' job data so that they can expand programs where their recent graduates are in high demand, even if it means shrinking some majors that are not leading to jobs.

Another healthy sign is that this issue has been largely exempt from political polarization. For example, I was at a meeting supporting funding for the National Institutes of Health that was attended by Republican House Majority Leader Eric Cantor; former Speaker of the House Nancy Pelosi, who of course is a Democrat; and Senate Majority Leader Harry Reid, also a Democrat. Although they did not sit together, they did all attend the meeting to support the work the NIH was doing in the sciences. Although it's unusual, at least at the time of this writing, to have bipartisan support for, well, anything, it was heartening to see that there are both Republicans and Democrats who understand the importance of science. However, at the time of this writing, the fate of funding for the NIH had not been decided.

CORPORATE PROGRAMS

Let's return to the Siemens Corporation and my earlier contention that community colleges are a vital element in our future. Because the United States is the world's most lucrative market, Siemens is providing its employees with the type of training they need to succeed in today's world. True, this is putting the burden of remedial education on a private company, but—as people say—*it is what it is*. If you want to make money, you need to invest.

Siemens is approaching the challenge by sending many of its American workers to vocational schools. For example, the company is a participant in Apprenticeship 2000, a four-year program in Charlotte, North Carolina, that trains high-school juniors and seniors for careers with eight partner companies—five of which are German or Swiss. The academic partner is Central Piedmont Community College, which designed the customized curricula for this effort.

In this way, community colleges are augmenting the existing workforce by developing programs for companies. In the case mentioned above, the program focuses on training people to work in Siemens's wind-turbine businesses. Some of these programs are modeled on German apprenticeship programs, which have successfully trained workers in that country for decades. Those programs, which are jointly paid for by the government and the companies, are not that different from what Siemens has set up in North Carolina.

These programs are not cheap. Siemens's Spiegel estimates that a typical program costs the company as much as $150,000 per apprentice. But since the students are working for the company during their apprenticeship, and are expected to stay at the company after they finish, it is viewed more as an investment than a cost.

In addition to these apprenticeship programs, Siemens developed an alliance with Penn State University to conduct research and train people in STEM fields critical to the company's future.

All of the schools I mentioned—Texas A&M, Penn State, and UConn—are looking into the possibility of using digital programs to educate students and community-college teachers so they can do a better job of training students to work at companies like Siemens and its competitors, such as GE. As part of this program, the National Science Foundation will be providing funding to integrate community-college students, whose educational aims are vocational, with engineering students at elite universities.

Community colleges came into their own during the financial and economic crisis. Not only are they educating their traditional student base—people who want to transfer to four-year institutions, students who need to enhance their educational skills, and students who are vocationally oriented—but they are also training graduates of four-year institutions to work in the evolving workplace.

The importance of two-year colleges is well known. President Barack Obama, in his bid for reelection in 2012, set a goal of increasing enrollment in these institutions by 2 million people, mostly for technical and vocational training. So far, Congress has not funded this effort, which would have gone a long way toward filling the 3 million openings for STEM-trained personnel that Spiegel alluded to. But even if Congress refuses to fund the program, which would be lunacy, at least the individual states know better. In 2012, twenty-four states approved plans to increase training programs and to better align those programs with the needs of industry.

This is not new. As long ago as 2007, I worked with the American Association of Community Colleges, a national membership organization for community-college leaders, on this issue. They understood the need to enhance the skill level of the country's workers even before the financial and economic crises hit, and they began preparing for it back then. Many community-college presidents told me they were in active discussions with industrial firms to create programs to better fulfill the needs of companies. Even more interesting, they were already coordinating their efforts, working together through the association to provide ways for national companies to send their employees to training programs in more than one location, and even in more than one state, for the same curricula.

With machines getting more complicated, and jobs becoming more technical, it makes sense for community colleges to explore the idea of developing common curricula. In addition, through their association, community colleges could set up a nonprofit educational consulting firm to work with companies to train people around the country. If this happened, GE or GM could provide its workers with the same training programs wherever they operated.

Community colleges are educating some 8 million students, including 3 million full-time students and 5 million part-timers, at a fraction of the cost of four-year institutions. And, because many of the two-year systems are big—Chicago's system has 120,000 students; Phoenix's Maricopa Community College system has 260,000 students; and Florida's statewide system has 900,000 students—decisions can be made centrally that affect thousands of students overnight.

For example, in Chicago, the decision was made by Mayor Rahm Emanuel to make the curriculum of the city's community colleges more relevant to today's high-tech workplace. Almost immediately, the leaders of the colleges began meeting with companies—a total of eighty-four companies so far—and new curricula were put into place, including what is now called "College to Careers," which trains people to work in specific organizations, such as hospitals. After a two-year planning period, the program is turning out students who leave school and go straight to work in a number of areas, including health care, logistics, manufacturing, and other fields. Companies have partnered with these institutions and offer internships along the way so that students can gain real-world experience. Other states and cities have similar programs in the works or already in operation.

It's tempting when bombarded with bad news by politicians and members of the media to despair. And not everything is rosy, by any means. But it would be incorrect to assume that responsible leaders in the United States are unaware that we need better-trained workers, and that we need them quickly. America is responding to the need for a higher-quality STEM-based workforce. It is doing it at the highest levels, at institutions such as Stanford and Caltech and MIT, and it is doing it at more generalized levels, too, through programs with community colleges.

HUGE OPPORTUNITIES

We should view education as an investment, not just a cost. No Child Left Behind, followed by Race to the Top, provided federal funds for states that assess educational progress and implement new programs to increase attainment. Both programs appear to be working—though it is still early. Many states have seen test scores in math and English increase, and thirty-four states have applied to join Race to the Top, even though its requirements—which include curriculum changes— are demanding. In addition, at the time of this writing, twenty-four states and the District of Columbia evaluate teachers by how their students perform, thirty-two states and the District of Columbia provide some form of support for charter schools, and forty-five states and the District of Columbia have accepted the "common core" curriculum, which is designed to promote proficiency in math and science and enables gifted students to gain college credit.[14]

When changes are made in K-12 education, it takes a long time to measure how well they are working. But the fact that so many states have changed their approach to education, have reformed their curricula, and are providing vouchers, so parents can select the schools their children attend, is remarkable, especially because these changes have taken place over a period of just roughly ten years. All of these efforts show that America is not sitting idly by while a disaster is in the making, as so many commentators want us to think. Rather, it shows that the concerns of parents are being listened to, and new approaches are being tried.

In the United States, there are thousands of schools and districts that are performing well. Massachusetts, for one, has an educational system that produces students who are the equal of those in any other country. But not all states are Massachusetts, and many need help. Those states that need help have been seeking it. And, although each state has its own set of challenges and unique circumstances, there is no reason why they cannot mirror the success of Massachusetts and of the best individual districts in the country. These successes show that investing in education pays off.

One piece of evidence supporting education as an investment, as noted earlier, is that 28,000 businesses have been started by MIT students and faculty since the school's inception as a land-grant school. These businesses create jobs, pay taxes, buy services from other companies, and have invented products that have made our lives better and more secure.

The investment comes from several primary sources. MIT students pay tuition, the state of Massachusetts provides funds to the school, and the federal government provides funds. This money has been multiplied many times over by students as they have put their education to use doing all kinds of things: designing new medical devices or computers or robots, for example. This is a unique attribute of educational institutions—it's not unique to MIT. Hundreds of colleges and universities in the United States spin off businesses and make our lives better. Millions of people have received the gift of education—although that gift is far from free.

Economists point out that if you provide government money— which is our money, after all—to consume what people produce, it adds less to the economy than if you invest in people, processes, and infrastructure that supports production. For example, if you invest in medical education, once a person becomes a doctor she adds a lot to society by curing sick people who can then produce more themselves. A dollar spent saving someone's life enables that person to create many more dollars that ripple through society. And, if some of these doctors join research teams that develop drugs, they might save the lives of thousands or even millions of people. The benefits from doing this are immeasurable.

Think about Jonas Salk, who discovered the first polio vaccine. Before the vaccine was introduced, in 1955, polio was a scourge. In 1952, one the worst years for the polio epidemic, 58,000 people, mostly children, were stricken with the disease in the United States. That year, 3,000 died and 21,000 were disabled. The population of the country was half what it is today. The cost of that disease in terms of loss of life, heartache and pain, and money is incalculable. But after Salk developed his vaccine, at the University of Pittsburgh, the process of eradicating polio began. And not just in the United States, but globally.

How do you measure the value of Salk's medical education? As a cost? As an investment? In retrospect, the answer is clear. Whatever it cost to send Salk to medical school, the gain returned to society was astronomical. Not only are we no longer losing 3,000 children and adults a year to this dreaded disease, or having to care for 50,000 gravely ill Americans, or providing for 21,000 disabled children and adults, but we are also reaping the benefits of all the things the people who were spared this disease have done over the years.

Almost every American since 1955 has received some version or descendant of Salk's polio vaccine. That includes some of our society's greatest contributors, and it includes you and me. If it weren't for the polio vaccine, thousands of Americans, perhaps millions, over time, would have been lost.

So is education a cost or an investment? Consider the contributions to society and the economy made by members of the Greatest Generation, after they went to college on the GI bill.

If you ask me, education is an investment unlike any other, because its payback is so large. Depending on the job and region, for each dollar you spend building a road or a bridge, or any other part of our infrastructure, economists argue, the economy as a whole gets that amount back only multiplied by known amounts.

So, what is the payoff from investing in education? It is measured in everything we do.

HIGH-TECH JOBS

STEM education and high-tech industry go hand in hand, especially when one of those hands is a robot's. An example of how high-tech ideas and STEM literally drive our economy to new heights is found in SpaceX, a company started in 2002 with the audacious plan of replacing

NASA's Space Shuttle with a series of new, inexpensive rockets. It was founded by Elon Musk, a South African–born entrepreneur and member of the "PayPal mafia," a small group of entrepreneurs—mostly foreign born—who came to the United States to complete their education and ended up starting PayPal. They then sold PayPal, one of the first online payment systems, to eBay for a whopping $1.5 billion. Ever since, members of the PayPal mafia have been investing in each other's projects and seeding other projects with cash from the eBay deal.

Musk, who is forty-two, knew how to develop software, not rockets, but what he really knew how to do was hire the best talent—people not just with the best educations, but who could put that education to work. Using his own money, funding from fellow PayPal mafia members, and money from some outside investors, Musk put together a team to design and build rockets in California.

Designing rockets is in the sweet spot of anyone who has an interest in the STEM set of subjects. It is an ultra-high-tech pursuit requiring sophisticated knowledge of aeronautical engineering, physics, aerodynamics, metallurgy, hydraulics, computer software and control systems, fuels, and many other fields. Musk had to assemble a group of people with all of those talents in order to begin the project. His decision to compete against rocket-building giants such as Boeing and Lockheed, which employ thousands of engineers, many with decades of experience, takes a lot of, well, moxie.

Musk took on the challenge, though, and during its sixth year in operation the company successfully launched its first rocket into orbit, the smallish Falcon 1. This was followed two years later by the launch of the Falcon 9, which is capable of sending cargo and even humans to the International Space Station. SpaceX is working on even larger rockets capable of orbiting the moon.

At the same time it was designing its rockets, SpaceX developed the Dragon capsule, which was for cargo and eventually humans. The Dragon successfully docked with the International Space Station in March 2013, 251 miles above Australia. When the rocket was fired, the Dragon capsule contained 1,270 pounds of supplies for the space station crew. When the capsule was sent back down to earth, it was filled with twice that amount of stuff that had been packed and sent home by the ISS crew.

Oh, and by the way, while Musk was getting SpaceX off the ground—literally—he was also starting Tesla, the electric automobile company, whose second car, the Model S, was the one *Consumer Reports* called the best car it ever tested. Trust me, I'm repeating this fact for a reason.

So here you have the quintessential American story. A group of foreign-born geniuses, from Ukraine, Germany, Poland, Taiwan, and South Africa, along with some home-grown talent, starts a few small companies. Then they join forces to start PayPal. But instead of retiring after the deal with eBay (which was also started by a foreign-born entrepreneur), they go on to invest in or build even more companies, including Facebook, LinkedIn, Zynga, Yammer, and others, all of which are technology dependent. And, although not all of the PayPal mafia worked in all of these companies, or even invested in all of them, as a group they all acted either as entrepreneurs, investors, or enablers, helping some very valuable companies get off the ground.

Just three of these companies—Facebook, LinkedIn, and Zynga—are worth a combined $84 billion at the time of this writing, fifty-six times the value of PayPal at the time of the sale to eBay. This is a powerful example of what can happen when a group of bright, entrepreneurial people come together in a creative, high-tech environment, where there is almost unlimited access to capital, access to talent, and access to the myriad of STEM resources at our great universities.

The PayPal mafia is a standout crowd. But think about what Musk has achieved—and he's only forty-two years old. He started a successful space exploration company, and he started a successful and highly valued automobile company, all within the space of a few years. No one else has ever done this. But he's not done yet. In the summer of 2013, Musk proposed building what he called the "Hyperloop," a train that travels inside a tube so that it can reach speeds of 798 miles per hour, cutting down the trip from Los Angeles to San Francisco to 35 minutes from what can only be called "endless" now.[15]

So, ask yourself this. If Musk had stayed in South Africa, where he was born, or hadn't had a STEM education and access to other people who had also had the opportunity of receiving that kind of education, could he have been involved in starting companies as big and important as PayPal, Tesla, or SpaceX? Could he have met the kind of talented people required to get these companies off the ground? Could he have raised the capital necessary to launch a space exploration company or a new car company, or even an electronic payments system? And, if not in South Africa, where else in the world could he have gone to do what he did?

That's a trick question, of course, since there is only one right answer. He could only have achieved his dreams in the United States.

▼▼▼▼

Since all of the companies started by Musk and other members of the PayPal mafia were by definition new, they had no choice but to hire people to get them up and running. As a result, not only did this group of friends and colleagues create $84 billion in value, they also directly created 11,565 jobs at SpaceX, Tesla, Facebook, and Zynga. If we use the software jobs multiplier[16] of 4.3 for San Jose, as described in Chapter 6, this means that this small group of entrepreneurs was responsible for the creation of another 49,729 jobs indirectly, for a total of 61,294 jobs created.

This is the reason why America is still the land of opportunity. Our universities, which are the best in the world, attract the world's best students. These students become energized by what they learn at institutions such as Stanford, Carnegie Mellon, and Berkeley—and from breathing the nation's entrepreneurial air. And then they are propelled forward by the so-called animal spirits of entrepreneurism, a term coined by economist John Maynard Keynes, to start companies that hire lots of people. It's also why we need to invest more to make sure our kids have a strong foundation in the STEM subjects.

Unlike many other countries, Americans think of entrepreneurs as heroes. We believe that striking out on your own to start a company is a noble pursuit. That's not a commonly held view around the world. On my last visit to Spain, for example, I learned that what college graduates want most is to become civil servants. That suggests that Americans and people in other countries have different views about how much risk is acceptable in business and in life. (On the other hand, in Spain people still run with the bulls in Pamplona, and fight them one on one, without protective equipment, in bullrings.)

But entrepreneurs need more than a high level of tolerance for business risks. They need an infrastructure of highly educated and motivated people who will help them get their businesses off the ground. They especially need the well-developed venture capital industry, something else that is lacking in most of the world. In addition, unlike many countries, we have many lawyers, consultants, accountants, banks, and search firms that specialize in working with young firms.

These firms are often flexible regarding how they get paid. Sometimes, in lieu of cash, a search or consulting firm will take its fees in shares of stock. It's risky, but when it pays off, the results are spectacular all around.

The ecosystem we've built to support new companies is the best in the world. There are startups in Britain, Canada, Sweden, and Finland. But none of these countries has the infrastructure of America. In fact, the greatest firms servicing startups are almost all American. What other country has the equivalent of a Kleiner, Perkins, Caufield & Byers, the venture capital firm, or Sequoia Capital, or Greylock Partners, or Draper Fisher Jurvetson, or any of dozens more? What other country has the equivalent of Wilson Sonsini, Goodrich & Rosati, a law firm specializing in startups? Or Silicon Valley Bank? The list goes on and on.

▼▼▼▼

This is a very potent mix—the world's best schools attracting the world's best talent and being able to support them as they start companies. It is the reason why America's job creation has outpaced Europe's and Japan's for decades. But it needs constant replenishment and care.

We need a steady supply of talented people to start, build, and work in our companies, many coming from outside the United States. But that has always been the case. If it had not been the case, then why would Henry Ford have started a school near his factory in 1914 to teach English to his immigrant workers? We need to make sure that the most gifted students who come to study in the United States have the opportunity to stay.

But we also need to grow more of our own talent. That means not only doing a better job of educating our students, but doing a better job of educating all Americans about the importance of education. It also means reminding people that the needs of the workplace shift as technology advances, and that each time that happens, jobs change. As a result, "getting our jobs back" no longer has any meaning, since the jobs that left, years or decades ago, no longer exist. New jobs, requiring new skills, have replaced them.

CHAPTER EIGHT

CALIFORNIA DREAMING

I began this book with a visit to Cambridge, Massachusetts. Let's take a second trip, this time to the West Coast to a part of California, and get another view of why America is entering its second great century with the capabilities it needs to remain on top. I love Massachusetts, have a home there, and love to talk about its virtues, one of which is its fiercely intellectual climate.

But I also have a home in California, a state that, with 38 million people, has almost six times the population of Massachusetts. And, although we walked through the streets of Cambridge, since the distances in California are so much bigger, we'll have to make this trip by car. So, hop in the sleek, signature red Tesla Model S that I rented this morning, the all-electric, California-designed and -built automobile that performed better than any other car on the National Highway Safety Administration's safety tests, and let's drive.

As we head toward the 101 Freeway, south through San Francisco, we pass the headquarters of the six-year-old company Dropbox, directly across from the San Francisco Giants stadium. Dropbox was started by two MIT engineering students and already has 100 million customers around the world using the service to share their files. From its inception, Dropbox has grown to earn $250 million in revenues, with a valuation of more than $1 billion.

A few blocks away, we come to Market Street, located at one end of the city's cable-car line. Market Street is home to Square, a new transaction service that enables your smartphone to take credit-card payments. The company, which was started by Jack Dorsey, is located here so he can be near the other company he started, Twitter, which is one block away.

A little ways past Dropbox is Salesforce.com, a fourteen-year-old, $3 billion company. This fast-growing firm focuses on helping small companies keep track of their customers so they can service them better. It was started by Marc Benioff, who used to work at Oracle, the huge database company, which we'll pass a little later.

Threading our way through the city, with its artisan bakeries, coffee shops, and tony restaurants, we arrive at the Mission District. This part of town was once the city's skid row. It was a maze of empty warehouses, people sleeping in doorways, and sidewalks strewn with wine bottles.

But now this part of town is teeming with startups. One of those companies is on our right, the world headquarters of Rdio, a startup founded by the group that started Skype, which it sold to eBay, which sold it to Microsoft for $8.5 billion. The founders of Skype, one Danish, the other Swedish, pocketed about $1.9 billion for their efforts, which they have been investing in cool new ventures. One of those ventures, Rdio, has a library of more than 20 million songs, which it streams to tablets, smartphones, and computers. Rdio occupies a floor in a refurbished old warehouse building that is filled with startups. The lobby area of the warehouse, which once held cargo for the holds of ships docked at San Francisco Bay, is now filled with dozens of bicycles owned by the people working in the building—software geeks, marketing mavens, content developers, and other inhabitants of the startup world.

Continuing into South San Francisco, we come to the headquarters of Zynga, the big online game company, which has more than 100 million users. Zynga, which has more than 2,000 people working for it in San Francisco, operates out of a less-than-elegant seven-story building nicknamed the "dog house." It is called the dog house because the company took its name from a bulldog once owned by one of the company's founders, Mark Pincus.

As we continue onto the 101, with the blue-gray, windswept, San Francisco Bay on our left, past Candlestick Park, and then the San Francisco Airport, the first thing you notice is that this state is big, compared to Massachusetts—which explains the traffic and why, even though we're in this fast, zero-emissions electric car, we're traveling so slowly.

Around the airport we seem to be surrounded by the Japanese and South Korean high-tech and electronics companies that have located their research and development centers or their US headquarters here.

If California were a country, its economy would be somewhere between the world's eighth and ninth largest—bigger than India's, with its 1.2 billion people, but slightly smaller than Italy's. If some California governor were to convince Walmart to move its headquarters from Bentonville, Arkansas, to, say, Bakersfield, California, the state's economy would suddenly become even bigger—nearly the size of Britain's.

And, let's be honest. Whereas Massachusetts punches way above its weight—given its stellar research universities, highly educated workforce, high-performing schools, and entrepreneurial zeal—its weather, while not exactly as cold as North Dakota's, is no match for California's sunshine.

Massachusetts is like a pint-sized terrier (its economy is somewhere between Thailand's and South Africa's in size) barking and yapping at California's Great Dane. Even so, *little* Massachusetts is second only to *big* California in innovation and investment in startups, and Massachusetts ranks first in venture-capital spending per capita. But, of course, if you've ever spent time at Fenway Park, the state's cathedral to the Boston Red Sox baseball team, you would quickly grasp two things. First, no citizen of Massachusetts is content to be number two. And second, as smart as people in that state are, no one in Massachusetts understands geography, because no one actually thinks the state is small. To those of us who love Massachusetts, we are certain the state must be at least the size of New York. Really, we are.

As we continue down the 101, past the San Francisco Airport, we pass the sprawling glass headquarters of the Oracle Corporation, the massive, global database company. A little farther south we pass another glass office park. One of those offices is occupied by VantagePoint Capital Partners, one of the venture firms that was an early investor in the company that made our Tesla car.

We continue our drive by pulling off the 101 and driving west, toward the ocean and the hills, and the three-city complex of Cupertino, Santa Clara, and San Jose. The streets in this area are tree lined and leafy, with rows of tract houses built in the aftermath of World War II. But don't mistake this area for a sleepy bedroom community. It is home to Apple, Intel, Adobe, Cisco, eBay, and dozens of other high-tech companies and corporate research centers.

California has some of the greatest research universities in the world. Stanford University, in Stanford, California, adjacent to Palo Alto and nearby Menlo Park, where Facebook headquarters is located, and Mountain View, where Google has its "Googleplex," is a short drive from San Jose. Stanford is located a few miles from Sand Hill Road, home to the world's largest concentration of venture capital investors.

If we drive down Sand Hill Road, it's interesting what we see. Rather than looking like billion-dollar financial institutions with lots of marble, glass, and steel, the offices on this road resemble the kinds of suites doctors or architects like to rent—low-key, made of wood, with plenty of trees out in front. Silicon Valley continues to hum, albeit not as in-your-face as in the past, but it's growing nevertheless. Stanford and the nearby University of California campuses at San Francisco, Berkeley, and Davis form the nucleus of one of the world's most powerful hubs of creativity and innovation. When it comes to digital technology, no other place in the world even comes close. Silicon Valley is in a class by itself.

One of the most interesting recent developments to come out of Stanford is called MOOC—for "massive open online course." Many MOOCs are free—though you typically don't receive college credit for them—and the selection of courses is educationally rich, with compelling subject matter. Online courses have been around for years, but MOOCs are different. Rather than taking a class online with thirty or so other people at the private, for-profit University of Phoenix, for example, where you're charged a lot of money to gain access to the material, MOOCs are big and available to everyone with an Internet connection.

When Stanford professor Sebastian Thrun launched a STEM-based MOOC called "Introduction to Artificial Intelligence," 150,000 students signed up, a group ten times the size of Stanford's undergraduate and graduate student population. Because of its success, universities around the country, and a few in Europe, began offering MOOCs of their own. They had the same results—tens of thousands of students, studying intently, without receiving credit, in the hopes of learning something new, important, and relevant to their careers. That number—150,000 students—is bigger than many school districts in the country and around the world.

Because of this success, a number of companies were started to provide MOOCs to students around the world, and to do so for profit, including Coursera, Udacity, and Edex. And many of these new companies received investments from the venture capitalists on Sand Hill Road.

The economics are there for this made-in-America innovation. It costs not much more to present an online course to 150,000 or even 1 million students than it does to present it to 30 students. That means that if you're responsible for the budget of a university system—whether in China, with its 20 million college students, or in the United States, with its 20 million—it might dawn on you that costs can be lowered for your students if you use MOOCs to teach basic required courses, including in the STEM subjects.

Required subjects such as math or physics—and even English and history—are now taught by thousands of professors, with varying levels of competency, in thousands of schools. There are more than 6,700 institutions of higher learning in the United States.[1] Each of these institutions has to pay its faculty, classroom space, and so on. If a professor in each of these institutions is paid $10,000 to teach a mandatory math class each quarter (in reality they are paid more) it will cost the country $67 million a quarter, or $268 million a year, to offer that course to students at each of our institutions of higher education.

Let's say the incoming freshman class in America's institutions of higher learning numbers some 7 million students. If we did a search and found the best introductory math teacher in the country—or even in the world—and paid that professor $1 million to teach the class, and all college freshmen took that class at home in a MOOC—we would make that professor rich and save $267 million a year. (I'm not including savings from not having to heat, cool, or clean classrooms for the course.)

This strategy is already working. At the time of this writing, Coursera had 3.68 million students around the world—ten times the number of students at the for-profit University of Phoenix and fifty times the number at Arizona State University, the largest public university in the nation. A typical Coursera class has 37,000 students. In addition, Coursera has new contracts with a number of universities to educate another 1.25 million students. What's interesting about Coursera's model is this: its MOOC program provides the basic educational content of a course in, say, physics, which frees up the professors at schools around the world to either conduct research—one option—or turn their courses into discussions to help their students arrive at a deeper understanding of the subject matter. Either way, this made-in-America model will change education in profound ways, not just in the United States, but globally.

If a few dozen colleges banded together and paid $2 million to someone to teach each basic, required college course in a MOOC format, we would be considered lavish, maybe even foolish, in our spending. But the schools would still save $266 million a year per course, if it was provided nationwide. And if we offered *all* basic, required college courses as MOOCs, the country would save billions of dollars a year on education—with each student learning from the world's best professors. These savings could help students graduate from college without being hobbled by debt.

If every student in Asia, Latin America, and Europe could take these classes to satisfy their requirements, it would not increase costs. The world would be saving tens of billions of dollars teaching basic courses, with every student learning from the best professors.

This is what Coursera, Udex, and the other startups are betting on.

But, let's face it, sitting alone at your computer and taking a class online is not what most students are looking for from their college experience. Nor is it ideal for older people who want to go back to school to be retrained. You can only see the professor, the whiteboard, and the backs of the heads of a few people sitting in front of the video camera (out of hundreds of thousands). The temptation to pull up another screen when you should be paying attention, or to talk on the phone, or to start texting or watching TV, or eating, might be excruciating. But, as the TV commercial says, "there's an app for that," which is to say, there's a software solution to the problem.

MOOCS AND VIRTUAL REALITY

Let's pull our nearly silent Tesla into a parking lot on the sprawling Stanford campus. The first thing we notice, after emerging from the beautiful, tree-lined Palm Drive onto the campus proper, are the broad lawns and low, almost Spanish-style buildings. The red tile roofs, arches, small inner courtyards, and domed Hoover tower draw from the Spanish Colonial Revival and Mission Revival styles.

If we walk from the parking lot along Serra Street and turn right, we come to Serra Mall, where Stanford professor Jeremy Bailenson runs Stanford's virtual reality lab—formally called the Virtual Human Interaction Lab. It is probably the best lab of its kind in the world for linking cognitive research with computerized animation. In fact, in contrast to most other virtual reality labs, Bailenson's lab emphasizes the cognitive side of research rather than the computer side.

Bailenson, a compact man in his early forties, has dark eyes and long black hair, which he combs straight back. He looks more like an artist or musician than someone running a lab at one of the best research universities in the world.

But Bailenson is doing amazing things. For example, when some colleagues and I visited his lab, we were taken up to the second floor, into a square room that was about 20 by 20 feet. The room was painted a muted beige, with a 2.5-foot-wide, straw-colored band around its circumference about 4 feet above the floor. There was a door on one side along with a dark, tinted window, behind which was a control booth. Special motion-capture TV cameras were installed every few feet just below the ceiling. Each of these high-tech motion-capture cameras cost $5,000, Bailenson said.

When the lab's research manager joined us, he brought with him one of the lab's experimental virtual-reality helmets. This apparatus makes someone wearing it look like Jeff Goldblum in the movie *The Fly*. The black, triangular-shaped helmet has two eye-sized color TV monitors inside. It has electronic sensors on top, and eye cups designed to keep out all of the room's light. There are mechanisms that you can adjust to keep the headset comfortably and firmly in place. In addition, the researchers gave us bands to attach to our ankles. The ankle clips combined with the equipment in the headgear send a signal to the computers to give the exact location of a person in the room. We were also given small cylinders to hold, which kept track of the location of our hands.

As soon as I put the headset on I was dazzled by the images I saw, which were of the room. The walls, door, tinted window, floor, and straw-colored band on the walls were exactly where they were supposed to be. But the people I was with had vanished from view.

If I turned my head to the left, I saw the door. If I turned my head to the right, I saw the wall and window. If I looked up, I saw the ceiling, and when I looked down, I saw the carpeted floor. It didn't look like an exact copy of the room, but it was close enough to look real. If I turned my head or walked around, the images I saw would adjust accordingly, just like in real life.

But as I stood in the virtual room, one of the graduate students asked me if I could see a wooden plank on the carpeted floor. When I looked down, a wooden plank appeared.

"Yes," I said. "I see it." It was about 10 inches wide, on the floor to my right. Judging by its color and grain, it looked like pine—but it was virtual pine.

"Step on the plank," the student said.

"Okay," I said.

Dutifully, I walked over to where I saw the plank and stepped on it.

I stood there and then heard a deep *thunk* or clang, and the floor began to vibrate, thanks to special effects. As it did, the carpeted floor abruptly parted below my feet, reminding me of a scene in the movie *Raiders of the Lost Ark*. Suddenly, I was standing on a plank looking down into what appeared to be a deep, cement-lined pit. The pit seemed to be at least 20 feet deep—enough to break my bones if I fell into it. It looked real enough to make my heart race.

"OMG!"

It's difficult to explain how I felt. Logically, I knew I was in a virtual world, but apparently my brain did not. My stomach grew queasy, and my legs kept adjusting so I could keep my balance. (I kept telling myself that I was standing on the floor, not on a plank, but my brain did not agree!) I could feel my palms begin to sweat. My brain was creating the same sensations I would feel if I were walking across a narrow plank over a 20-foot-deep hole in the ground. And yet, in-tellectually I knew I was at Stanford wearing a headset and looking at two miniature TV screens in front of my eyes. I was in Stanford's version of the *Matrix*.

I worked my way across the plank carefully, heart racing, arms extended, trying to keep my balance. And when I made it to the other side, having prevented myself from falling into the pit, I felt relieved, as if I had accomplished something dangerous. But what had I accomplished, really? Not much. I had walked 10 feet across the lab's carpeted floor. And yet, I felt I had survived a life-and-death test.

When the people I was with took their turns walking the plank, they had the same reaction. Some of them screamed. One man tried to jump from the plank to the edge of the pit, and by doing so managed to jump into one of the room's very-real, very-solid, walls (that's why the graduate students were there, to prevent accidents). It was an incredible experience.

When we finished, we went back to Bailenson's office. He stood in front of us and discussed his research.

"The cameras use the ankle and head sensors, and the ones you were holding in your hands, to locate where you are in the room," he said. "The computer captures that information and redraws you and the room 120 times a second to account for any movements."

Given how real the scenes looked, and how the room was drawn and redrawn, I imagined some big mainframe computer clicking and flickering behind the glass wall.

As if reading my mind, someone asked, "What kind of computer equipment does all this run on?"

"It's an off-the-shelf Dell with a few modifications. Nothing fancy," he said, which tells you something about how quickly computer technology has advanced.

"I am not a computer scientist," Bailenson said. "As an engineer, I'm just okay. My primary field is cognitive psychology. That's where I have my PhD. I'm interested in the experience, how we feel, how our brains process information. That's why our lab is not in the computer science department."

▼▼▼▼

I am discussing MOOCs and virtual reality together for a reason, and not only because they are both Stanford's brainchildren. As I mentioned, MOOCs, as they currently are delivered, are impersonal. But what if virtual reality and MOOCs were to be merged? What if basic STEM courses were taught using virtual technology?

Bailenson said one of his projects is to construct a virtual classroom. In that classroom you would have an avatar—a virtual likeness of yourself with a virtual body. He showed us a program that uses the camera on your computer to take pictures of your face, and then uses those images to create a virtual *you* that moves, has expressions (your expressions!), can open and close its mouth when you speak, and can do all this in real time, all from the computer on your desk at home.

Now, if you have an avatar, and I have an avatar, we can seat them next to each other in a virtual classroom—one that Bailenson's lab can design—even though you may be in Beijing and I may be in Menlo Park. Using existing networks, we can log on and communicate with each other by text or voice.

If I am looking at my computer screen or monitor, my avatar, with its brown eyes, glasses, and sadly thinning hair, can look at your avatar, which is sitting next to me in the virtual classroom. We can shift our heads and look at Professor Thrun standing at the whiteboard as he lectures to the class about artificial intelligence. We can do all this in a virtual environment that makes it seem *as if* we were in the same place, doing the same thing, side by side.

Bailenson explained that soon virtual reality will not need big headsets, ankle clips, and handheld cylinders to make the technology work. Startups like Occulus VR are already making smaller virtual reality goggles. And new ultrasensitive sensors, far better than the sensors used in Microsoft's Kinect and other games, will capture motion so your laptop or tablet device (or perhaps even your phone) can redraw your location many times a second as you move. These movements will enable your onscreen avatar to duplicate what you do next to your virtual friends.

PUTTING IT TOGETHER

So there you are, in class, listening to Professor Thrun. But instead of 150,000 people sitting alone at home, looking at their computer screens and trying to stay awake, virtual reality can convert this mass

MOOC experience into something much more personal, even intimate. Virtual reality will place you in a classroom with other people, so that when you get up to go to the bathroom, your seat will look empty to all the people who have their avatars sitting in your area of the class. And then, when you return to your seat, your fellow students will see you return.

As schools change, students will sit in a myriad of different (and changeable) virtual reality classrooms filled with avatars of students from their own schools, watching and listening to the world's best professors. As schools change, professors will spend more time with students one on one, less time in the classroom, and more time in the library or lab.

As the technology develops, students will take these classes in virtual 3D—a technology that is under development at the Electronic Visualization Laboratory at the University of Illinois at Chicago— which might be combined with online multiplayer educational games. Over time, these students could come together to meet in person.

This kind of learning is not yet in existence, but I am convinced that this scenario, or something quite like it, will begin taking shape shortly. All the elements are there. As it takes shape, America will do what America does best—change reality, upset the status quo, make a lot of people angry, and force the rest of the world to adapt, adjust, join with us, or be left behind. As this happens, it is likely that some smart professors will figure out how to make a killing with MOOCs and virtual reality, and that one of the venture capital firms on Sand Hill Road will back her or him. It is also likely that other professors, at more traditional institutions, will decry this evolution as vile, and as further evidence of our decline.

But the truth is, virtual reality is already becoming a reality. I have seen it with my own eyes. And when it is fully developed, education—and a generation's experience of it—will be unlike anything that has come before.

THE ROOTS OF OUR PROWESS

In 1969, Peter Drucker, a student of history, philosophy, organizations, and business, published an important book called *The Age of*

Discontinuity.[2] This book carried forward some of Drucker's earlier, path-breaking concepts. Among those was his idea that a "knowledge economy" was forming that would be run by what he called "knowledge workers." Knowledge workers would deal with concepts, ideas, strategies, and relationships that could be used to construct new things, but also had value in and of themselves. When a consulting firm sells ideas that a hedge fund might use to construct its investment portfolios, nothing tangible changes hands, and yet wealth can be created.

In his book, Drucker also discussed what he called the "global shopping center," which we now simply call globalization. He discussed how globalization would influence our lives and fortunes. Though he knew nothing about MOOCs, Drucker did discuss where our educational system was failing. And, though he died in 2005 at the age of ninety-five, before the National Security Agency could eavesdrop on everyone's smartphones, and before there were millions of video cameras linked to law-enforcement agencies via the Internet, Drucker warned about our loss of privacy. Our technology would change how we think about ourselves, he said.

In his discussion of globalization, Drucker put forward a concept that is interesting. He said that in the immediate aftermath of World War II, political leaders in Europe, the Soviet Union, and elsewhere thought that each country would develop in its own unique way. For example, Soviet leaders thought there would be no appetite for private cars in Russia. British leaders did not think Germany would be able to manufacture products for a consumer society, or even be interested in doing so. Britain, following the war, saw no urgent reason to join Europe, and France dropped out of the North Atlantic Treaty Organization (NATO) because its leaders believed France would be a world power equal to the United States. After World War II ended, very few people thought Japan's tradition-bound society would become a consumer-oriented country. What leaders back then didn't realize, Drucker said, was how different the post–World War II era would be from the pre–World War II era.

The implication was that while political, economic, and even religious beliefs are important, *artifacts*—inventions or creations of one kind or another—matter more. Some social scientists in Drucker's day also understood this. The Canadian historian Harold Innis and one of Innis's students, the nearly incomprehensible philosopher of communication (of all things!), Marshall McLuhan, understood that technology changes society and then people change.[3] They understood that politics and other forms of ideology *followed* technology— they did not lead it. Feudalism arose, Innis wrote, because someone invented stirrups so that knights could fight on horseback. Since each horse required a certain amount of pastureland, feudal lords arose to farm and protect that land. Next came castles. Feudalism was not a theory first, and then a fact. It was the result of changes in technology. Virtual reality and MOOCs (McLuhan coined the term "classroom without walls" in 1960, decades before the first MOOC) could have similar effects.

▼▼▼▼

My point is that the first American Century was built largely around the power of weaponry, while the second American Century is being built around technology more broadly defined.

American inventions, or inventions Americans perfected, such as computers, commercial jet airplanes, and consumer electronics and games, change us, and they will change how we view ourselves. A student sitting at home in a virtual-reality classroom studying calculus or physics or basic engineering concepts with 150,000 other freshmen is likely to have a different take on the world from those of us who were educated in more traditional ways. America's inventiveness will change people's heads.

Humanity has always been shaped by its creations, and today's creations are products of the always-fertile American mind. It wasn't a book by Adam Smith that brought down the Soviet Union. It was the fact that capitalism was capable of producing an endless supply of stuff. The Berlin Wall didn't fall because of a philosophy that wore out, it fell because capitalism could make an inexhaustible supply of what people wanted.

America's inventiveness is what the second American Century will be based on. But we can't make the mistake that Europe's leaders made when they thought that after World War II ended, countries would go back to the way they were. As Harold Innis pointed out, even a simple piece of technology, like the stirrup, can change the way millions of people organize their lives.

Now, take the impact of a simple device like the stirrup, and multiply it several million times over to accommodate the treasures being turned out at labs like Stanford's virtual reality lab. That's the impact America will be having on the world.

CHAPTER NINE

OPPORTUNITIES ABOUND

My enthusiasm for the United States and its economy is not shared by all those pundits who make a living trashing what we do. People who mindlessly repeat the phrase "We don't make anything here anymore" are ill informed or want to stir up trouble. Politicians of both parties and at all levels who refuse to compromise on budgetary issues for ideological or personal reasons have not so much damaged the economy as retarded its growth. As I noted in Chapter 2, the results of the most important academic paper arguing that government debt retards growth, written by Carmen Reinhart and Kenneth Rogoff, has been called into question. Errors in the computer model, when corrected, show that government debt has little or no effect on growth. As a result of all the hot air that has been expelled regarding the debt, people have become nervous and reluctant to invest. But when their confidence returns, so will growth.

The biggest negative factor affecting the economy is the perception that we are weaker than we are, that our problems are bigger than they are, and that no one is doing anything to get us ready for the future. These perceptions are not based on reality, they are based on fears that are constantly fanned. Even our most vexing problem—educating our youth—is being dealt with.

Anyone who pays attention understands that the United States is not a nation in decline. The economic issues being confronted by Brazil, India, China, Russia, and a growing list of other countries around the world were dealt with by Americans generations ago.

I've heard it said wistfully by more than one American business leader who should know better that in China, if the government needs a road built, it simply condemns everything in the roadway's path and gets to work building the road. "Why can't we be that efficient?" these business leaders ask.

The answer to that question is that we were that efficient at one time. And it was at a time when most Americans were poor, like most people still are in China. It was then that we built the interstate highway system, dozens of dams, hundreds of bridges, and our national parks. The result of that effort over the past one hundred years is all around us. We already have a sophisticated national infrastructure. We don't need to build one from scratch. True, our infrastructure needs about $2 trillion worth of upgrades over the next decade, but the elements are all in place.

We should not mistake China's efficiency with something that can be sustained long term. No one is happy—whether American or Chinese—when his house is condemned or his farm is seized to make way for a new roadway. No one likes the Chinese-style march of progress when it results in having lead in toothpaste, arsenic in the water, and lead in children's toys.

Already, China has thousands of demonstrations a year, many against property seizures by the government and the criminal degradation of the environment. Some of these demonstrations involve tens of thousands of people, and some are violent. And, although it is true that the majority of Chinese people who live in poverty want to have a better life, they do not want to become wealthy at any cost.

In the 1950s and 1960s, when large parts of California were condemned so freeways could be built, it was by and large a peaceful process. The state paid fair prices for homes that lay in the path of the planned freeways, and protests almost never took place. The same has been true in other parts of the country. Homeowners and farmers in Arizona, Texas, New Mexico, and much of the so-called New South sold their property to make way for progress, all without the need for teargas or police in riot gear.

So let's not beat up on ourselves or long for greater governmental authority so that property can be condemned in the name of progress.

America built its infrastructure quickly and efficiently and without the kind of protests that are underway in China. To move forward now, we only have to refurbish what our parents and grandparents put into place.

A CLEARER LIGHT

We may mindlessly bicker about whether our best days are behind us, but the rest of the world sees us in a different light. The rest of the world is betting on the United States—and doing it unabashedly. Why else would so many people in other countries buy our debt, or flock to the dollar? People in one country don't buy the debt of another country if they think that country is in decline unless they are rewarded handsomely for taking the risk. But people are content to lend money to the US government even though they receive almost no interest in return. Why would the Chinese government lend us its hard-earned money at a near-zero interest rate? Because the Chinese have faith in our ability to grow.

Think about it. China and the United States have been at odds lately over a number of issues—from the Iranian embargo, to disputed islands near Japan, to North Korea. Even so, that hasn't clouded China's perception of the US economy and its prospects. In January 2013, China owned $1.3 trillion worth of US government debt, according to the US Treasury Department.

China didn't buy those Treasury notes and bonds by accident or on a whim. It bought them after careful deliberation. Nor did China buy that debt to gain control of our economy, as people with a conspiracy bent might believe. China bought our debt because it has a lot of cash from running trade surpluses for years, and we have the only economy big enough to absorb that money and pay a return. And, in spite of our rivalry, China needs the United States to be economically strong so we can buy their products. While China is our largest foreign creditor—it owns about 7 percent of our debt—foreigners, in general, own less than half our debt (46 percent) with the remaining amount, 54 percent, owed domestically.[1]

▼▼▼▼

People outside the United States have high levels of confidence in our private sector as well. In 2000, foreign companies had about $1.3 trillion invested in the United States in the form of property, plants, and equipment. By 2008, the latest year for which data are available, that figure had nearly doubled, to about $2.5 trillion.[2] That increase took place despite 9/11, despite the wars in Afghanistan and Iraq, and despite the housing bubble. Companies located in the United States, but owned by interests from abroad, employ about 5.5 million workers. Of those employed, 2 million work in manufacturing, which is a powerful indicator of what this country has to offer in terms of market size, talent, and expertise.

Unlike many other countries—Brazil, for instance—the United States doesn't force companies to locate here to sell into our market. It doesn't force foreign companies to form joint ventures with American companies, and it only imposes import quotas and tariff restrictions on a handful of imports, such as sugar. Foreign firms come to the United States after they make a detailed analysis of the opportunities we provide now and the opportunities they can expect in the future. The staggering size of their investment indicates that after they conduct their analyses, these companies like what they see.

This investment comes from a very sophisticated group of companies—many of which are household names. The majority of these companies are headquartered in Switzerland, Britain, Japan, France, and Germany, where the standards for quality and return on investment are very high. Neither BMW nor Toyota is expanding their operations in the United States in order to lose money, or to gain a foothold in a new market. They are here because of what we have to offer.

Investing in American property, plants, and equipment represents a small share of the world business community's vote of confidence in the United States. If we look at all foreign investments in the United States, including financial investments in stocks, bonds, and other instruments, as well as government debt, foreigners owned about $25 trillion worth of American assets[3] in 2012. (American companies and investors owned $21 trillion of foreign assets in the same year.) No one invests so much money in a single place, especially when interest rates are so low, unless it's a sure thing.

People look at China's investment in the United States as if it were a bad thing. It's not. It's a vote of confidence, prickly relationship or not. China understands that America's prospects are exceptionally good and that it will pay back what it borrowed.

People living outside the United States are not investing in the United States under duress. They are investing their pension funds and savings in American assets for one simple reason: they know we are good for it. Why else would they buy our government debt, or our stocks, or our real estate? Would citizens of China, Japan, South Korea, Taiwan, Britain, Germany, and so many other countries invest in America if they thought we were a has-been nation?

Of course not.

FORETELLING THE FUTURE

No one can foretell the future. I know that firsthand. I have correctly forecast a number of events, but on occasion I have also been wrong. Surprise plays a big role in our lives, and whenever there are trends, there are countertrends as well.

Surprises can go either way. The night before 9/11, I was at a dinner in New York, in a venue that had once been a firehouse. Kofi Annan, who was secretary general of the United Nations, was there, and so was Klaus Schwab, the founder of the World Economic Forum. Before dinner, there were speeches about the positive changes taking place that would remake the world for the better. And yet, the next day, all of those hopes were dashed because of the devastating events that took place.

Surprises can also be good, though. No one forecast the natural gas revolution, or foresaw that the American chemical industry would be transformed. In only a few years, that industry has been transformed from one that imported more than it exported into one that is increasingly export led. That change took place overnight, thanks to natural gas.

Alone among developed countries, the United States did not sign the famous Kyoto Protocols of 1997, which set the goal of reducing emissions of greenhouse gases to 1992 levels. And yet, because the

United States is transitioning its electrical utilities from using coal as a fuel to burning cleaner natural gas, our greenhouse gas emissions have fallen to 1994 levels. As this unexpected transition proceeds, the United States could be the first country to meet Kyoto's goal of reducing emissions to 1992 levels. If that happens, it will have happened without anyone having to draw up a plan.

The natural gas revolution didn't come out of a government lab—which is no reason to cut funding for government labs. Those labs have put science at the service of the country and done so in a big way. Even so, we need to stand back and look at what's happened since about 2005. Nothing happens exactly as planned. And yet, we do know some things. For example, I doubt that in the near term there is much money to be made from natural gas *itself*. The money is downstream, as they say.

At prices below $4.30 or so per million BTUs, natural-gas producers lose money, according to energy investor Boone Pickens. Even at the break-even price of $4.30, natural gas is still significantly cheaper than all petroleum-based fuels and coal.

This tells me that investors need to look to the long run when it comes to this fuel. The companies best poised to profit from such long-term vistas are the big oil companies, all of which have large investments in natural gas. With such large resources and enough revenue from other sources, they can be very patient investors.

Fracking is complicated to do and it is easy to get wrong. Big oil companies are likely to be better at it than small ones, since they are large, slow-moving targets when it comes to lawsuits, and approach engineering problems carefully. Still, big oil can get it wrong. One need only look at the 2010 BP Horizon drilling platform disaster in the Gulf of Mexico to be reminded of just how wrong.

In a way, that's good news, because it means that these big companies have the motivation to do fracking procedures correctly. If something does go wrong, they have a lot to lose. When these companies team up with large oil services companies, such as Halliburton, GE, Fluor, and others, they will probably figure out the safest way to bring natural gas and nonconventional oil to the surface and then follow these best practices. Oil services firms are just as invested, because they are likely to make money more quickly than the big oil companies when things are done right.

At the time of this writing, a battle is brewing in Washington about whether natural gas should be exported. On the one hand, as mentioned in Chapter 4, there are the chemical companies, which want natural gas to stay at home so that prices remain low for their firms in the future, thanks to limited demand. That way, they can turn natural gas into products more cheaply. This side argues that every $1 of natural gas kept at home can be turned into $6 of chemicals for export, and that by exporting these products instead of natural gas, America can improve its trade balance at a far faster clip than if it exports natural gas. On the other hand are the oil companies, which are in favor of more exports to drive up prices. As a result, two powerful industries are going head-to-head over policy. In the end, natural gas will probably be exported. The truth is, either way, America wins.

Natural gas is expected to change things dramatically, first because energy and fuels are such a big part of the economy. But it will also change things because these industries require a lot of well-trained talent. To that end, we are seeing the effect already. Chevron, the oil and natural gas giant, has begun hosting job fairs once again to attract new workers. In the first six months of 2013, the company hosted four of these fairs in an effort to hire enough engineers to oversee drilling for natural gas and oil.

These workers will be spending the money they earn, which will propel the economy forward. And, while it may take years before demand for natural gas is sufficient to increase the price to $4.30 per million BTUs, in the immediate term the opportunities are on the demand side, as Boone Pickens says. If a company uses oil as a feedstock or source of energy, transitioning to natural gas will save it a lot of money. Those savings create profits and opportunities that will be good for the United States.

OTHER POCKETS OF OPPORTUNITY

Much of the business and technology world I've described in this book is fragmented. There are dozens of robot manufacturers, for example, each doing highly creative work, though none of these companies are very big. Still, the market for these products is growing. Already, robots are hard at work vacuuming our rugs, and soon they will be washing our floors. But rather than investing in these small companies, it makes more sense to focus on the companies that will benefit from the robotics revolution.

Consider Kiva Systems, a maker of robots and computer systems. Kiva's sturdy, orange robots read barcodes, pluck products off of warehouse shelves that weigh up to 3,000 pounds, and transport those items to stations where humans, or robots like Baxter, can ship them.

Kiva began in the robotics cluster around MIT in North Reading, Massachusetts. The company's squat orange electric "bots" race around warehouses, stop when a human gets in the way, and go back for recharging when they need a pick me up. Kiva's robots lack Baxter's anthropomorphic charm, but they have increased the efficiency of company distribution efforts multifold. Companies such as Staples, Crate and Barrel, Dillard's, Walgreens, Gap, Toys "R" Us, and many others use systems made by Kiva to get products to customers fast. Even Amazon has come on board with using robots.

Amazon, the world's largest online retailer, did not use robots or automation in its warehouses until 2011. When Amazon executives got to know Kiva, they began the process of automating some of the company's largest warehouses. The collaboration worked so well that, in 2012, Amazon bought Kiva for $775 million. "Amazon Prime," which provides free two-day shipping for Prime members who pay an annual fee, among other benefits, is based around Kiva's technology.

Kiva, like many other robotics companies, may be growing quickly, but it's Kiva's big customers—the Gap, Amazon, Staples—that reap most of the benefits.

The revolution is raging most intensely in health care and security. Even now, surgeries are being performed by robots with hands far steadier than those of any human. For many types of prostate surgery, the use of robots has become routine. Robots can even be used at a distance, something that was first tried in 2001, when a surgeon in New York successfully conducted laparoscopic surgery on a patient in Strasbourg, France. New York and Strasbourg were connected via a dedicated fiber-optic line to minimize the chances of a "dropped call," which could result in a situation with terrible consequences. In the future, perhaps remote surgeries will take place frequently, and not just in New York, but in countries all over the world, even in emerging market countries.

When the fiber-optic communications system in the United States was built, mostly in the 1990s, there were complaints that it had actually been overbuilt. Stories abounded about fiber-optic cables that hadn't been "lit," owing to overcapacity. But as the surgery example shows, bandwidth for medical procedures will be increasingly needed, and some unlit fiber-optic cables are likely to be pressed into service. Some of this bandwidth will be needed for the vast amounts of data that new genetic mapping techniques will make available as that data is sent around the country for analysis and interpretation.

Increasingly, inside of hospitals, you can hear the whirr of American-made robots as they wheel themselves carefully down the hallways and into rooms to deliver meals. Other robots perform tests, or remove waste materials and biological substances. These robots are only now joining the workforce, but make no mistake about it, this is just the beginning.

Years ago, I went for my annual checkup and was instructed by the nurse to sit in a special chair, which I did. The nurse, who was from the Philippines, turned around before leaving the room to tell me my blood pressure would be taken by what I heard as "Miss Shin." I waited in the chair for Miss Shin to arrive, and as I did I felt a metal band clasp my arm and apply pressure. Then I realized that the nurse hadn't said "Miss Shin," she had said *"machine"*—as in, your blood pressure will be taken by machine.

Increasingly, there will be other Miss Shins coming into the world of medicine. Some will take vital signs, while others will be programmed to do physical therapy; some will lift recovering patients out of their beds, while others change the sheets.

In oil-rich Abu Dhabi, one of the wealthiest nations on earth on a per capita basis, I visited a new hospital for the treatment of diabetes, which is prevalent in that country. That hospital, designed and managed by Britain's Imperial College, a well-regarded research university, was filled with advanced American-made medical equipment, and equipment from other countries as well. None of the equipment seemed all that revolutionary compared to, say, what you would find in an advanced American hospital—with one exception. Almost all of the equipment was *connected*.

What I mean by that is that when Abu Dhabi's version of Miss Shin took someone's blood pressure, the data from that test was automatically transferred from the machine to the patient's chart. Machines analyzing blood sugar and other components of blood chemistry also delivered the information directly to a person's chart.

After all the measurements and vital signs were taken, when the patient finally met with the physician, the doctor would be carrying an iPad-like device displaying the patient's data. It had all been transmitted directly, without any human intervention, from the various machines to the patient's medical record. People can make medical errors by copying a letter or number incorrectly—and physicians notoriously have illegible handwriting, whatever language it is. With this digital, networked system, every health-care professional looking at a person's chart is able to access the original data, as captured by the machines.

The immediate impact of these robots will be to make money for the small firms that produce them, which are then likely to be bought by bigger firms. But in the long term, these devices will lower the cost of medical care, if not in absolute terms, than at least in relative terms as a share of GDP. With a new health-care system taking shape in the United States, innovations that save money will be highly prized, and robotic devices will be in demand.

Security is another big area where robots are excelling. In addition to aerial robots—drones and various types of autonomous and remotely piloted aircraft—there are undersea and land-based robots employed by police departments, the FBI, intelligence agencies, and the Pentagon.

In the aftermath of the tragic bombing at the Boston Marathon on April 15, 2013, the Boston Police Department and officers from neighboring areas used a security robot to go into the area behind a house in Watertown, Massachusetts, where one of the bombing suspects was believed to be hiding in a boat. The robot, a PackBot made by MIT-spinoff iRobot, had HD TV cameras and other sensors. PackBot, which fits into a backpack, went behind the house under its own power and used its articulated arm to grab a plastic tarpaulin covering the boat, lift it up, and catch a glimpse of the wounded suspect. Once it successfully completed this task, the police and suspect exchanged gunfire, which led to Dzhokhar Tsarnaev's arrest. During the four-day pursuit of the suspects, other PackBots were used to probe inside a car to look for explosives.

For security robots, such as PackBot, this is just the beginning.

INEXHAUSTIBLE OPPORTUNITIES

For the United States, the future looks bright. The country has abundant new sources of energy, high levels of creativity, the world's largest manufacturing base—which is getting larger—and enough private capital to turn anyone's plan into reality.

Each of these dynamic forces by itself could be transformative. But we also need to know where we stand. We are not, as many would like us to believe, impaired. The American system is working the way it was designed to work, for the most part. And those areas that need attention, such as K-12 education, especially in the inner cities, and infrastructure investment, are being addressed not simply by means of traditional approaches, such as putting fewer students in the classroom, or adding longer hours to the schoolday, but by changing curricula and investing in STEM education. Community colleges are partnering with business to prepare students for the new jobs. And new technological applications, such as MOOCs, will further change the status quo in education.

In addition, the housing market is slowly coming back, with prices returning to pre-crises levels in many parts of the country. When you buy a house, coop, or condo, there are a myriad of other purchases and transactions that go with it. Buying a house creates business for banks, insurance companies, lawyers, and escrow companies as well as an army of inspectors, surveyors, estimators, appraisers, and movers. When I sold my last house, the new buyer even brought in a white-coated mycologist, who carried a microscope to check for mold.

Then there are the after-sale purchases. Once you buy a new house, you quickly find that nothing from the old place seems to fit—or look good. That means purchasing furniture, carpets, window treatments—and more paint.

Then there are all those sales of American-made white goods—refrigerators, wine coolers, trash compactors, washing machines, dryers, and dishwashers—not to mention TVs, stereos, and, more recently, computerized music servers.

In addition, people who own property pay taxes.

Trust me, once housing recovers, the result will be a rapid drop in unemployment among the members of the most afflicted group—young males without much education—followed by increased employment and longer work hours for skilled workers such as plumbers, masons, electricians, and plasterers.

Housing exerts a powerful pull-through effect on the entire economy.

RETURN TO FINANCIAL HEALTH

In April 2013, the Federal Reserve completed an annual "stress test" of the American banking system. Periodic stress tests were instituted after the financial crisis and are compulsory.

The results of the tests were encouraging. According to Federal Reserve Chairman Ben Bernanke, American banks have enough financial strength to withstand risks greater than those they normally sustain in the course of business. The risk banks were supposed to successfully sustain were what the Fed calls "severely adverse." These risks include how banks would fare during an economic slowdown, during periods of rising interest rates, and during a time of increased inflation.

The good news from the 2013 test was that all but two American banks had a sufficient capital cushion to survive the tests satisfactorily. Two other banks were required to increase their capital before undertaking the buyback of their publicly traded stock. The even better news was that, since the first stress test was administered in 2009, banks have doubled the amount of capital they hold. They have done so as they repaid roughly 90 percent of the cash injected into the banking system to keep it solvent during the darkest days of the crisis.[4]

This is good news and has much greater significance than the fact that our banks are regaining their strength. What it really means is that soon these banks will begin to take slightly greater risks. As that happens, they will make housing loans, which will work their way through the economy, as already mentioned.

But even more importantly, Americans can't take full advantage of our soaring levels of creativity, or our vast energy resources, or our strong manufacturing capacity, without banks feeling confident enough to take risks. The country may be awash in capital, but if that capital is not invested, it may as well not exist.

A stronger banking system means that banks will begin lending, drawing down their excess reserves. This is important. The meager amounts of growth that the economy produced since the twin crises began came from larger companies that refinanced their debt in the public markets, thereby reducing their costs. But as we know, although big companies are responsible for a lot of economic activity, they do not create as many jobs as small companies do. That's because large companies increase profits by increasing efficiency, or by acquiring other companies, while small companies increase profits by adding to their capacity.

As banks become more confident, because of successfully completing stress tests and by becoming convinced that the recovery will hold, they will lend more money, at better terms, to smaller, capital-starved firms, resulting in more hiring.

In some ways, you could argue that the banks have been the economy's missing link between a tepid recovery and robust growth. Now that this sector is healing—with the Fed saying 99 percent of banks are considered strong—lending will return. As that happens, we will watch the American economy do what it does best, which is to say, it will once again amaze the rest of the world.

MY OUTLOOK

Like so many Americans, I'm impatient. But when the economy collapsed, and people with experience said it could take as long as a decade before America began to grow again in a powerful but sustainable way, I was filled with frustration. Like every other hyperactive

American, I thought ten years was just too long. We can do better than that. And we are.

Five years ago, Lehman Brothers collapsed, and now almost all of the economic indicators that matter are good.

America has money.

It has vast reserves of cheap, cleaner-burning energy.

It has millions of talented people in a broad array of fields, including the most advanced sciences and every aspect of technology.

America has five years of pent-up demand for housing.

And, on top of all that, I can only recall *one* master entrepreneur who left the country in search of a better place to start a company.

As I survey the economy and our society, and as I look at our capabilities, my firm belief is that America's best days are yet to come.

The second American Century is about to arrive.

NOTES

PREFACE

1. *"North America, with the U.S. in the lead . . ."*: George P. Shultz, "The North American Global Powerhouse," *Wall Street Journal*, July 11, 2013, http://online.wsj.com/article/SB10001424127887324637504578566192 239796864.html.

INTRODUCTION: "NO ONE EVER MADE A PLUGGED NICKEL BETTING AGAINST THE USA"

1. *Profits for the company in Cupertino:* "The Facts About U.S. Manufacturing Investment Abroad," n.d., National Association of Manufacturers, www.nam.org/~/media/61BAC542ACBD454F89252160FAB6FE33 /Facts_About_US_FDI.pdf.
2. *The world's gross domestic product:* "International Macroeconomic Data Set," Historical Data Files, US Department of Agriculture, Economic Research Service, June 13, 2013.
3. *Our companies have in the bank:* Bloomberg, May 23, 2013.
4. *Catastrophe since at least the 1980s: 2014: The Next Financial Meltdown Begins,* video presentation by Harry S. Dent, available at http://harry dentpredictions.com/.
5. *Unemployment above 20 percent:* "Obama Approval Drops as Fears of Depression Rise," CNN Poll, June 8, 2011.
6. *"Economic headwinds":* William Safire, "On Language," *New York Times*, October 3, 2008.
7. *Net energy exporting nation by 2025:* ExxonMobil, *2013: The Outlook for Energy. A View to 2040,* 2013, www.exxonmobil.com/corporate/files /news_pub_eo2013.pdf.

CHAPTER ONE: A STROLL THROUGH THE INNOVATION CORRIDOR

1. *Number of qualified engineers:* "Growth and Competitiveness in the

United States: The Role of Its Multinational Companies," June 2010, McKinsey Global Institute, www.mckinsey.com/insights/americas /growth_and_competitiveness_in_us.

2. *Ranked the world's top twenty-five schools:* US News & World Report, "World's Best Universities," 2012. For the full list, see www.usnews.com /education/worlds-best-universities-rankings.

3. *Six areas of focus:* "Areas of Focus," n.d., Broad Institute, www.broad institute.org/what-broad/areas-focus/areas-focus (italics in original).

4. *"Capable of capturing key health metrics . . .":* "Qualcomm Tricorder XPrize: Healthcare in the Palm of Your Hand. Overview," n.d., Qualcomm, www.qualcommtricorderxprize.org/competition-details/overview.

5. *Employing 3.3 million people:* Edward B. Roberts and Charles Eesley, "Entrepreneurial Impact: The Role of MIT," February 2009, Kauffman Foundation, www.kauffman.org/uploadedfiles/mit_impact_full_report .pdf.

6. *None of this was happenstance:* Vannevar Bush, "Science, the Endless Frontier: A Report to the President by Vannevar Bush, Director of the Office of Scientific Research and Development, July 1945" (Washington, DC: US Government Printing Office, 1945), is available online at the National Science Foundation website, www.nsf.gov/od/lpa/nsf50 /vbush1945.htm. Vannevar Bush, "As We May Think," *The Atlantic*, July 1, 1945, is archived at www.theatlantic.com/magazine/archive/1945/07 /as-we-may-think/303881/.

7. *New MIT buildings:* Scott Kirsner, "Construction Report: 10 Buildings That Will Change the Innovation in Boston and Cambridge," *Boston Globe*, July 25, 2012, www.boston.com/business/technology/innoeco/2012/07 /construction_report_10_project.html.

8. *Clusters form over time:* Michael E. Porter, "Clusters and the New Economics of Competition," *Harvard Business Review*, November-December 1998, http://hbr.org/1998/11/clusters-and-the-new-economics -of-competition.

9. *ENCODE project was managed:* For a description of ENCODE, see Gina Kolata, "Bits of Mystery DNA, Far from 'Junk,' Play Crucial Role," *New York Times*, September 5, 2012, www.nytimes.com/2012/09/06 /science/far-from-junk-dna-dark-matter-proves-crucial-to-health .html?pagewanted=all; or the National Human Genome Research Institute's description of the project, "ENCODE Pilot Project," n.d., found at www.genome.gov/26525202.

10. *In fact, 13.4 percent:* Vivek Wadhwa, Anna Lee Saxenian, and F. Daniel Siciliano, *Then and Now: America's New Immigrant Entrepreneurs*, Part VII, Ewing Marion Kauffman Foundation Research Paper, Kauffman:

The Foundation of Entrepreneurship, October 2012, www.kauffman
.org/uploadedFiles/Then_and_now_americas_new_immigrant
_entrepreneurs.pdf.

11. *26 percent of the Americans:* Ibid.

CHAPTER TWO: THE RICH MAN'S DEPRESSION

1. *"It's clear we're one step away . . . ":* Joe Bel Bruno, Christopher S. Rug-
aber, and Martin Crutsinger, "Crises Roil Wall Street," *Denver Post* (from
the Associated Press), September 15, 2008, www.denverpost.com
/headlines/ci_10465966.

2. *Florida, Arizona, and California:* Peter Y. Hong, "Home Values Dip Past
Forecasts," *Los Angeles Times*, November 19, 2008, quoting a study by
MDA DataQuick, a San Diego–based real-estate research firm, http://
articles.latimes.com/2008/nov/19/business/fi-homes19.

3. *Average household income:* These figures are based on various estimates,
including those by Angus Maddison, University of Groningen; Em-
manuel Saez, University of California at Berkeley; and Thomas Piketty,
Paris School of Economics.

4. *The average age of America's appliances:* These figures are based on an
analysis of data from the Bureau of Economic Analysis made by Mark
Perry and posted on his blog, "Carpe Diem," December 7, 2012, in
"With Average Age of Consumer Durables at 49-Year High, Replacement Cycle Boom Could Boost Economic Growth," AEI Ideas, www
.aei-ideas.org/2012/12/with-average-age-of-consumer-durables-at-49
-year-high-replacement-cycle-boom-could-boost-economic-growth/.

5. *About 125 million homes:* These figures are from statistics compiled in
2012 by the housing website Zillow. Zillow says that 29.3 percent of
all homes are owned outright, as quoted in Alejandro Lazo, "Nearly
One-Third of U.S. Homeowners Have No Mortgage," *Los Angeles Times*,
January 10, 2013, http://articles.latimes.com/2013/jan/10/business
/la-fi-free-and-clear-20130110.

6. *Mathematical study:* Carmen M. Reinhart and Kenneth S. Rogoff, *This
Time Is Different: Eight Centuries of Financial Folly* (Princeton, NJ: Princeton University Press, 2009).

7. *As high as $200 a barrel:* Louise Story, "An Oracle of Oil Predicts
$200-a-Barrel Crude," *New York Times*, May 21, 2008, www.nytimes
.com/2008/05/21/business/21oil.html?_r=0.

8. *At the bottom of the income ladder:* Figures based on data from the Federal Reserve and the US Department of Commerce, Bureau of Economic Analysis. Data shows income growth for most months of 2008
was below 1 percent.

9. *Add it all up:* Figures based on data from the Federal Reserve and the US Department of Commerce, Bureau of Economic Analysis.
10. *Ditto for Japan:* International Monetary Fund, World Economic Outlook database archives, www.imf.org/external/ns/cs.aspx?id=28.
11. *Electronics components as well:* Nikolaus S. Lang and Stefan Mauerer, et al., *Winning the BRIC Auto Markets: Achieving Deep Localization in Brazil, Russia, India and China* (Boston: Boston Consulting Group, 2010).
12. *18 percent a year:* Charles Fishman, "The Insourcing Boom," *The Atlantic*, November 28, 2012, www.theatlantic.com/magazine/archive/2012/12/the-insourcing-boom/309166/.
13. *Grew at a rate of 4.2 percent:* Michael R. Brill and Samuel T. Rowe, "Industry Labor Productivity Trends from 2000 to 2010," July 2013, US Department of Labor, Bureau of Labor Statistics, www.bls.gov/spotlight/2013/productivity/pdf/productivity.pdf.
14. *20 percent in that year alone:* IHS Global Insight, *Global Manufacturing Compensation Watch, 2010.*
15. *Switch to new homes being built:* Urban Land Institute and Ernst & Young, Real Estate Consensus Forecast, April 2013.
16. *The problem . . . is real:* US Department of Labor, Bureau of Labor Statistics, Current Population Survey, "Labor Force Statistics from the Current Population Survey," Table 3, "Employment Status of the Civilian Noninstitutional Population by Age, Sex, and Race," 2012, last modified February 5, 2013, http://bls.gov/cps/cpsaat03.htm.
17. *People with professional degrees:* US Department of Labor, Bureau of Labor Statistics, Current Population Survey, "Employment Projections," "Earnings and Unemployment Rates by Educational Attainment," 2012, last modified May 22, 2013, www.bls.gov/emp/ep_chart_001.htm.
18. *Making it the world's largest producer:* Russell Gold and Daniel Gilbert, "US Is Overtaking Russia as Largest Oil and Gas Producer," *Wall Street Journal*, October 2, 2013. www.wsj.com/news/articles.

CHAPTER THREE: THE UNITED STATES OF CREATIVITY

1. *Volunteered for something at least once:* US Department of Labor, Bureau of Labor Statistics, "Volunteering in the United States—2012," www.bls.gov/news.release/pdf/volun.pdf.
2. *"Action is with the scholar . . . ":* Ralph Waldo Emerson, "The American Scholar," 1837.
3. *"A declaration of intellectual independence":* Robert Watson Gordon, ed., *The Legacy of Oliver Wendell Holmes, Jr.* (Palo Alto, CA: Stanford University Press, 1992).
4. *Descriptions of that methodology:* George Heilmeier, who directed DARPA in the early 1970s, came up with what is called "Heilmeier's

Catechism" for innovation at DARPA. The catechism contains the following questions to be asked before beginning any project:

- · What are you trying to do? Articulate your objectives using absolutely no jargon.
- · How is it done today, and what are the limits of current practice?
- · What's new in your approach and why do you think it will be successful?
- · Who cares?
- · If you're successful, what difference will it make?
- · What are the risks and the payoffs?
- · How much will it cost?
- · How long will it take?
- · What are the midterm and final "exams" to check for success?

5. *Willing to pack up the car:* Alexander Janiak and Etienne Wasmer, "Mobility in Europe: Why It Is Low, the Bottlenecks and the Policy Solutions," European Commission Economic Paper 340, September 2008.
6. *With commercial companies:* It is important to recognize that there are opportunities for conflicts of interest in these relationships. Most companies and academics guard against these abuses and they are actually quite rare.
7. *Urban residents in China:* National Bureau of Statistics in China, "Income of Urban and Rural Residents in 2011," January 30, 2012, www.stats.gov.cn/english/pressrelease/t20120130_402787464.htm.
8. *Foxconn said that within three years:* David J. Hill, "1 Million Robots to Replace 1 Million Human Jobs at Foxconn? First Robots Have Arrived," Singularity Hub, November 12, 2012, http://singularityhub.com/2012/11/12/1-million-robots-to-replace-1-million-human-jobs-at-foxconn-first-robots-have-arrived/.
9. *As of November 2012:* These numbers come from the Swiss-based, global website Robohub (http://robohub.org/), which provides news and information for researchers, enthusiasts, and people working in the robotics industry. They were posted on November 26, 2012, by Frank Tobe, publisher and owner of The Robot Report (www.therobotreport.com/), which tracks global trends in the robotics industry.
10. *Ten most innovative robotics companies:* These were: (1) iRobot, which makes Roombas and military equipment; (2) Recon Robotics, which makes tiny robots that can search through dangerous environments; (3) Google, which is experimenting with autonomous vehicles that can find a destination on their own and navigate through traffic; (4) Mazor

Robots (Israel), which makes surgical robots; (5) SpaceX, which makes rockets and autonomous vehicles that can navigate to destinations in space, such as the International Space Station (ISS); (6) Lockheed Martin, which makes robots for military purposes, including many that fly; (7) PV Kraftwereker (Germany), which makes robotics equipment for the solar power industry; (8) Boston Dynamics, which makes autonomous products such as Petman; (9) Ekso Bionics, which makes robotic exoskeletons to "augment human strength, endurance and mobility"; and (10) Seegrid, which makes autonomous industry trucks, primarily to fill customer orders in warehouses.

11. *Started by Rodney Brooks:* See Antonio Regalado, "Small Factories Give Baxter the Robot a Cautious Once-Over," *MIT Technology Review*, January 16, 2013, www.technologyreview.com/news/509296/small -factories-give-baxter-the-robot-a-cautious-once-over/

12. *Granted 811 patents:* Hannah Seligson, "Hatching Ideas, and Companies, by the Dozens at M.I.T.," *New York Times*, November 24, 2012, www.nytimes.com/2012/11/25/business/mit-lab-hatches-ideas-and -companies-by-the-dozens.html?pagewanted=all&_r=0.

13. *An inclusive nation:* There is a saying that "the French copy no one and no one copies the French." The point is not to pick on the French, but to show how different we are. Openness to new ideas and collaboration in the United States is a strength. No country can succeed for long if it thinks its own ideas are superior to those of others and chooses to live in intellectual isolation.

14. *In the high-tech sector alone:* Vivek Wadhwa, *Kauffman Thoughtbook, 2009* (Kansas City, MO: Ewing Marion Kauffman Foundation, 2009).

15. *Concepts Emerson had expressed:* There were no specific plans in the "American Scholar" for institutions of any kind, which is why I use the word "concepts." Another word that could work as well in this regard is "inspired," as in "inspired by Emerson."

16. *338 Nobel Prizes:* Through 2012, Nobel Prizes have been awarded a total of 555 times to 863 people and organizations worldwide. As the Nobel Prize website explains, "With some receiving the Nobel Prize more than once, this makes a total of 835 individuals and 21 organizations" (see "All Nobel Prizes," www.nobelprize.org/nobel_prizes /lists/all/index.html). Adding up America's share of Nobel Prize winners is no small task, given that many of them were born in other countries. In some lists, a Nobel Laureate is counted more than once—in his or her country of birth, and also in his or her country of residence. For example, Henry Kissinger, who won the Nobel Peace Prize in 1973, is often counted in America's tally of laureates as well

as in Germany's, even though he fled Germany as a child to escape Nazi persecution.

17. *Spent about $436 billion:* These figures are from *2012 Global R&D Funding Forecast*, sponsored by Battelle and *R&D* magazine, December 2011, available at http://battelle.org/docs/default-document-library/2012 _global_forecast.pdf.

CHAPTER FOUR: ABUNDANT, CHEAP ENERGY

1. *The IMF thought would happen:* International Monetary Fund, World Economic Outlook, 2011, www.imf.org/external/pubs/ft/weo/2011/01/.

2. *Overtaken the United States economically:* Arvind Subramanian, *Eclipse: Living in the Shadow of China's Economic Dominance* (Washington, DC: Peter G. Petersen Institute for International Economics, 2011).

3. *Number one by 2027:* Jim O'Neill, *Growth Map: Economic Opportunity in the BRICS and Beyond* (New York: Portfolio/Penguin, 2011).

4. *Number one in 2030:* National Intelligence Council, "Global Trends 2030: Alternative Worlds," December 2012, http://globaltrends2030. files.wordpress.com/2012/11/global-trends-2030-november2012.pdf.

5. *Gas prices from gas exports:* The original study, focusing on liquid natural gas (LNG), was released for comments on December 5, 2012. Its purpose was to forecast how "U.S. LNG exports could affect the public interest, with an emphasis on the energy and manufacturing sectors." The conclusion of the report was unambiguous: "Across all these scenarios, the U.S. was projected to gain net economic benefits from allowing LNG exports." Subsequent to the release of the document, thousands of documents from a myriad of groups were filed opposing the conclusions of the report. A subsequent update by NERA, released on April 23, 2013, concluded, "There were net economic benefits to the U.S. economy across all the scenarios that we examined in which the global market would take LNG exports from the U.S." See US Department of Energy, Office of Fossil Energy, "LNG Export Study," http://energy.gov/fe/services/natural-gas-regulation /lng-export-study.

6. *As much as $16 for an equivalent amount:* Prices vary by season and demand. At the time of this writing, according to BP's authoritative natural gas price comparisons index, prices for 1 million BTUs of natural gas were about $2.99 in the United States, $9.22 in the United Kingdom, $11.60 in Germany, and $17.10 in Japan.

7. *2.5 million barrels of oil a day:* US Energy Information Administration, Annual Energy Outlook 2012, June 2012, www.eia.gov/forecasts/aeo /pdf/0383(2012).pdf.

8. *Convert some of these facilities for export use:* Jim Snyder and Edward Klump, "Gas Export Approval Not Seen Signaling U.S. Permit Flood," Bloomberg, May 17, 2013.

9. *Funded by the National Science Foundation:* R. D. Vidic, S. L. Brantley, J. M. Vandenbossche, D. Yxtheimer, and J. D. Abad, "Impact of Shale Gas Development on Regional Water Quality," *Science*, May 17, 2013.

10. *Sensation around the world:* Donella H. Meadows, Dennis L. Meadows, Jørgen Randers, and William W. Behrens III, *The Limits to Growth* (New York: Universe Books, 1972). Updated editions were later published.

11. *"Service companies are developing . . . ":* National Intelligence Council, "Global Trends 2030: Alternative Worlds," December 2012, http://globaltrends2030.files.wordpress.com/2012/11/global-trends-2030-november2012.pdf, 36.

12. *Net energy exporter by 2025:* ExxonMobil, *2013: The Outlook for Energy. A View to 2040*, 2013, www.exxonmobil.com/Corporate/files/news_pub_eo.pdf, 47.

13. *35 percent compared to the present:* Ibid., 1.

14. *Will jump from $33 billion:* Sherle R. Schwenninger and Samuel Sherraden, *The Promise of (and Obstacles to) America's Emerging Growth Story* (Washington, DC: New America Foundation, Economic Growth Program, 2012), http://newamerica.net/sites/newamerica.net/files/policy docs/America_Emerging_Growth_Story.pdf.

15. *Received scant attention:* Roger J. Stern, "United States Cost of Military Force Projection in the Persian Gulf, 1976–2007," *Energy Policy* 38, no. 6 (2010): 2816–2825.

16. *Scoring toward the bottom:* See Transparency International's "2012 Corruption Perceptions Index" page at www.transparency.org/cpi2012, as well as the clickable map at www.transparency.org/cpi2012/results. As Transparency International explains, the index rates perceptions rather than the level of corruption directly because "corruption generally comprises illegal activities, which are deliberately hidden and only come to light through scandals, investigations or prosecutions. There is no meaningful way to assess absolute levels of corruption in countries or territories on the basis of hard empirical data. . . . Capturing perceptions of corruption . . . is the most reliable method of comparing relative corruption levels across countries" ("What Is the Corruption Perceptions Index," www.transparency.org/cpi2012/in_detail#myAnchor2).

17. *Largest oil producer by 2020:* International Energy Agency, World Energy Outlook, 2012.

18. *Twice as much ethanol as Brazil:* "World Fuel Ethanol Production," 2012, Renewable Fuels Association, http://ethanolrfa.org/pages /World-Fuel-Ethanol-Production.

19. *Used more energy than it produced:* Todd Diemer, "Al Gore Mea Culpa: Support for Corn-Based Ethanol Was a Mistake," *Politics Daily*, January 23, 2011, www.politicsdaily.com/2010/11/23/al-gore -mea-culpa-support-for-corn-based-ethanol-was-a-mistake/.

20. *According to the US Energy Information Administration:* US Energy Information Administration, "Frequently Asked Questions," accessed May 16, 2013. www.eia.gov/tools/faqs/faq.cfm?id=93&t=4.

21. *"Spurred by signs of economic improvement":* David Bird, "U.S. Oil Futures Surge as Economy Improves," *Wall Street Journal*, March 27, 2013, http://online.wsj.com/article/SB2000142412788732478950457838401 1642706352.html.

22. *Rose on expectations:* I sometimes think you could write the equation for what sets oil prices like this: Real demand, plus fear of Middle East instability, plus future expectations of demand, multiplied by the manipulation of supplies by OPEC, or $(RD + F + ED) \times M(S) = P$.

CHAPTER FIVE: MONEY TO BURN

1. *My colleagues at the Milken Institute:* James R. Barth, Tong Li, Wenling Lu, and Glenn Yago, *2009 Capital Access Index: Best Markets for Business Access to Capital*, April 2010, Milken Institute, www.milkeninstitute. org/pdf/CAI2009.pdf.

2. *Fifth in the lineup:* The reason the United States didn't fall further in the rankings was that after "freezing" for a period of months, the corporate bond market began functioning once more, at least for the biggest American companies. This meant that big companies could borrow money at very favorable rates. However, smaller businesses and individuals still suffered. The newly chastened banks either stopped lending to them or lent money to them at high rates of interest, sometimes even requiring equity to limit their risks. In the United States, the bottom line was that big companies continued to have access to capital, while others did not.

3. *All things being equal:* See Joel Kurtzman and Glenn Yago, *Global Edge: Using the Opacity Index to Manage the Risks of Cross Border Business* (Cambridge, MA: Harvard Business Publishing, 2007).

4. *At the time of this writing:* David Sterman, "10 Companies with the Biggest Cash Stockpiles in America," September 21, 2012, StreetAuthority .com, www.streetauthority.com/energy-commodities/10-companies -biggest-cash-stockpiles-america-459772.

5. *We pay between 15 and 39 percent:* The global accounting firm KPMG uses the figure of 40 percent as an average for America's corporate tax rate, with 25.5 percent the average for all developed countries.

6. *$1.9 trillion:* Sherle R. Schwenninger and Samuel Sherraden, *The Promise of (and Obstacles to) America's Emerging Growth Story,* July 2012, New America Foundation, Economic Growth Program, http://newamerica .net/sites/newamerica.net/files/policydocs/America_Emerging_ Growth_Story.pdf.

7. *Debt-to-GDP ratio:* "National Debt Graph by President," n.d., zFacts, http://zfacts.com/p/318.html.

8. *Five times greater:* "SIPRI Military Expenditure Database," Stockholm International Peace Research Institute (SIPRI), www.sipri.org/research /armaments/milex/milex_database/milex_database. SIPRI is an authoritative nongovernmental organization in Sweden.

9. *In medieval England:* Peter Corless, "Medieval Agriculture Yields and Equivalents," December 10, 1994, ibiblio, www.ibiblio.org/london /agriculture/general/1/msg00070.html.

10. *Collectively, Americans had:* Research and Statistics, Weekly Money Market Mutual Fund Assets, September 5, 2013, Investment Company Institute, www.ici.org/research/stats/mmf.

11. *Mutual fund investments at the end of 2012:* Investment Company Institute, *2013 Investment Company Fact Book,* 53rd edition, www.icifact book.org/fb_ch1.html.

12. *Additional $1.3 trillion:* Ibid.

13. *$7 trillion deposited:* "Total Savings Deposits at All Depository Institutions," Federal Reserve Economic Data, http://research.stlouisfed.org /fred2/series/SAVINGS.

14. *To at least $22 trillion:* "Market Capitalization of Listed Companies (current US$)," World Bank, http://data.worldbank.org/indicator/CM.MKT .LCAP.CD.

15. *Collectively owned about $64 trillion:* This number underreports total household net worth. "Financial Accounts of the United States: Flow of Funds, Balance Sheets, and Integrated Macroeconomic Accounts," a Federal Reserve Statistical Release, for the first quarter of 2013, puts household net worth at an even higher amount, $70 trillion. However, I will stick with the lower and more conservative amount for safety's sake. See www.federalreserve.gov/releases/z1/current/z1.pdf.

CHAPTER SIX: AMERICA MAKES THINGS

1. *They make an average of $33.77:* There is a difference between salary and benefits and labor costs. Labor costs include salary, benefits, and long-tail liabilities, such as health-care costs for retirees. Salary is typically

a pay-per-time unit, plus benefits, which vary, and other factors. However, not everyone computes these numbers the same way, given how complex the variables can get. As a result, it is rare for two analysts to come up with exactly the same numbers for either figure. The numbers quoted here are from a paper published by Kevin C. Brown, PhD, "A Tale of Two Systems," December 21, 2011, on *Remapping Debate*, an online journal of economics, www.remappingdebate.org /article/tale-two-systems.

2. *American wages are too low:* During the automobile industry bailout, in the aftermath of the bankruptcy of GM, Chrysler, and some suppliers, entry-level wages and benefits were negotiated downward. For example, a summary of the United Auto Worker's 2011 contract by Abby Ferla, published on the *Remapping Debate* website on September 21, 2011 ("Putting the New GM-UAW Contract in Historical Context"), shows that an average veteran autoworker hired before 2006 will make $25.94 an hour in 2015, while one hired after 2007 will make between $16.86 and $17.79 an hour (www.remappingdebate.org/map-data-tool /putting-new-gm-uaw-contract-historical-context).

3. *$2,000 a car:* Sean P. McAlinden and Yen Chen, *After the Bailout, Future Prospects for the U.S. Auto Industry*, December 2012, Center for Automotive Research, available at www.cargroup.org /?module=Publications&event=View&pubID=98.

4. *J. D. Powers Initial Quality Study:* Jeff Youngs, "2013 Initial Quality Study: Top-Ranked Models," J. D. Power: McGraw Hill Financial, http://autos. jdpower.com/content/blog-post/FCRnIHl/top-ranked-models-in-the -j-d-power-2013-initial-quality-study.htm.

5. *Most productive country in the world:* "2011 International Comparison of Labor Productivity," February 16, 2012, Japan Productivity Center, www.jpc-net.jp/eng/research/2012_02.html.

6. *Theft of $45 million:* Mark Santora, "In Hours, Thieves Took $45 Million in A.T.M. Scheme," *New York Times*, May 9, 2013, www.nytimes. com/2013/05/10/nyregion/eight-charged-in-45-million-global-cyber -bank-thefts.html?pagewanted=all&_r=0.

7. *American firms with operations in China:* Mandiant, *APT1, Exposing one of China's Cyber Espionage Units*, February 2013, http://intelreport .mandiant.com/Mandiant_APT1_Report.pdf.

8. *Given the research I have conducted:* See various papers relating to the Opacity Index by Joel Kurtzman and Glenn Yago between 2000 and 2011.

9. *"Malicious implants . . . ":* "Investigative Report on the U.S. National Security Issues Posed by Chinese Telecommunications Companies Huawei and ZTE: A Report by Chairman Mike Rogers and Ranking

Member C. A. Dutch Ruppersberg of the Permanent Select Committee on Intelligence," US House of Representatives, 112th Cong., October 8, 2012, http://intelligence.house.gov/sites/intelligence.house.gov/files/Huawei-ZTE%20Investigative%20Report%20(FINAL).pdf.

10. *Focused on the Spartanburg plant:* Horatiu Boeriu, BMW Blog, January 10, 2013, www.bmwblog.com/2013/01/10/bmw-spartanburg-plant-reports-record-production-volume/.

11. *A staggering amount:* Tom Orlick, "Rising Wages Pose Dilemma for China," *Wall Street Journal*, May 17, 2013, http://online.wsj.com/article/SB10001424127887324767004578488233119290670.html.

12. *Economic Research Service:* "Farm Labor: Background," "Hourly and Annual Earnings, Selected Occupations, May 2011," table, United States Department of Agriculture, Economic Research Service, www.ers.usda.gov/topics/farm-economy/farm-labor/background.aspx#wages.

13. *0.7 percent of America's workforce:* Central Intelligence Agency, *The World Factbook*, "The United States, Economy, Labor Force, by Occupation," https://www.cia.gov/library/publications/the-world-factbook/geos/us.html.

14. *20 percent of our economy:* US Department of Agriculture, National Agricultural Statistics Service, "Farm Labor: Number of Farms and Workers by Decade, US," n.d., www.nass.usda.gov/Charts_and_Maps/Farm_Labor/fl_frmwk.asp.

15. *Thanks to new manufacturing techniques:* "Increasing Global Competition and Labor Productivity: Lessons from the US Automotive Industry," November 2005, McKinsey Global Institute.

16. *Priciest places to live:* "Worldwide Cost of Living Index 2013," *The Economist*, Intelligence Unit, https://www.eiu.com/public/topical_report.aspx?campaignid=Wcol2013.

17. *People will need office space:* David Segal, "A Missionary's Quest to Remake Motor City," *New York Times*, April 13, 2013, www.nytimes.com/2013/04/14/business/dan-gilberts-quest-to-remake-downtown-detroit.html?pagewanted=all&_r=0.

18. *Over the past four years:* World Bank, "Foreign Direct Investment, Net Inflows (BoP, current US$)," 2013, http://data.worldbank.org/indicator/BX.KLT.DINV.CD.WD, shows that between 2008 and 2012, China received about $250 billion in outside investment, while the United States received about $205 billion.

19. *And ours is just 313 million:* World Bank, "Population, Total," n.d., http://data.worldbank.org/indicator/SP.POP.TOTL.

20. *Location is as important:* Enrico Moretti, *The New Geography of Jobs* (Boston: Houghton Mifflin Harcourt, 2012).

21. *Has a multiplier of 7.8:* Rob Sentz, "Job Multipliers: Silicon Valley vs. The Motor City," August 31, 2012, EMSI, www.economicmodeling.com/2012/08/31/job-multipliers-silicon-valley-vs-the-motor-city/.

22. *Mitt Romney, for example:* Mitt Romney, "Let Detroit Go Bankrupt," *New York Times*, November 18, 2008, www.nytimes.com/2008/11/19/opinion/19romney.html?_r=0.

23. *The book . . . shows so well:* Matthew B. Crawford, *Shop Class as Soulcraft: An Inquiry into the Value of Work* (New York: Penguin, 2009).

24. *"Outsourcing that is based . . . ":* Jeffrey R. Immelt, "The CEO of General Electric on Sparking an American Manufacturing Renewal," *Harvard Business Review*, March 2012, http://hbr.org/2012/03/the-ceo-of-general-electric-on-sparking-an-american-manufacturing-renewal/ar.

CHAPTER SEVEN: NOT EVERYTHING'S PERFECT

1. *$23,520 versus $51,108, on average:* US Department of Commerce, US Census Bureau, 2009.

2. *Versus $72,000:* US Department of Commerce, Economic and Statistics Administration, US Census Bureau, "Field of Degree and Earnings by Selected Employment Characteristics: 2011," October 2012, www.census.gov/prod/2012pubs/acsbr11-10.pdf.

3. *Only 800,000 people:* US Department of Labor, Bureau of Labor Statistics, "Databases, Tables and Calculators by Subject," www.bls.gov/data/.

4. *Tough-minded automobile testers:* "2014 Chevrolet Impala Is Consumer Reports' Highest Scoring Sedan," *Consumer Reports*, www.consumer-reports.org/cro/2013/07/2014-chevrolet-impala-highest-scoring-sedan-consumer-reports/index.htm.

5. *National Highway Safety Administration:* Harold Maass, "Tesla's Model S is the Safest Car Ever," *The Week*, August 20, 2013, http://theweek.com/article/index/248468/why-teslas-model-s-is-the-safest-car-ever.

6. *Led to the establishment:* The National Science Foundation was established by Congress in 1950. At present it makes about 10,000 grants a year for scientific research. Its research has led to breakthroughs in supercomputing, nanotechnology, astronomy, mathematics, biology, and many other areas.

7. *"There must be a steady stream . . . ":* Vannevar Bush, "Science, the Endless Frontier: A Report to the President by Vannevar Bush, Director of the Office of Scientific Research and Development, July 1945" (Washington, DC: US Government Printing Office, 1945), Chapter 3 (n.p.), available online at the National Science Foundation website, www.nsf.gov/od/lpa/nsf50/vbush1945.htm.

8. *Going to college was rare:* "Educational Attainment in the United States, Population and Characteristics, 2009," February 2012, US Department of Commerce, US Census Bureau, www.census.gov/prod/2012pubs /p20-566.pdf.

9. *Sites around the country:* "Professionals: Manufacturing Opportunities," n.d., Siemans, www.usa.siemens.com/en/jobs_careers/professionals /manufacturing_and_production_opportunities.htm.

10. *9.8 percent for non-STEM jobs:* David Langdon, George McKittrick, David Beede, Beethika Khan, and Mark Doms, "STEM: Good Jobs Now and for the Future," July 2011, US Department of Commerce Economics and Statistics Administration, Office of the Chief Economist, www .esa.doc.gov/sites/default/files/reports/documents/stemfinaljuly14.pdf.

11. *By the McKinsey Global Institute:* James Manyika, Scott Nyquist, Lenny Mendonca, Sreenivas Ramaswamy, and Susan Lund, "Game Changers: Five Opportunities for US Growth and Renewal," July 2013, McKinsey, www.mckinsey.com/Search.aspx?q=stem.

12. *Enrollment in engineering schools:* "Science & Engineering Indicators," National Science Foundation, www.nsf.gov/statistics/seind12/.

13. *"Demand for engineering education . . . ":* Christopher R. O'Dea, "The Graduates: How to Fill Three Million Jobs," *Korn/Ferry Briefings: Talent + Leadership* 4, no. 15 (2013): 28–35, www.nxtbook.com/nxtbooks/kf /briefings_2013q3_v2/index.php?startid=29.

14. *Gain college credit:* One of the best reports on Race to the Top was done by the Center for American Progress: Ulrich Boser, "Race to the Top, What We Have Learned from the States So Far," March 2012, www .americanprogress.org/wp-content/uploads/issues/2012/03/pdf/rtt_ states.pdf. There are other studies as well that chart the impact of states adopting the common curriculum program and tougher standards.

15. *Called "endless" now:* Elon Musk, "Hyperloop," Tesla Blog, www.tesla motors.com/blog/hyperloop.

16. *Software jobs multiplier:* I'm using the Economic Modeling Specialists International figure of 4.3 as an average for software, IT, high-tech, Internet, and related jobs. SpaceX is a manufacturer, which has a higher multiplier, but my aim is to be conservative in these estimates.

CHAPTER EIGHT: CALIFORNIA DREAMING

1. *6,700 institutions:* "Database of Accredited Postsecondary Institutions and Programs," June 2013, US Department of Education, http://ope .ed.gov/accreditation/GetDownloadFile.aspx.

2. *Student of history:* Peter Drucker, *The Age of Discontinuity: Guidelines to Our Changing Society* (New York: HarperCollins, 1969).

3. *And then people change*: See Harold Innis, *Empire and Communications* (Toronto: Dundurn, 1950); Harold Innis, *The Bias of Communication* (Toronto: University of Toronto Press, 1951); Marshall McLuhan, *Understanding Media: The Extensions of Man* (New York: Routledge, 1964); Marshall McLuhan, *The Gutenberg Galaxy* (Toronto: University of Toronto Press, 1962).

CHAPTER NINE: OPPORTUNITIES ABOUND

1. *Owed domestically:* "Federal Debt Basics," n.d., US Government Accountability Office, www.gao.gov/special.pubs/longterm/debt/debt basics.html.

2. *About $2.5 trillion:* James K. Jackson, "Foreign Direct Investment in the United States: An Economic Analysis," October 26, 2012, Congressional Research Service, www.fas.org/sgp/crs/misc/RS21857.pdf.

3. *$25 trillion worth:* "U.S. Net International Investment Position at Year-end 2011," June 26, 2012, US Department of Commerce, Bureau of Economic Analysis, www.bea.gov/newsreleases/international/intinv /2012/intinv11.htm.

4. *Darkest days of the crisis:* According to the Federal Reserve, the largest banks performed well on the 2013 "stress tests," which models the impact of a large drop in economic activity on the strength of the banking system. According to Federal Reserve Governor Daniel K. Tarullo, "Significant increases in both the quality and quantity of bank capital during the past four years help ensure that banks can continue to lend to consumers and businesses, even in times of economic difficulty." Tarullo was quoted in a March 7, 2013, press release that is archived at the website of the Board of Governors of the Federal Reserve System at www.federalreserve.gov/newsevents/press/bcreg/20130307a.htm.

INDEX

Joel Kurtzman is a senior fellow at the Milken Institute, a nonprofit, nonpartisan think tank, where his research focuses on energy globalization and its risks. Kurtzman is a member of the editorial board of *MIT Sloan Management Review*, a senior fellow at the Wharton School's SEI Center for Advanced Studies in Management, and editor-in-chief of *Korn/Ferry's Briefings on Talent & Leadership*. He is the author of many books and articles. Earlier in his career, Kurtzman was the editor-in-chief of *Harvard Business Review*, founding editor-in-chief of *Strategy + Business* magazine, a business editor and columnist at the *New York Times*, and global lead partner for thought leadership and innovation at PriceWaterhouseCoopers. Kurtzman was also an international economist at the United Nations. He divides his time between Santa Monica, California, and Concord, Massachusetts.

PublicAffairs is a publishing house founded in 1997. It is a tribute to the standards, values, and flair of three persons who have served as mentors to countless reporters, writers, editors, and book people of all kinds, including me.

I. F. STONE, proprietor of *I. F. Stone's Weekly*, combined a commitment to the First Amendment with entrepreneurial zeal and reporting skill and became one of the great independent journalists in American history. At the age of eighty, Izzy published *The Trial of Socrates*, which was a national bestseller. He wrote the book after he taught himself ancient Greek.

BENJAMIN C. BRADLEE was for nearly thirty years the charismatic editorial leader of *The Washington Post*. It was Ben who gave the *Post* the range and courage to pursue such historic issues as Watergate. He supported his reporters with a tenacity that made them fearless and it is no accident that so many became authors of influential, best-selling books.

ROBERT L. BERNSTEIN, the chief executive of Random House for more than a quarter century, guided one of the nation's premier publishing houses. Bob was personally responsible for many books of political dissent and argument that challenged tyranny around the globe. He is also the founder and longtime chair of Human Rights Watch, one of the most respected human rights organizations in the world.

．　　　．　　　．

For fifty years, the banner of Public Affairs Press was carried by its owner Morris B. Schnapper, who published Gandhi, Nasser, Toynbee, Truman, and about 1,500 other authors. In 1983, Schnapper was described by *The Washington Post* as "a redoubtable gadfly." His legacy will endure in the books to come.

Peter Osnos, *Founder and Editor-at-Large*